CONTENTS

LONGMAN SOCIOLOGY SERIES

Frontiers of Identity

The British and the Others

Robin Cohen

LONGMAN
London and New York

Longman Group Limited,
Longman House, Burnt Mill,
Harlow, Essex CM20 2JE, England
and Associated Companies throughout the world.

Published in the United States of America
by Longman Publishing, New York

© Robin Cohen 1994

All rights reserved; no part of this publication may be
reproduced, stored in a retrieval system, or transmitted
in any form or by any means, electronic, mechanical,
photocopying, recording, or otherwise without either the
prior written permission of the Publishers or a licence
permitting restricted copying in the United Kingdom issued
by the Copyright Licensing Agency Ltd.,
90 Tottenham Court Road, London W1P 9HE.

First published 1994

ISBN 0 582 24577 X CSD
ISBN 0 582 24576 1 PPR

British Library Cataloguing-in-Publication Data

A catalogue record for this book is
available from the British Library

Library of Congress Cataloging-in-Publication Data
Cohen, Robin,
    Frontiers of identity : the British and the others / Robin Cohen.
      p.   cm. – (Longman sociology series)
    Includes bibliographical references and index.
    ISBN 0–582–24577–X. – ISBN 0–582–24576–1 (pbk.)
    1. Great Britain – Ethnic relations. 2. Immigrants – Great Britain – Social
conditions. 3. Great Britain – Emigration and immigration. 4. Refugees – Great
Britain – Social conditions. 5. Aliens – Great Britain – Social conditions. 6. National
characteristics, British. 7. Great Britain – Race relations. I. Title. II. Series.
DA125.A1C64 1994
305.8'00941 – dc20
                                                94–11852
                                                  CIP

Set in Times Roman 10/11
Produced by Longman Singapore Publishers (Pte) Ltd.
Printed in Singapore

UNIVERSITY COLLEGE
LIBRARY
SWANSEA

UNIVERSITY OF WALES SWANSEA
PRIFYSGOL CYMRU ABERTAWE
LIBRARY/LLYFRGELL

Classmark HT221 COH

Location Miners' Library

1004408017

LIST OF FIGURES AND TABLES

SERIES EDITOR'S PREFACE

The Longman Sociology Series aims to provide an alternative to the standard texts in the field. Although most of the books in the series are designed with sociology undergraduates in mind, the editors will include books that are of wider interest, both to students, researchers and scholars in cognate fields and to a more general readership who actively use the social sciences.

The series is forward looking and reflects key controversies and debates in sociology and social policy in the 1990s. Each book will be theoretically informed, use new empirical material and have some relevance to political and social policy. The focus of each volume will be upon theoretically informed empirical work. As the volumes are intended for an international audience they frequently contain comparative material.

One can hardly imagine a more live controversy than that tackled by Robin Cohen in this volume. The nature and contours of British identity and the way in which national identities intersect with racial and ethnic identities form the basis of his conceptual and theoretical contribution. But he has also used the notion of a 'fuzzy frontier' to look at how, in practice, exclusion takes place. Home Office data, interviews with detainees, deportees and those in sanctuary are supplemented with case workers' files and extracts from European newspapers.

The author compares British patterns of exclusion with those in Germany and France. His conclusion provides an indictment of those who covertly and secretly define who will be admitted into the gilded European cages, while his recommendations invite new policy alternatives in the treatment of asylum-seekers, migrants and minorities.

Robert G. Burgess
University of Warwick

LIST OF ABBREVIATIONS

ADWG	Anti-Deportation Working Group
AI	Amnesty International
AR	Armée Révolutionnaire (Revolutionary Army, France)
BBC	British Broadcasting Corporation
BIVS	Berlin Institute of Comparative Social Research
BRC	British Refugee Council
CIA	Central Intelligence Agency (US)
CNRS	Centre National de la Recherche Scientifique
CRE	Commission for Racial Equality
DHSS	Department of Health and Social Security
DPs	displaced persons
EEC	European Economic Community (see EC and EU)
EC	European Community (see EEC and EU)
EFTA	European Free Trade Area
ELR	Exceptional Leave to Remain
EU	European Union (see EEC and EC)
EVWs	European Volunteer Workers
FN	Front Nationale (National Front, France)
GDR	German Democratic Republic
IAD(s)	Immigration Act Detainee(s)
ICIHI	Independent Commission on International Humanitarian Issues
ILO	International Labour Organisation/Office
IO(s)	Immigration Officer(s)
IND	Immigration and Nationality Department (Home Office)
ISU	Immigration Service Union
IIIU	Illegal Immigration Intelligence Unit (Scotland Yard)
JCRV	Joint Committee for Refugees from Vietnam
JCWI	Joint Council for Welfare of Immigrants
JP(s)	Justice(s) of the Peace (Magistrates)
MEP(s	Member(s) of the European Parliament
MP(s)	Member(s) of Parliament
NAFTA	North American Free Trade Agreement
NATO	North Atlantic Treaty Organisation

OAS	Organisation de l'Armée Secrète (Secret Army Organisation, France)
OECD	Organisation for Economic Co-operation and Development
ON	Ordre Nouveau (New Order, France)
OFPRA	Office Français de Protection des Réfugiés et Apatrides
PC	'politically correct'
POWs	Prisoners of War
PRT	Prison Reform Trust
PTA	Prevention of Terrorism Act
RCG	Revolutionary Communist Group
RLE	'Refused Leave to Enter' (the UK) (those so refused)
RSG	Religious Support Group (see VMDC–RSG)
RSPCA	Royal Society for the Prevention of Cruelty to Animals
SCPS	Society of Civil and Public Servants
SEA(s)	Secondary Examination Area(s)
TREVI	Terrorism, Radicalism, Extremism and International Violence
TUC	Trades Union Congress
UKIAS	United Kingdom Immigration Advisory Service
UMIST	University of Manchester Institute of Science and Technology
UN	United Nations
UNHCR	United Nations High Commission for Refugees
VMDC	Viraj Mendis Defence Campaign
VMDC–RSG	Viraj Mendis Defence Campaign–Religious Support Group
WASP(s)	White Anglo-Saxon Protestant(s)
WEF	World Economic Forum

ACKNOWLEDGEMENTS

The writing of all books incurs debts. I would like warmly to acknowledge the help of a number of friends, colleagues and respondents.

Malcolm Cross provided a detailed critique of the manuscript at a crucial stage. Paul Kennedy and David Goldberg wrote incisive comments in the margins of the draft of my first chapter. Various anonymous readers who acted for the publisher gave me invaluable assistance by quickly pointing to the gaps in my reading and, sometimes, in my logic.

Mandy Little sorted out the contract in her usual, efficient way. Heather Lynn and Ann Shaw were sympathetic librarians. Bob Burgess, Charlie Carman and Chris Harrison piloted the book through Longman. The Home Office Research and Statistics Department checked my figures and updated some with unpublished data. Viraj Mendis and the family of Rajwinder Singh acceded to lengthy interviews. Anton (Manfred) Obholzer kindly sent me Hansards of debates in the House of Lords on the 1993 Asylum Bill. Once again, Selina Cohen provided practical help and moral support even when very pressed with her own work.

Finally, I want to thank members of the Study Leave Committee of the University of Warwick who gave me the time to complete this book. As Britain advances inexorably towards mass higher education combined with lower resources, the possibility of being granted leave to undertake research and to write is a precious privilege that keeps many academics going. Let us hope we can cling on to at least this one remnant of the *ancien régime*.

INTRODUCTION

This book is concerned with the historical, social and political construction of a British identity. The nature and contours of such an identity are exceptionally difficult to describe and analyse. The impenetrability of a specifically *British* (as opposed, for example, to an *English*) identity confronts an author at many turns, and may indeed constitute one of its intrinsic elements. A good example of the opacity of my subject-matter is shown by the recognition of no less than six categories of British nationality in Acts passed during the 1980s – British citizenship, British Dependent Territories citizenship, British Overseas citizenship, British Subject status, British Protected Person status and British National (Overseas) status.

Multiplicity and obscurity at the legal level is paralleled by confusion at the level of public discussion and private belief. How then to proceed? My starting point is that a complex national and social identity is continuously constructed and reshaped in its (often antipathetic) interaction with outsiders, strangers, foreigners and aliens – the 'others'. You know who you are, only by knowing who you are not.

Between the familiar (a word tellingly close to 'familial') and the strange (note again the linguistic affinity to 'stranger'), lies a set of frequently unexplored and unstated frontiers. These boundaries can be crossed at several points of access and linkage, but they also may constitute a formidable barrier to integration and the development of a pluralist society. The more open the frontier the higher the levels of tolerance and association, the more closed the higher the level of xenophobia.

Those who are hostile to the expression of an exclusive British identity – or to the narrower English identity with which it is frequently conflated – often denounce a high level of xenophobia as 'racist'. While I use this term in the text, I do so with caution and discuss my reservations more fully in the concluding chapter. My wariness derives from a belief that the expressions 'racist' and 'racism' are often used thoughtlessly, as mere epithets. If so abused, the terms can serve to mask the dynamic and chameleon-like inventions and re-inventions of a complex social identity. We will need a finely-whetted rapier, not just a clumsy blunderbuss, to penetrate the enigmatic nexus of unease, affinity, antipathy, empathy, conflict and distaste between the British and the rest of humankind.

By analysing the 'frontiers of identity' – frontiers being seen in both a metaphorical and more literal sense – by investigating the outstations, checkpoints and turnstiles where these boundaries are policed, defended and defined, I seek to discern how a Briton gets separated from an alien, an insider from an outsider, a 'self-hood' from an 'other-hood'. In practice, this exercise has involved a combined plan of attack. While the first and last chapters of this book are largely conceptual and theoretical, the bulky filling in the sandwich (Chapters 2–6) remains resolutely historical, empirical and comparative.

It seems odd to have to draw attention to historical evidence and the presentation of actual data, but so many books (in philosophy, sociology, literary theory, politics and cultural studies) are these days pasted together from a few neologisms, a word processing package and some similar books, that my observation appears to be necessary. Certainly, so quixotic and inexact a subject as a British identity cannot be addressed merely by abstract reasoning. Nor can it be apprehended by summarising other writers' 'representations' of reality under the guise of post-modernism, or some other form of non-engagement with the complexities of the contemporary world.

By contrast, I insist that there are *real* agencies and agents involved in the management of the processes of acceptance and rejection of 'the Other': the 'frontier guards', so to speak, of the national identity. These frontier guards include everyone from immigration officers and judges to newspaper editors, Home Office ministers and other politicians, as well as social and political movements that seek to influence the ideological and legal parameters of nationality, citizenship and belonging. Again, there are *real* policies, structures and institutions that constrain the frontier guards' and their victims' freedom of action, and *real* changes in the way these actors, policies and structures have interacted over time. These realities are given full expression in the text.

In summary, the design of the book is as follows:

- In Chapter 1, I provide a conceptually led narrative, tracing the boundaries between British identity and six other identities (those of the Celtic fringe, the Dominions, the Empire and Commonwealth, the Atlantic, the European and the Alien) with which it is intimately connected.

- In Chapter 2, I show how the targets of deportation and expulsion shifted historically and how these changes influenced the definition of who was 'English', then 'British'.

- In Chapter 3, I deal with the issue of asylum. I suggest that the grant of asylum is often less driven by humanitarian impulses, and that Britain's record on asylum is far more equivocal than is commonly believed.

- In Chapter 4, I show how since the effective policing of the frontiers has been established, the detention (and sometimes the subsequent deportation) of non-acceptable strangers has been common. I examine the wartime internments, detentions under the Prevention of Terrorism Acts and the detentions arising from the enforcement of the modern immigration acts.

- In Chapter 5, I investigate the sanctuary and anti-deportation movements in the UK. Regardless of its biblical and Norman sanction, Home Office officials argue that the right of sanctuary does not legally exist in Britain. Based on first-hand observations and interviews, the sanctuary and subsequent deportation of Viraj Mendis is described and analysed.

- In my sixth chapter, the British experience is set within the European context as the immigration practices of the members of the European Union (EU) coalesce around the defence of 'Fortress Europe'. In particular, I examine the migration histories and current levels of tolerance towards immigrants, guest-workers, illegals, refugees, asylum-seekers and diasporic communities in France and Germany. I suggest that an embryonic cross-European status order dividing 'citizens' from 'denizens' (privileged foreigners) and 'helots' (underprivileged aliens), is in the process of developing.

- My final chapter comprises two elements. First, I draw together the theoretical implications of my study in relation to recent discussions of racism, otherness and difference, boundary formation, nationalism and social identity. Second, I include a more personal note showing how classical descriptions of the stranger-host interaction resonate with my own experience.

CHAPTER 1

Six frontiers of a British identity

> ... the English children she met said that colonials couldn't be
> ladies and gentlemen. They weren't English either – only
> British, which was quite different. And they had an awful
> accent. 'I never liked their voices any more than they liked
> mine,' Jean wrote. 'I'm glad to remember I slapped one little
> English girl good and hard once.'
>
> – Angier (1992: 19)

The 'Jean' in my opening quote was the novelist Jean Rhys, whose
biographer depicts her childhood at the turn of the century in the small
Caribbean island of Dominica. Jean was white, but her father apparently had no class, national or racial prejudices, treating white and
black, poor and rich, exactly the same ('he even liked the French').
Her mother, on the other hand, tried to 'make her English' by such
bizarre stratagems as substituting porridge for mangoes at the breakfast
table and forcing her to wear woollen vests in the tropical climate. It is
perhaps not surprising that Jean became more like her father. None the
less she was conscious that 'British' was different from 'English' and
that 'English' carried connotations of class, linguistic and cultural
superiority, from which some people of the same genotype and phenotype were, apparently, excluded.

Jean's line between British and English was drawn in a colonial
setting, but clearly this is just one of several contexts in which a British
identity separates from other sorts of identity. Looking at boundary
divisions within such settings ultimately was to give me my principal
technique to investigate the nature of British identity. But it is perhaps
instructive to note why other possible lines of enquiry led up blind
alleys. Why was it not possible, for example, to evoke some legal
notion of citizenship, or to distinguish some widely-held ideology of
'Britishness' or to turn to some formal constitutional principles? If,
again, it was possible to read off an approximate notion of French
identity from the revolutionary constitution and the *code civil* – which
enunciate unequivocal notions of citizenship and nationality with their
accompanying rights and responsibilities – why was such an endeav-
our so flawed in the case of Britain?

Defining Britishness through citizenship proved particularly fruit-
less. Most inhabitants of the UK attained their 'citizenship' by a legislative sleight-of-hand in the 1948 Nationality Act, not by public
discussion, agitation or revolution. Indeed, we would have to use
inverted commas around the word 'citizenship' precisely to signify

that unlike the French case, where the very notion implies active participation in the body politic, in the UK we are observing a passively-received legal categorisation.

Prior to 1948, those in the British Isles and those in the British Empire were, formally, equal 'subjects' of the Crown. With the impending independence of India and the insistence by the Canadian government that it wished to develop its own immigration practices which might involve the exclusion of British subjects, a more up-to-date and separate status had to be invented for the inhabitants of the UK. Again, as recently as 1 January 1983, most Britons who had been previously described in their passports as 'British Subject: Citizen of UK and Colonies' suddenly acquired the label 'British Citizen'. Nearly all were unaware that any change had been made. Indeed so vague is the understanding of British citizenship among the people who hold it that census-takers have avoided the issue in their decennial exercises. Their pilot questions on the subject had generated confusion and uncertainty.

Given how obliquely legal 'citizenship' had arisen, it is not perhaps surprising that many residues of a prior legal status, 'subject-hood', remain. Even the national government is said to belong to Her Majesty, while ministers of state exercise 'the royal prerogative' in respect of their powers. The Post Office can lose your parcels and (until recently) hospital kitchens could poison you under the protection of 'Crown Immunity'. It may be argued that these are mere historical residues and denote only token power by the Crown. But if we are talking about mere residues, why is it so difficult to provide a simple, up-to-date, definitive statement of the limits to constitutional monarchy, the nature of parliamentary power, the rights and responsibilities that attach to British citizenship and, above all, the parameters of a national identity?

Such an elucidation is hard enough to make even in legal and formal terms, let alone in social scientific terms,[1] and any attempts at definition appear to be strongly resisted by dominant political actors. Perhaps concealment of such matters is deliberate, or at least functional? In his vehement critique of the 'blanketing English fog' that obscures 'any social and historical reality', Perry Anderson (1992: 31) advances just such a suggestion:

---

1 The very notion of a social scientific analysis – commonplace in the USA – jars on the British political élite's ears. This may be because of the need to obscure the real workings of national institutions. Whether this is intentional or merely habitual, it is normal to disavow that the British polity and society can be subjected to a logical and precise analysis. One example must suffice. The first Tory minister of education in the Thatcher government, Sir Keith Joseph (held to be the leading intellectual in the Conservative Party at the time), sought to weaken or close down the Social Science Research Council. When the investigating committee he set up under Lord Rothschild failed to provide any grounds for this action, he extracted his revenge by forcing the organisation to change its name to the Economic and Social Research Council, thereby eliding the politically unacceptable expression 'social science'.

The hegemony of the dominant bloc in England is not articulated in any systematic major ideology, but is rather diffused in a miasma of commonplace prejudices and taboos. . . . Traditionalism and empiricism henceforward fuse as a single legitimating system: traditionalism sanctions the present by deriving it from the past, empiricism binds the future by fastening it to the present. A comprehensive conservatism is the result, covering society with the pall of simultaneous philistinism (towards ideas) and mystagogy (towards institutions), for which England has justly won an international reputation.

If there is 'mystagogy' and 'philistinism' among the English ruling class, it has ramified into both legal definitions and élite and popular understandings of the idea of 'Britishness'. Restated in my terms, the boundaries of British nationality, identity and citizenship are only very imprecisely drawn and understood. This indeterminacy can be thought of as a series of blurred, opaque or 'fuzzy' frontiers surrounding the very fabrication and the subsequent recasting of the core identity.

What do I mean here by 'fuzzy'? I suggest that ambiguity often characterises the boundaries between an English and a British identity (the internal frontier) and between a British and supranational identities (the external frontiers). The concept of 'fuzziness' also draws on the notion of 'fuzzy logic' used by natural scientists, particularly mathematicians, who have a method of proceeding by eliminating the uncertain edges of a problem. This method seems to get results, despite not conforming to formal logic. In aspiration, my notion of a 'fuzzy frontier' has something of the same methodological intent. At the same time, it is important to emphasise that some frontiers (for example, the line that divides Britons from aliens) are less fuzzy than others. Moreover, rather as one can twist the lens of a manual camera to secure greater or lesser definition, the degree of focus along different frontiers of identity can be varied situationally and temporally.

In this chapter I discuss six fuzzy frontiers in turn. First, the Celtic fringe. Second, the heritage of the Dominions. Third, the Empire and non-white Commonwealth. Fourth, the continuing Atlantic and anglophone connection. Fifth, the relationship to an emergent European identity. Finally – a concern that is pursued at greater length in subsequent chapters – the British notion of and relationship to 'aliens'. These six frontiers are illustrated in Figure 1.1 overleaf.

The Celtic fringe

The first fuzzy frontier of identity is within the British Isles itself – where I need to set out the extent of association or distanciation between the Scots, Welsh and Irish (the Celtic fringe) on the one hand and the English on the other.

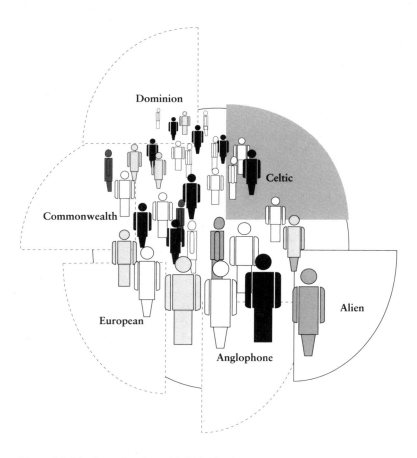

Figure 1.1 The fuzzy frontiers of British identity

The Scots

The Scots have always been regarded with an element of fear and not a little incomprehension by the English. Antoninus's and Hadrian's walls sought to limit the incursions from the northern frontier but failed to prevent wars between the English and the Scots in the Middle Ages. The Crowns of Scotland and England were united in 1603, but not until over a century later (in 1707) were the two parliaments joined under the Treaty of Union.

It is illuminating that it took what at first looked like a photo-finish British election in 1992 for Prime Minister Major to recognise that the long-articulated and widely held Scottish demand for devolution (the nationalists want independence) constituted a significant constitutional crisis. It was not the Scots who were 'sleepwalking' into the new situation, as the prime minister asserted, but the English who, at all key decision-making levels, had been totally oblivious to the nationalist undercurrents of the previous twenty years.

In his path-breaking study of ethnic nationalism within Britain, Nairn (1977: 96–8) traced the origins of separatist and nationalist movements to the uneven impact of industrial capitalism as it spread from its heartlands in England and France around 1800. Nationalism, in Nairn's view, was an inevitable outcome of this uneven development. It is perhaps better to say that it was an inevitable *demand* for, as Nairn himself accepted, a successful nationalism requires a powerful bourgeoisie and an active intelligentsia to act as the medium through which the dilemma of underdevelopment is refracted and articulated. Ignoring the now all-too-frequent cases of sheer revanchism and atavism (seen, for example, in the post-1990 disintegration of Yugoslavia), nationalism thus normally has some practical component. It draws popular and powerful opinions into the idea that a materially-beneficial outcome might result from some form of separatism. The prospect of oil revenues flowing to Edinburgh rather than London, together with the idea of bypassing Westminster in order to effect a direct relationship to Brussels, provides just such a horizon for the Scots in the intermediate future.

The Welsh

The prospect of material advance through separatism is notably less likely in the case of Wales. As Colin H. Williams (1982: 145) has argued:

Generally the advantages of co-operation, even incorporation, outweigh the disadvantages of loss of autonomy for minorities who benefit from access to wider markets, increased standards of living and unfettered participation in the central political system. The interesting feature of Welsh nationalism is not its chequered progress during the twentieth century, but that it should exist at all, given a period of state-wide participation when Welsh-based politicians, and those which [sic] they represent, have enjoyed a disproportionate influence in the development of the United Kingdom.

The perceived benefits gained from the incorporation of Wales have meant that its nationalism has predominantly taken a romantic, cultural form, in contrast to the more hard-headed Scots variety.

The Welsh are also unable to draw on a long history of independence. Despite various military uprisings led by Lord Rhys (in the twelfth century) and Owain Glndwr (in the fifteenth century) the expression of nationhood and independence remained elusive. It was eroded again when the Tudors, a Welsh family based in Anglesey, succeeded to the English throne at the end of the Wars of the Roses. Though providing a line of English monarchs, the Welsh never had an uncontested monarchy themselves. We thus have the paradox that Wales is popularly included in the expression 'United Kingdom', though unlike Scotland it was not a kingdom at all, but, at best, a principality. Again, while it has been many decades since a Welsh family ruled England, Prince Charles, an English Prince, is Prince of Wales.

Without the possibility of Scottish oil-wealth and given the interdependence, indeed virtual complete overlap, of the English and Welsh economies and polities, the pockets of nationalist resistance represented by Plaid Cymru are not regarded as serious threats to the unfettered expression of an English identity. Though resident English families often manifest their resentment at having to learn Welsh in school, this rarely transmutes to a positive recognition of the legitimacy of their neighbours' cultural, linguistic or separatist demands. The Welsh National Eisteddfod – the key annual cultural event founded, it is believed, by Lord Rhys in 1177 – is normally regarded by the English in Wales as quirky, eccentric, or the object of humour. The event is ignored in the English popular media.

One other aspect of nationalism affecting both the Scots and the Welsh is the development of intense sporting competition. As Holt (1990: 7) has shown in his stimulating history of British sport, sporting patriotism did not unify the British nations; rather it resulted in an often bitter reaction to English dominance:

The rise of a new kind of popular 'Welshness' and 'Scottishness' and its expression through rugby and football make British sport unique – in certain events Britain and Northern Ireland compete as a united nation, in others the UK is a federation of four nations each with its own teams; it is as if the French sent representatives from the Languedoc, Britanny and Provence alongside a team from 'France' on the basis that these 'countries' had once been self-governing states.

The Irish

If the force of Scottish nationalism has barely gained recognition in England and Welsh nationalism is regarded as almost harmless, Irish national consciousness has always presented a far greater conundrum to the English. The English incursion stretches as far back as 1171, when Henry I declared himself to be lord of Ireland. Irish resistance to English domination was only suppressed by the brutal campaign of Cromwell (1649–50). Rebellion flared up again in the eighteenth and mid-nineteenth century when the starvation and mass emigration that followed the potato blight were blamed on the rapacious English land-lords. (Ireland has not yet recovered demographically from these events.)

An important barrier between the two nations – and one that prevented a Scots-type union – was the long hostility of the English Crown, and (after Henry VIII) of the newly-established Anglican Church, to Catholicism. Here was the taproot of the English perception of the Irish as troublesome dissenters. The Catholic Relief Act of 1829 (which gave Catholics the opportunity to sit in the central parliament) failed to stem nationalist demands. Gladstone produced two Home Rule Acts and a third that never came into existence because of the outbreak of the First World War. For Sinn Féin this was the moment for armed rebellion and the proclamation of a republic.

Partition, dominion status, then finally, independence followed for the 'south'. The 'north' was allowed to opt out of independence and six of the nine counties of the old Ulster province (mainly Protestant in religious affinity) exercised this right in 1925. Northern Ireland, with its own parliament, was then bolted on to the UK, but in a characteristically nebulous way. The Westminster parliament continues to allow the direct representation of Northern Ireland constituencies (implying that it is an intrinsic part of the UK), yet the mainstream mainland political parties have not so far organised there (implying the opposite). The suspension of the Ulster parliament and the advent of direct rule from Westminster might suggest yet another constitutional status – that of a colony – though this characterisation would be fiercely repudiated by all but the Republicans.

Violence continues on a more or less daily basis in Northern Ireland between the mainland occupying army, the Republicans (proclaiming their defence of the interests of the Catholic minority and their link to the Irish revolutionary tradition) and the Loyalists (who declare their largely unreciprocated fidelity to the UK – or should it be 'the rest of the UK'?)

Despite frequent constitutional tinkering, since 1925 there has been little political discussion on the mainland as to how the communal violence in Northern Ireland is ultimately to be resolved. Only the frequent bombs disrupting life in parts of England – including, in recent years, a mortar shell at 10 Downing Street, a fatal and massive bombing at the Conservative Party conference in Brighton and the murder of two innocent children in Warrington in April 1993 – met with more determined efforts to promote peace towards the end of that year. The limited attempts to effect a settlement in the previous 25 years probably had less to do with the famed English phlegmatism in the face of danger than with their incomprehension of, and impatience with, the Celtic fringe and particularly its Irish component.

In the light of the English governing class's hostility to the Irish, it is especially notable that all the Irish, *including* Eire citizens, have enjoyed both a largely free right of entry to the UK and the right to cast their votes in a UK election. This concession was granted after the split in 1925 and long before the UK and Eire both joined what is now called the European Union (EU). (There were some modest restrictions enforced during the Second World War when some Irish sympathy for the Nazis was evident.) This extraordinary constitutional anomaly seems to have been adopted and accepted over the years with virtually no public discussion of its merits or logic.

Free movement *and* voting rights in national elections for other EU nationals now look visionary in the context of an emerging Europe, despite the normal continental perception that the UK is 'dragging its feet' on European constitutional matters. I can well remember the incredulity of some continental political scientists when I described the arrangement at a conference in Paris in 1992. (Le Pen, the French right-wing populist, proclaims in his campaigns that a vote for 'foreigners' means no less than 'the end of France'.) Is the favourable electoral situation of the Irish on the mainland attributable to tolerance, to the much self-advertised intuitive political skills of the English ruling class, or simply to Perry Anderson's 'blanketing English fog'? I can advance no definitive answer here. However, what we might be observing is a largely unconsidered response to the fuzzy frontier between the southern Irish and the northern Irish on the one hand, and the English on the other.

The Celtic fringe, in short, is a familiar but inexplicit internal boundary. For the English, the boundary is marked by irresolution, un-certainty, incongruity, derogation or humour. 'Humour' (if such it be called) is still directed against the 'dumb Irishman', derogation is still aimed at the Welsh though, in the case of the Scots, ethnic humour has been in rapid decline since North Sea oil has started flowing.

In subsequent sections of this chapter, I concentrate my attention on the interaction between 'the British' and people whose origins or settlement lie outside the British Isles. This does not mean I am insen-sitive to the fact that many of my observations hold by analogy *within* the British Isles. For example, attitudes of extreme xenophobia have been applied by the English to the Irish as well as to external racial minorities and aliens. Formally, however, Section 32 of the 1948 British Nationality Act declared that British protected persons *and* citizens of Eire were *not* aliens. Despite this backhanded compliment, many Irish people understand their history as a 'colonial' one – involving subjection to an alien government. When they live on the mainland, they often do so as invisible sojourners, part of the landscape, but rarely active members of civil and political society.

By contrast, I am also aware that (depending crucially on the period and circumstance discussed) the attitudes and conduct towards outsiders I have described sometimes as 'English' have their larger British manifestations – in so far as these attitudes are shared by others within the Celtic fringe. However, where this is possible, I try to use the terms 'English' and 'British' with some precision.

Class and gender dimensions

Before I turn to the world outside the British Isles, two special features of British identity need comment. First, the expansion of the British abroad in the form of colonies of settlement and Empire often had a differential impact on different classes. It was true that all classes were drawn into expressions of patriotism or jingoism at particular moments – as, for example, in the anti-French sentiments at the time of the Napoleonic wars, during the Fashoda crisis, the Crimean war, at the outbreak of the First World War and during the Falklands crisis.

But the Empire was often an upper- and middle-class quest. Even the colonies of settlement were, for many working-class people, outposts that they were condemned to by poverty, unemployment, orphanhood, homelessness or a vicious judge, rather than being 'undiscovered' frontiers for the brave and patriotic spirits among them. Moreover, the ineptitude and callousness of the British generals towards the conscript troops during the First World War (in the memorable phrase 'Lions led by Donkeys'), often propelled the working-class movement to an insular nationalism rather than to an expansionist jingoism.

If anything, the evolution of a British national and imperial consciousness was even more unevenly articulated in the case of women. The most penetrating accounts of women's national consciousness are confined to English, rather than British, women. In her discussion of the reactions to Governor Eyre's brutality in suppressing the Morant Bay Rebellion in Jamaica in 1865, Catherine Hall (1992: 255–95) shows how two intellectual currents came to be emblematic of two conceptions of an English identity. The first, but weaker, strand was led by John Stuart Mill who had intuited the political connection between the bondage of slavery and the bondage of womanhood. His was a more egalitarian, more feminised and less racist version of an English identity. He and his supporters wanted to prosecute Eyre for his killing and flogging of the Jamaican protesters, who included many women.

By contrast, the other narration of the Jamaican events, supplied by Thomas Carlyle, described Eyre as a 'brave, gentle and chivalrous' man. Despite being a Scot, Carlyle called on the English nation 'which never loved anarchy, nor was wont to spend its sympathy on miserable mad seditions' to be grateful for Governor Eyre's prompt action in overpowering the rioters (p. 283). As Hall argues, the woman, the child, the servant, the employee and the slave were all the brutalised 'others' separated from the manly, independent 'self'. That self was in turn identified with proudly inarticulate but doughty John Bull figures like Eyre who sustained a masculine, ethnocentric and conservative version of Englishness.

But, if Englishwomen were excluded from the John Bull version of Englishness, the unfolding of their public personae was none the less closely associated with expressions of patriotism. As Linda Colley (1992: 236–81) shows, despite many formal restrictions on their civic rights, in practice many Englishwomen gained a separate and recognised voice by supporting the wars against Revolutionary and Napoleonic France. When a small French expeditionary force landed at Fishguard in 1797, it had to be protected from the fury of the local villagers, the women being 'more clamorous and making signs to cut their throats' (pp. 256–7). Throughout the nineteenth century, making flags, banners and warm clothing for the troops, raising wartime subscriptions and providing relief to wounded seamen and soldiers were the principal means whereby women could transcend their confinement in the domestic sphere. With Victoria's accession to the throne, the female Roman emblem for Britain, Britannia, was increasingly clad in sword, shield and armour. In the process Victoria von Saxe-Coburg-Gotha had smoothly moved from German princess to Queen of England and Empress of India.

Fortunately, there were intimations of a less bloodthirsty role too. The male organisers of boycotts of slave-produced sugar found a ready response from many women who refused to serve 'slave sugar' at home and shopped only for 'free sugar'. In this early example of a consumer boycott, women's private and public domains were united but, suggestively, only in the context of an emergent women's and national consciousness articulating with its larger imperial surrounding.

The English and British abroad, the creation of colonies of settlement, plantation colonies and later, a massive Empire, were to be intimately bound up with the construction of the British identity in general, to the frontiers of which I now turn.

The Dominions

The xenophobic right is prone to describe the British Isles as under siege from a horde of restless foreigners about to invade their histori- cally undisturbed homeland. This is a curious myopia as it takes little account of the many early invasions of Britain by the Vikings, the Normans, the Romans and others, or the fact that the British have themselves been highly energetic colonisers of other people's lands. Many of the population invasions of the last 250 years started, not ended, in Britain.

British expansion abroad commenced with the plantation economies initiated under the aegis of mercantile capitalism. The plantations predominantly deployed slave, indentured and contract labourers from Africa and Asia who were regarded as racially inferior. Their subordi- nation was regarded as morally permissible. However, it is perhaps important to remember Eric Williams's (1964: 7) non-racial corrective that, 'Unfree labour in the New World was brown, white, black and yellow; Catholic, Protestant and pagan'. He shows how 'redemption- ers', convicts and white servants from Ireland, Britain, Portugal, Madeira and elsewhere, were sent to the West Indies before the plan- ters turned to Africa. (Small, pathetic communities descended from these groups, like the 'Red Legs' of Barbados, still survive today.)

However, the bulk of British migrants went not to plantation colo- nies, but to the United States and to what are sometimes described as 'the colonies of settlement'. These were New Zealand, Canada, Australia, Rhodesia and South Africa. What linked these countries together was that in each territory the British migrants were ultimately numerous enough or powerful enough to assert, or try to assert, inde- pendence from the motherland and hegemony over the indigenous populations. In short, the settlers captured the political institutions from the colonial power (sometimes only for a short while) and sought to deny access to those institutions to the local inhabitants. Most of the countries mentioned became Dominions in a formal sense between the two world wars, but the description can be used more analytically (dominions with a small 'd'), as it aptly captures the superordination that the settlers sought to assert.

The USA is probably the most successful example of a dominion society in this latter sense, in that it relatively easily shook off vacillat- ing British rule during the American Revolution and widened its frontiers to include large parts of Spanish Mexico. Other settler domin- ions also established their right to self-government, in each case (and like in the USA) with deleterious effects to the indigenous populations. The British in Australia killed the Aborigines and virtually destroyed their way of life; the British in New Zealand crippled Maori culture; the Canadians forced the Inuit peoples into reservations. To each of these three countries the British government accorded formal Domin- ion status – i.e. self-government and a franchise to the settlers – while showing only token regard for the native peoples.

In all the dominions, a 'British' identity became hegemonic. English and Welsh law, the English language, the Anglican church, English sporting traditions,[2] and Westminster-style political institutions either became paramount or were accorded a high status.

Settlers fared less well in the remaining dominions and colonies to which the British migrated. In Kenya, the Mau Mau put paid to a wild attempt by the tiny settler group to declare 'white independence'; instead decolonisation placed power in the hands of the black élite. In Rhodesia, Ian Smith managed to sustain a Unilateral Declaration of Independence for about a decade, but he too was finally laid low by the force of an armed African struggle.

In South Africa, that most difficult of countries to classify and typologise, the construction of a pure dominion society was inhibited by the contrary pulls of Boer and British ambitions (demonstrated by the Anglo–Boer War of 1899–1902), and by the counterforce of African arms. Whereas the Boers organised successful shooting parties against the helpless San and Khoi-khoi (known in politically incorrect days as the Bushmen and Hottentots), the Zulu impis proved rather more formidable opponents. The fate of settler society in South Africa now hangs in the balance. Whereas the European population's political monopoly is now nearly at an end, its social and economic dominance is nevertheless likely to remain important.

Given the highly variable and often costly outcomes of the movement of European settlers to dominion or aspirant-dominion societies and the historical association between large populations and big-power status, it is perhaps worth reflecting for a moment why British governments generally encouraged the movement of Britons abroad. In essence, emigration to the settler countries was seen both as a solution to social problems at home and a means of expanding English interests abroad. This notion was first advanced in a state paper delivered to James I by Bacon in 1606. He suggested that by emigration England would gain, 'a double commodity, in the avoidance of people here, and in making use of them there' (cited E. Williams 1964: 10). The poor rates and overpopulation would be relieved and idlers, vagrants and criminals would be put to good use elsewhere.

---

2   English rather than British here, as the sporting traditions of the Celtic fringe diverge radically. The Gaelic Athletic Association, for example, banned all non-indigenous games from 1887. Holt (1990) maintained that sport provided the crucial function of promoting loyalty to the Empire by colonial whites (and also by native élites). Cricket, athletics and rugby – the sports of the *English* public schools – were vigorously promoted in the Empire and Dominions. (Football was too 'working-class'.) Partly because of the presence of non-British whites, the French Canadians, these sports did not 'catch on' in Canada. On the other hand, despite John Buchan's disparaging remark that the Afrikaners of South Africa 'were not a sporting race', the Boers took to rugby with such avidity and determination that the mauling scrum became a crucial ritual through which their deep resentment against the British was expressed.

Once established, the principle was extended laterally. Scottish crofters, troublesome Irish peasants, dissident soldiers (like the Levellers) all were shipped out with careless abandon. Even the reverses of British power in the United States were attributed not to a design fault in its pro-emigration policies, but to the incompetence and capriciousness of the German monarch on the British throne at the time of the American Revolution (the first in his line, incidentally, who could speak some English). The movement to encourage the export of the surplus British population reached its apogee in the work of the Cambridge professor of history, Sir John Seeley, who, in his book *The Expansion of England* (1883), identified emigration as the key means of effecting British imperial designs.

The relationship between the British at home and their dominion–diaspora abroad has been cemented by ties of kinship, economic interdependence and preferential trade arrangements, by sport, by visits and tourism, and by the solidarity wrought by the sharing of arms in two world wars and other encounters like the Korean conflict. Until quite recently many New Zealanders, Canadians, Australians and white South Africans and Rhodesians/Zimbabweans stubbornly clung on to British passports as a means of affirming their British identity and hedging their political bets. Young men and women from the British diaspora abroad still often spend a *rite de passage* year in England. (They concentrate with a remarkable lack of imagination in Earl's Court in London: the nearest area between Heathrow and central London with a large rental market.)

Education, legal training and certification also bonded the dominions (and the Commonwealth more generally) to 'the mother country'. One small example is the Rhodes scholarship programme, which draws young men from the white dominions and the United States to Rhodes House in Oxford. The programme was endowed by the famous British imperialist to celebrate the achievements of the British abroad and secure a cohort of key administrators for the Empire. (Only a miniscule number of black and female Commonwealth scholars were accorded recognition.)

The attempt to cling to a linked British home and diasporic identity defined primarily by descent and racial phenotype, was, however, to be severely challenged on a number of fronts.

First, it proved difficult to be too racially specific – the wider Commonwealth comprised a brown and black Empire as well as the zones of white settlement. Indeed the very *raison d'être* and guiding vision of the post-1948 Commonwealth was that it was a *multiracial* association of states with a common historical link to Britain. So crucial was the ideological commitment to multiracialism that the 'white' members of the Commonwealth had to concur in the decision to expel South Africa for its apartheid policies in 1961. Continuing Commonwealth boycotts and sanctions against South Africa and the denunciation of Ian Smith's ultimately doomed attempt to declare unilateral white rule in Rhodesia reinforced the message. (On the other hand, the continuing pull of racial affinity was shown in the British government's reluctance to send UK troops to Rhodesia to put down the rebellion of its own 'kith and kin', a phrase that gained currency at the time.)

Second, with the postwar movement of Commonwealth citizens from India, Pakistan and the Caribbean to Britain, it became increasingly difficult to uphold the idea that a British identity was exclusively a white identity. In short, with decolonisation and non-white Commonwealth immigration, another fuzzy frontier had appeared. Although I will expand on this theme in other chapters, here it should be noted that a number of determined attempts were made in postwar British immigration law and practice to bolster the myth of a racially exclusive British identity. In brief, the four main legislative interventions were:

- In the British Nationality Act of 1948 the status of a 'Citizen of the UK and Colonies' was invented. This was distinguished from the older category of 'British subject' (who still had rights of abode in the UK), and also from a 'British subject without citizenship'. This last category applied mainly to people from India and Pakistan, who were henceforth subject to immigration controls.
- The 1962 Commonwealth Immigrants Act was introduced as a means of controlling non-white Commonwealth immigration. Henceforth, most Commonwealth citizens were subject to immigration control and had to obtain a Ministry of Labour employment voucher in order to enter the UK.[3]
- The intriguing concept of 'patriality' – a word apparently not previously in any dictionary, but rather coined by an official in the Home Office – was introduced in the 1971 Immigration Act. It allowed the right of abode in Britain to citizens of the UK and Colonies and Commonwealth citizens who had a parent or grandparent who was *born* in the UK. This massively widened, on essentially racial grounds, the categories of non-patrial citizens of the UK and Colonies, non-patrial Commonwealth citizens and British Subjects without citizenship, who henceforth had no right of entry to the UK.

---

3   In his Conservative Political Centre pamphlet published seven years later, William Deedes (1968: 10), a minister without portfolio in 1961, explicitly admitted: 'The Bill's real purpose was to restrict the influx of coloured immigrants. We were reluctant to say as much openly. So the restrictions were applied to coloured and white citizens in all Commonwealth countries – though everybody recognised that immigration from Canada, Australia and New Zealand formed no part of the problem.' Deedes's racially tinted glasses saw dominion immigration as 'no part of the problem' even though in the early 1960s the total number of migrants admitted and embarked and the total number of immigration 'evasions' were greater for the three old dominions named than for the rest of the Commonwealth combined (Patterson 1969: 31–5).

- The British Nationality Act of 1981 (which came into force on 1 January 1983) proliferated the number of British 'citizenships' without right of entry and also introduced, for the first time in British immigration history, the notion of *jus sanguinus* (the law of blood). Since 1983, people born in Britain of non-British citizens do not automatically acquire British nationality and citizenship. Though small numbers are involved, the compelling and long-standing principle that birthplace confers citizenship (*jus soli*), has been breached.

Despite these and other zealous measures designed to buttress a racially-based British identity which fused white Britons to their diaspora in the dominions, a third and final factor undercut any neat correspondence between Britishness and whiteness. I allude to seismic shifts in the postwar international political economy, which impacted both on the UK and on the white British diaspora.

The UK's historic decision to enter the European Economic Community (now the EU) swept away any realistic possibility (though not the pretence) that it could maintain an independent world role. Public rhetoric that Commonwealth interests would be safeguarded was recognised, even at the time, as empty and tokenistic. As discussed below, British identity was now to be entangled and constrained along another fuzzy frontier – that of a European identity.

Events of similar impact were affecting the old white dominions. For the Canadians, already heavily intermeshed with the USA, although with a distinctive state ideology of multiculturalism, negotiating the North American Free Trade Agreement (NAFTA) in 1991 was seen as a sad though inevitable result of their geopolitical situation. The minority British diasporic communities in Zimbabwe, and increasingly in South Africa, are gradually being corralled into accepting black majority rule. Thousands, perhaps even tens of thousands, may take up their opportunity to live in the UK, but over the next generation many will lose their 'patrial' rights and will slowly adopt a single, local citizenship. Australia and New Zealand still have close cultural, familial, sporting and linguistic ties to 'the mother country', but the entry of the UK to the European Economic Community (EEC) represented a brutal familial rupture. Wool, butter and lamb exports were immediately affected, but the abandonment of the Commonwealth as an economic unit also had a profound psychological effect, particularly in Australia. Prime Minister Keating's angry outburst in April 1992 that Britain had deserted Australia in the Second World War by its precipitate withdrawal from the Far East was yet another slash at the old umbilical cord. New Australians from southern Europe and Asia rarely share the British link, republican sentiment is growing and the country increasingly relates more to the Pacific Rim and *its* hegemonic power, Japan.

The diasporic identity

Until these more recent events, the British abroad provided a crucial expression of (and gave vital reinforcement to) the evolution of a British identity in general and an English identity in particular. Like other diasporic communities, exaggerated mannerisms and demonstrations of patriotism often made the English abroad more English than the English at home. And, despite the distinction that Jean Rhys found in Dominica at the turn of the century, the separate English and Celtic identities were more easily overcome abroad than at home.

The exaggeration of metropolitan manners, particularly in the case of the English, but not forgetting instances like the 'kilt culture' of the overseas Scots, derived directly from the imperial heritage – the heritage of the quasi-aristocratic rule over 'the natives'. Again Perry Anderson (1992: 32) provides a penetrating insight into the origins of this manifestation of overseas 'Britishness':

> The administration of an empire comprising a quarter of the planet required its own special skills. Imperialism automatically sets a premium on a patrician style. . . . Domestic domination can be realised with a popular and egalitarian appearance, colonial never: there can be no plebeian proconsuls. In an imperial system, the iconography of power is necessarily aristocratic.

Those old enough to have observed the British colonial administration at work would be struck by the force of Anderson's observation. In remote regions of Africa, Asia and the Caribbean middle-class English administrators affected the manners of lords. Even working-class Britons who fled postwar Britain for the easy lifestyle available in southern Africa in the 1950s and 1960s soon adopted the overbearing *hauteur* of a racial élite. The misapprehensions derived from the colonial experience of patricianship were also demonstrated by African and Asian students and visitors to the UK who were often surprised to find a normal occupational structure (white rubbish collectors, milkmen, etc.), and shocked to see the circumstances to which their former overlords had been reduced in their home country.

As to excessive patriotic devotion in the British diaspora, let me use a family story to illustrate this feature. My wife was born into an anglophone family in South Africa, one side of which had strong British connections. Her grandfather, an English colonel who had served in the Cape Mounted Rifles in the Boer War, gathered his six South African-born grandchildren around him to listen to the commentary on the Queen's coronation in 1953. 'Salute, damn you,' the red-faced old man thundered. The six bemused children had to stand to attention and solemnly salute the crackly valve-radio.

The automatic and unthinking affinity between the British diasporic communities and 'home' as evidenced by the colonel is now largely gone. It addressed a vital nerve centre in the British identity, one that crucially coupled patricianship abroad to upper-class pretensions and mannerisms at home. The Britain that the British diaspora looked to was dominated by English aspirations and signified by the monarchy, the gentlemen's clubs, the benign feudalism of P. G. Wodehouse's novels, the *Spectator* and the *Daily Telegraph* (for the 'intellectuals'), *Punch* and the *Daily Mail* (for the not-so-cerebral), cricket at Lords, Henley, Wimbledon, prep. and boarding schools, and the many other small nuances of dress, vocabulary, accent, manner and recreation that bipolarised the class structure. By signalling their putative association with the English, upper part of that class structure at home, the British abroad were thereby also engaging in the much-venerated, and sometimes deadly serious, pastime of upward social climbing.

The diasporic boundary of British identity, particularly that part powerfully impregnated with class pretensions, is rapidly fading without the sustenance wrought by the intimate connection between the mother country on the one hand and the Empire and dominions on the other. As it used to state on its banner-head, the *Daily Mail* was founded by Harmsworth to proclaim 'The Power, the Supremacy and the Greatness of the British Empire'. Its editorials now rarely rise above crude anti-EU and anti-Labour Party campaigns. *Punch* published its last issue in 1992. The library of the Royal Commonwealth Society, an old watering hole of dominion academics, sold up in the next year.

The echoes of worldwide racial bonding were still evident in the Falklands campaign and in the activation of the British diasporic vote for the Conservative Party in the 1992 general election. But black immigration to the UK, macro-changes in the world situation of Britain and its former dominions and the evolution of the Empire into a multiracial Commonwealth have fragmented the unquestioned nature of the racial boundary of British identity. It is to the non-white Commonwealth frontier that I next turn.

Empire and Commonwealth

Global British economic supremacy in the nineteenth century was not solely based on the export of its population abroad. Mercantilism, then dominance in international free trade, had already given British manufacturers a decisive competitive advantage in key commodities – tobacco, sugar, slaves, cotton and early manufactures.

What is called the 'high' imperialism of the 1870s and 1880s was not so much an economic apotheosis (as Lenin supposed), as an ideological and political one. This was dramatically affirmed by Queen Victoria being accorded the vainglorious title of Empress of India, while the Indian Durbar was indigenised and reconstituted as a home grown Jubilee (P. Anderson 1992: 25).

The Empire functioned, therefore, not only or not even primarily to cement Britain's economic interests: indeed the amount of non-Empire investment in Argentina, the USA and Russia exceeded the total invested in the Empire at the turn of the twentieth century. What empire did was to establish a cultural and national superiority of worldwide proportions: an empire where, truly, the sun never set. The British were the new chosen people. Their assigned task was to conduct a civilising mission at the frontiers of all humanity. They were enjoined to shoulder, in Kipling's famous phrase, 'the white man's burden'.

At first, the British expansionists abroad seemed incapable of rising to Kipling's task – English pirates in the Caribbean seemed almost excessively bloodthirsty; they plundered and stole as well as any Spanish *conquistador* and often engaged in more gratuitous violence. In the Far East, the depredations of the East India Company and the corruption and conspicuous consumption of the Nabobs reached historic heights. With rare exceptions of cultural broad-mindedness, such as that exhibited by Governor-General Warren Hastings, the Company's officials in India manifested a crude social Darwinism in their treatment of others. As a nineteenth-century correspondent for *The Times* (cited Little 1947: 213) declared:

I must say that I have been struck with the arrogant and repellent manner in which we often treat natives of rank and with the unnecessary harshness of our treatment of inferiors. The most scrubby mean little representative of *la race blanche* . . . regards himself as infinitely superior to the Rajpoot with a genealogy of 1,000 years.

This report is telling also both because of the careful note that there *were* Indians of rank and because of the apparently ingenuous lapse into French – the hidden implication being that it was already somehow shameful for a British person to be exhibiting naked racial sentiments, an explicitness best left to foreigners.

Shameful it may have become, but only because the British in India were given a painful lesson they never forgot. In 1857 what the Indians call the 'Indian National Rising' and the British 'the Mutiny' totally shattered the aplomb of the Company officials. This was a watershed event which ramified throughout colonial administrations for decades. From then on, it was apparent to all, not least the British officials themselves, that an empire could only be maintained by the cultivation of the local élites, the practice of honest government, the bestowing of equal justice and the appearance of non-racialism and non-sectarianism.

In announcing the end of Company rule in India and the immediate commencement of Direct Rule by the Crown, Queen Victoria's Proclamation of November 1857 exactly captured the post-Mutiny spirit:

We hold ourselves bound to the natives of our Indian territories by the same obligations of duty which bind us to all our subjects, and these obligations, by the Almighty God, we shall faithfully and conscientiously fulfil. ... We declare it to be our royal will and pleasure that none be in any wise favoured, none molested or disquieted, by reason of their religious faith or observances, but that all shall alike enjoy the equal protection of the law (cited Visram 1986: 7).

Like all colonialisms and imperialisms, British expansion abroad attracted its fair share of opprobrium from the nationalist movements, emerging particularly after the Second World War. This criticism was nearly always just. There was arrogance and cruelty, economic exploitation and a supreme indifference to suffering in the name of racial and cultural difference. Social Darwinism gained a new lease of life in Africa where the inhabitants were often conceived of as inferiors, brutes or naive children. And in the privacy of colonial clubs, prejudice and snobbery were rife.

But Queen Victoria's legacy was a powerful and, in the end, a dominant one. Her heritage is still acknowledged in former colonial countries in the reverence for the Indian Civil Service, the continuation of British judicial traditions and the deference paid to the culture of fairness, of equal access to the powerful and the courteous treatment of petitioners. The collapse of many Commonwealth African countries into one-party, no-party or military dictatorships would seem to belie this comment, but all these misfortunes prove is that people often aspire to far more than they achieve. The current movement for democracy in Africa demonstrates the still continuing attraction of the best parts of the colonial legacy. As Goulbourne (1991: 81), a political scientist with extensive experience in Africa and the Caribbean, contends:

... in the end the overwhelming majority of new and independent states have been proud to be part of the British Commonwealth of nations. ... [Through peaceful decolonisation] Britain has retained a paramount status whilst the former colonies have become respected members of the world community of 'nation-states'. In effect, the ex-colonies have been able to transform themselves and display the (British) ability for political compromise. Much goodwill remained (and probably still remains despite what is widely regarded by Commonwealth members as Margaret Thatcher's, paradoxically, non-British behaviour) between Britain and her former colonies.

Goulbourne's observations are pertinent in discussing one of the great counter-factual suppositions of the postwar period. Why did successive British governments not take advantage of the great opportunity offered to transform the prevailing goodwill, as well as the economic, sporting and cultural ties within the Commonwealth, into a powerful, global trading bloc?

Superficially, this would have been a highly attractive possibility. India's market alone is now three times the size of the EU's: its cottons and manufactures are making it into a formidable economic power. The energetic Commonwealth newly industrialising countries (Singapore, Malaysia, Hong Kong) have virtually rewritten the economic textbooks in being able to sustain high growth rates with minimal natural resources. The old white dominions, a South Africa under majority rule (the African National Congress will rejoin the Commonwealth), a minerals and resource-rich Africa: all this could have made the Commonwealth a global bloc more powerful than the three current contenders – NAFTA, the EU and the Pacific Rim under the hegemony of Japan.

Why did this not happen? One temptation is to attribute failure solely to malice, prejudice or incompetence in Britain. This would be unfair. When the first key turning point arrived, with the impending independence of India, Nehru and others in the Congress Party became suspicious of the British government's motivations, thinking that the Commonwealth could turn into a disguised perpetuation of Empire. A decade later, Nkrumah, then the dominant African nationalist leader, saw 'neocolonialism' as the main danger to Africa. Nearly all the newly emergent independent states of Africa and Asia looked towards a diplomatic future that was more diverse and nonaligned. Only the anglophone Caribbean countries were ideologically committed members of a greater Commonwealth. There too the notion of a Commonwealth citizenship survived for longer – though it finally collapsed in the face of UK indifference and micro-nationalism in the region.

While I argued that the British government should not be *solely* blamed for missing a great historic opportunity, this should not obscure the fact that there was a notable lack of conviction in the future of the Commonwealth in leading ruling circles in the UK. The Foreign Office was dominated by Atlanticists, Europeanists and Arabists. The military umbrella of the Americans, trade with Europe, unimpeded oil supplies from the Middle East – these were the sacred cows dictating foreign policy after 1945.

As with much else in Britain, issues of principle were also clouded by class sentiments. It would not, I think, be too much of an exaggeration to assert that the predominantly upper-class, Oxford-trained, Foreign Office officials despised the boys in khaki shorts and bush-hats from middle-class homes who staffed the Colonial Office. Much of this battle was internal, a silent class struggle, but it was not long before the victors emerged. The Colonial Office was closed as a separate entity, and absorbed (the relationship was too asymmetrical to be called 'merged') into its rival under the name of the Foreign and Commonwealth Office. Then, at least in popular usage, the embarrassing tail was dropped and the pristine redesignation 'the Foreign Office' emerged supreme.

It is well known that Prime Minister Thatcher had scant regard for the toffs in the Foreign Office, but they were treated with kid gloves compared to the contempt for the Commonwealth she displayed. Perhaps the most memorable incident was when she emerged from a Commonwealth conference in Bermuda with the announcement that she had rejected the demand for increased sanctions against South Africa. Forefinger opposing thumb, she intoned to the world's media that only the 'tiniest, tiniest' sanctions would be accepted by the British government. Not only had the British prime minister flagrantly violated the Commonwealth leaders' convention of 'agreed statements only', she had sent a clear signal to her followers. Decoded, the message read: 'No bunch of wogs are going to push *me* around; if I want to support the white South Africans, I'll bloody well do it.'

Even if other powerful British decision-makers were not so crude as the redoubtable Mrs Thatcher, the Commonwealth was regarded largely as of sentimental value only. In 1993, the Commonwealth Institute, the flagship building of the organisation in London, could not secure a Foreign Office grant adequate to keep its fabric from rotting away. Few – the Queen herself was a notable exception – saw the possibilities for using the Commonwealth to establish a competitive trading bloc. Instead, *realpolitik* dictated a continuing and enhanced alliance with the USA (Mrs Thatcher, a convinced Atlanticist, vigorously supported this tendency), or a fateful and final commitment to Europe (the line backed by the Foreign Office and most business and financial opinion). It is to the fuzzy frontiers of the USA and Europe that I next turn.

The Atlantic and anglophone connection

From 1820 to 1927 some 37 million migrants arrived in the United States, some 32 million of whom arrived directly from Europe (Power 1979: 10). They came predominantly from Great Britain, France, Germany, Russia, Austro–Hungary and Italy. The migrants and their descendants rapidly built up the population of the country. In 1800 the US population was only 5.3 million; by 1905 it had reached 105.7 million people (Potts 1990: 131). The newcomers immediately adopted their country of settlement as their own with scant regard to the rights of the native Americans and a certain disdain for settlers of non-European origin.

Although many scholars have rightly questioned the extent to which the newcomers were able or willing to discard their prior ethnic identities, the ideology of Americanisation was none the less powerful enough for the immigrants to assert a collective citizenship. The governing spirit is well captured by the monologue by the pogrom orphan of Israel Zangwill's 1908 hit play, *The Melting Pot*:

America is God's crucible, the great Melting Pot where all the races of Europe are melting and reforming! Here you stand ... in your fifty groups with your fifty languages and histories, and your fifty blood hatreds and rivalries, but you won't be long like that brothers, for these are the fires of God you've come to – the fires of God. A fig for your feuds and vendettas! German and Frenchmen, Irishmen and Englishmen, Jews and Russians – into the Crucible with you all. God is making the American (cited Glazer and Moynihan 1963: 289–90).

Perhaps it was divine intervention that fashioned the American, but God seems to have used a mould patented by the Virginia Company of London, whose charter for the 'Habitation and Plantation' of Virginia was granted by James I in 1606. Essentially, the design was that of a dominion society in the analytical sense I have outlined earlier. This was evidenced in the charter by the insistence that the king's subjects who settled in the colony *and* their offspring were to retain their 'Liberties, Franchises and Immunities, with any of our other Dominions, to all Intents and Purposes, as if they had been abiding and born within this our Realm of England' (cited Ringer 1983: 39).

As Ringer shows elsewhere in his account, the English created a society in the New World which was predicated on their racial, religious, national and linguistic heritage. In the Declaration of Independence, in the Constitution, in the processes that transformed the thirteen original colonies into a federated nation-state, the notion of 'We, the People' constituted an undisguised colonial presumption, an ethno-national putsch. For 'the People' were none other than the English settlers. The true First Nations, the native inhabitants (misleadingly labelled 'Indians' by Columbus, who thought America was India) were treated with violence, force or fraud. Africans were dehumanised and enslaved.

As the nineteenth- and twentieth-century mass immigration to the USA shifted the white ethnic balance from English to British, from British to northern European, from northern European to southern European, it became increasingly difficult for the English to maintain an unchallenged hegemony. Moreover, as historians of Hispanic America (for example, Samora and Simon 1977) have reminded us, a large part of the history of the USA consisted of the movement of Hispanic peoples into the southwest and did not simply comprise the settlement of the eastern seaboard and its subsequent westward expansion.

Despite this felicitous corrective, it is remarkable none the less how dominant the institutions developed by the English settlers remained. Cohort after cohort of bemused eastern and southern Europeans wrestled with the English language at night schools supported by public grants. (Leo Rosten's comic sketch, *The Education of Hyman Kaplan*, provides a hilariously painful account of the encounter between a Jewish immigrant and his English teacher.) Henry Ford employed sociologists and social workers to habituate and anglicise his workers. The courts, public education, the acknowledgement of the dominance of WASPs (White Anglo-Saxon Protestants) in the status hierarchy, the desperate genealogical searches for respectable English ancestors –all this signified the continuing potency of English colonisation. In a number of the snob 'Ivy League' universities, Jews and blacks were excluded from teaching appointments until the 1950s and 1960s.

The Boston Tea Party signalled the end of British political domination in the USA, but the frontier of identity derived from the dominance of the English language, together with the many institutions bequeathed by the English settlement, have left an indelible mark.

The English language itself was crucial to the continuing vitality of this frontier. Britain's nineteenth-century imperial mission and the twentieth-century corporate global reach of the USA have both been expressed in a tenaciously monoglot English. I accept, of course, that American English has now diverged considerably from BBC English – why else would Churchill utter his well-known aphorism that Britain and the USA were 'two countries divided by a common language'? However, this did not prevent 'the greatest living Englishman' from communicating with his American mother, just as the British manage to interact with American guests, tourists, politicians, generals, traders, bankers and industrialists. This ease of communication and the historic links between a former dominion society and its motherland largely account for the so-called 'special relationship' between the USA and the UK.

The fact that the English language has been made so dominant by Britain in the last century and the USA in the current century, has forced even powerful national actors – the Germans, the Japanese, the French, the Spanish and the Italians – on to the defensive. Despite their claims none of their languages, with the possible exception of Spanish, has the status of a world language: increasingly international commerce, law, business and (to the *chagrin* of the French) diplomacy, are conducted in English. In order to ensure fluency in the emergent global *lingua franca*, smaller nations like the Dutch are actively considering abolishing teaching in Dutch in the universities in favour of English.

The adoption of the English language and the continuing relevance of the British colonial period in US institutions and in its status order, has given to the British identity an ego injection of considerable potency. It would show utter naiveté for any British government to believe that US administrations do not act solely on behalf of the USA's own interests. The USA was reluctant to get into the Second World War and only did so when its Pacific claims were immediately threatened,

Eden's colonial adventure at Suez was denounced by the USA, George Bush quickly saw that the German government was the pivotal actor in Europe, not Whitehall. But despite these fallouts and the challenge from recent ideologies of multiculturalism, a cousin-hood between the British and many Americans remains: a fuzzy frontier somewhere between a self-hood and an other-hood.

As to the future of the English language, linguists propose two possible outcomes. The first is the Latin analogy, where languages of a common origin localise and become mutually unintelligible Creoles. The second can be called 'the amoeba scenario', with a comprehensible English spreading to all who are enmeshed in the nexus of an international society, polity, culture and economy. Without having the professional qualifications to assert this with certainty, I suspect the second outcome is far more likely. Major powers (the pre-1989 Soviet Union, China) were already constrained to run English-language radio stations to get their message across. Equally, travel and tourism, the electronic and printed media, software packages and instruction booklets – all are overwhelmingly dominated by the English language.

A curious disjuncture then arises: i.e. Britain's linguistic centrality gives to it the status of a fountainhead of primary, global significance. On the other hand the most expressive and ambitious uses of the English language are shifting outside England. (It is rare, for example, for an English-born writer to win the prestigious Booker literary prize.) Equally Britain's industrial and commercial strengths place it a little lower than halfway down the list of major industrial countries.[4] Put another way, Britain's international purchasing power is considerably lower than its communication power. Could this be the underlying reason why Britons abroad have to speak English a little louder when they are not clearly understood?

Britain in Europe

'Foreigners start at Calais' goes the blunt slogan of British and English nativism. This insular sentiment has indeed made a lasting impression

---

4   Using conventional economic measures, the 1992 figures issued by the Organisation for Economic Co-operation and Development showed the UK ranking as tenth out of the OECD's membership of eighteen. More complex measures are provided in the 1992 *World Competitiveness Report* produced by the Word Economic Forum (together with a Lausanne-based management school). In the overall ranking the UK came thirteenth out of twenty-two. These scores simply confirm the long-term relative decline of the UK noticed by economic historians, most of whom would date the start of this process to about 1900–1910. Fierce political discussion in Britain continues as to which administration, Tory or Labour, has delivered, or is likely to produce, a better growth rate. In fact, over the long term, there is little evidence to suggest that the mediocre performance of the economy varies greatly with either party.

on the continent of Europe. The British are seen by many on the continent – in political circles, in the continental media and in the popular
consciousness – as reluctant Europeans, stubbornly monolingual, still
tied to the dreams of Empire and to the apron strings of the USA.

The continental politician who expressed this most openly was
Charles de Gaulle, who was implacably opposed to Britain joining the
EEC. This opposition was predicated on a clear national interest – the
Franco–German alliance neatly protected German industry in
exchange for the subsidisation of French agriculture. But de Gaulle's
opposition was also based on a principled vision of Europe – a zone of
peace, a bloc between the blocs and, in particular, the bonding of a set
of countries that did not have to depend on the goodwill of the USA.
For him, admitting the UK to the European club was as foolish as the
Trojans breaking down their city walls to admit the wooden horse of
the Athenians.

It is difficult, in retrospect, to fault de Gaulle's logic. At the industrial level, much indigenous UK manufacturing capital has collapsed,
been switched to third countries or to speculative punting in the City.
Inward manufacturing investment to the UK came mainly from the
USA and Japan, countries anxious to establish an export platform in
Europe. One can perhaps understand the apprehensions and anger of
the French or Italian car manufacturers and buyers when they are
confronted with 'transplant' factories in the UK like Ford (always
owned by Ford USA), Vauxhall (acquired by General Motors in the
1970s), Jaguar (purchased by Ford in the 1980s), and the Honda–
Rover partnership (now challenged by Germany through BMW's
majority stake in the company announced in January 1994). The direct
transplants, Nissan and Toyota, are likely to be major players in the
European market. Even if the Volkswagens, Fiats, Peugeots and
Renaults compare favourably and sometimes compete successfully in
the British and continental markets, by encouraging the development
of the 'transplants', British industrial policy seems to have frustrated
the very purpose of the original EEC, i.e. to create a trading bloc
excluding Japan and the USA.

In respect of monetary policy, social policy, defence postures and
immigration matters, Britain is also frequently in a minority of one.
Indeed, for about a decade the UK government's posture was reminis-
cent of the proud mother's comment while she watches a military
parade: 'All out of step but my Jimmie,' she boasts. While space
forbids a full analysis of the British position on European issues, a few
comments on the broad differences between the postures of 'the 11
plus the 1',[5] will be illustrative:

---

5   I understand this was, at first, Jacques Delors's private phrase. *The Sun* showed its
    unerring grossness and lack of diplomatic sense by running a sustained nativist 'Up
    Yours, Delors' campaign in 1991/2. This, *inter alia*, featured a rally of readers at
    Trafalgar Square and an immense front-page photograph showing two 'patriotic'

- By defending an anachronistic role for sterling and showing a lack of interest in a common European currency, the current British administration has secured some immediate flexibility in *monetary policy,* but has lost any prospect of long-term support from the key continental central banks and was forced to accept that the new European bank would be located in Frankfurt rather than in the City.
- Britain's opposition to European *social policy* includes the principled position that British workers should be free to work more than 48 hours a week, a notion that the '11' think smacks of the nineteenth century. In so far as they can attribute rationality to the British government's hostility to the Social Chapter of the Maastricht Treaty, they assume it is to continue to cheapen the costs of British labour to attract further non-EU investment.
- In its *defence policy*, Britain is trying to buttress the North American Treaty Organisation (NATO) and the Western European Union (whose Standing Armaments Committee is tied closely into NATO) against Franco–German plans to set up an independent European command structure. In other words, the British government is doing just what de Gaulle predicted by refusing to co-operate in setting up a European army command. In frustration, the German and French governments have set up a small joint force.
- The foreign secretary (and former home secretary), Douglas Hurd, has made repeated statements that Britain's *immigration policy* will include the mounting of independent immigration checks on other EU nationals (excluding, as mentioned earlier, Eire citizens). The reason advanced for this flagrant violation of its treaty obligations was that Britain 'is an island'. This *non sequitur* is an unusually clear example of mystagogy that the '11' cannot penetrate.

Only in the matter of political union has Britain found itself joined by a somewhat unexpected ally, Denmark, whose electorate narrowly voted against the Maastricht Treaty in a referendum in mid-1992. Prior to this boost for those in Britain who oppose the political union of Europe, the British debate confusingly centred on the forbidden 'F-word', 'federalism', which a number of UK politicians and the popular media suggested meant the fusion of all power in Brussels. In fact, as any political science textbook, dictionary or encyclopaedia will reveal, federalism means the exact opposite – namely, the distribution of specified constitutional powers to national and regional governments

British fingers splayed in the 'fuck you' position. During 1991 and early 1992 the '11 plus 1' phrase was commonly used in European meetings as a gentle, but ironic, comment on the characteristic British posture on European policies. However, the anti-Maastricht referendum in Denmark and the narrow pro-vote in France dented the self-confidence of the 'Eurocrats' considerably. '10 plus 2' did not sound quite so auspicious a calculation, and the plans for a European Union were nearly scuppered.

and the co-operative pooling of certain powers at the centre. What the Danish referendum result has at last clarified is a debate on how much power is to be pooled and how much is to be retained and reserved at the national level.

Before 1993, the UK government had simply not been 'talking the same language' as many on the continent. Ironically, this problem was more acute in the figurative than in the literal sense. The '11' rushed to their dictionaries in an attempt to comprehend the British government's position on federalism and political union, but to no avail. For although the UK government may have disliked the *reality* of the sharing of power somewhat, it has had to accommodate to that harsh condition for many years. (The UK's defence policy, for example, has been predicated on American military power since 1943.) What the '11' were slow to appreciate is that the UK government's most profound fears centred on the loss of *the appearance* of power.[6] After many nods and winks during the course of 1991–92, the '11' finally got the message and left the dreaded F-word (which did not mean what the British thought it meant, but if they thought it meant that, then . . .) out of the Treaty of Maastricht. The substance of the Treaty changed not one whit, but Prime Minister Major was able to claim a victory for British 'common sense' – or should that be mystagogy.

The appearance of Denmark as an unexpected ally in the anti-Maastricht cause broke the neat asymmetry between the UK government and its continental counterparts. Where the major continental governments wanted to consolidate the EU around the existing core plus a few additional members, others, including the UK, want to add a substantial number of other members, the better to dilute the common enterprise and the effectiveness of Brussels. With the French franc under pressure and Germany preoccupied with reunification, the cement between these two core members is beginning to crack. The ratification of the Maastricht Treaty secured only narrow support in Germany and France while the most likely new members of the club, Finland, Austria, Norway and Sweden, all seemed to be closer to the

---

6   Crucial to this pretence is the illusion of sovereignty. This has two major dimensions: (a) *Military independence*. Successive UK governments, for example, held grimly on to the fiction that the UK had an independent nuclear deterrent, when its use was utterly conditional on Washington's assent; (b) *Parliamentary sovereignty*. This absurd notion was propagated by an English scholar, Albert Venn Dicey, whose views generations of 'Politics' and 'Government' students (like 'social science', the expression 'political science' is taboo) were expected to regurgitate. I nearly gagged in the attempt. It therefore comes as a considerable personal relief to learn through Mount's book (1992) that Dicey was a classifiable lunatic. His sovereignty-mania and ideas of absolute omnipotence for parliament were inversions of his own fear and impotence. As Nairn (1992: 27) comments, Dicey's psychopathology may have been taken to the British political élite's hearts precisely because 'it intuited something analogous about Great Britain. A multi-national state with no armature of reason depended on unchallengeable faith and doses of symbolism (like the monarchy)'.

British position in favouring very restricted powers for Brussels. Moreover, there have been strong disagreements over foreign policy, with
the Greeks, for example, being strongly opposed to NATO intervention in Bosnia. Unfortunately, the support Britain seemed to be
receiving from the new entrants withered in the spring of 1994, as the
UK government held simultaneously to the view that it was right to
enlarge the community, but not at the expense of Britain blocking
powers over new legislation. This left no room to *provide* votes for the
aspiring members; so some natural 'northern European' allies were
carelessly alienated.

The imminent enlargement of the Union and other shifts in national
interest have led to much more complex internal relations within the
EU, but this should not disguise the broad contrast in political styles
and language that still remains. The continental predilection for precision contrasts with the British preference for political intuition. The
'11' want transparency, openness, explicitness, legally binding and
enforceable obligations, the '1' wants opacity, impenetrability, imper-
viousness and vague 'understandings'. So potent are these differences,
that even after two decades of membership of the EEC and its
successor bodies an old dilemma can still be posed. Can the British
ever become Europeans? Can the gulf of mutual incomprehension
allow enough points of access and permeability for a British identity to
become subsumed in a wider European identity? No definitive answer
to these questions is yet possible.

On the one hand, the slow drip-feed of European integration is
influencing the younger generation – who increasingly study, work,
travel and holiday on the continent and who forget their kith and kin
abroad, deride the British Empire and neglect the idealistic notion of a
multiracial Commonwealth. The USA is still culturally hegemonic at
the level of popular music, cinema, television series and Mickey
Mouse artefacts – but the attractions of Rome, Barcelona, Berlin,
Amsterdam and Paris are ever more alluring. The sense of style and
design, the drugs scene, football, several kinds of music, architecture,
popular philosophy, fast hatchbacks, ski resorts and beach culture – all
these aspects of British youth culture are incrementally drawn as much
from European as American models.

On the other hand, the older British generation – in particular those
with wealth and power – are culturally resistant to the European idea
and find few inspiring or ideologically-compelling reasons for 'being
there'.[7] That is not to argue that there are not recognised *instrumental*

---

7   The contrast I make between young and old Britons was confirmed by a poll
    commissioned by the *European* (25–8 June, 1992). When asked if they would vote
    'yes' to the Treaty of Maastricht if accorded a referendum, the spread between the
    young (18–34) in Britain and the population at large was 8 points, the greatest in
    Europe. UK voters as a whole would have voted against the treaty – all other
    countries but Denmark suggested large majorities 'for'. But there were fewer com-
    mitted opponents of the EU in the young UK sample (20 per cent), compared to 30

reasons for having joined the European club. Businessmen want to sell in the wider market; the middle classes now have an excellent choice of pâtés, soft cheeses, sausages and yoghurts in their local branch of Sainsburys; it is easier to travel and to buy a second home in the European sun.

The Queen was not allowed to address the European parliament in Strasbourg during Mrs Thatcher's terms of prime ministerial office. When she finally did so, in May 1992, she managed to draw some inspiration from Churchill's celebration of the richness and vitality of Europe's achievements in the arts, culture and science and its need to avoid the succession of self-destructive conflicts which had scarred the history of the continent. Europe, she argued, if somewhat loftily, could be a force for civilisation and tolerance in the world.

It may be that Britain can still make its distinctive contribution to this vision of the future. But, at least so far, mean-spirited materialist and instrumental messages have drowned out any compelling and principled reason for Britain's membership. This is in notable contrast to the prior frontiers explored by the British. The shouldering of the white man's burden may have been both a paternalistic and self-assigned task, but it provided an ideologically sustaining reason for British expansion. Establishing dominions abroad may have been an arrogant putsch against the indigenous nations, but British political ideas and institutions undoubtedly spread the practice of liberty, representation and equal justice. The notion of a world association of black, brown, yellow and white peoples, which underlay the design of the post-1947 Commonwealth was perhaps the most utopian, but sadly the most underdeveloped, vision of all.

By being largely unable to articulate any uplifting reasons for being in Europe, successive British governments have enfeebled the frontiers of British identity at precisely its most vulnerable points. Instead of drawing lessons from the multiracial Commonwealth, the British are in danger of catching a resurgent racial virus from Germany and France. Instead of broadcasting Queen Victoria's message of religious tolerance, the British are in danger of accepting a narrow religious zealotry which isolates Muslims from Europeans in a demonology as outdated as the Holy Roman Empire. Instead of celebrating the real successes of the initiatives towards racial equality in Britain (the work of the Commission for Racial Equality, the Race Equality Councils, the anti-racist movements), the government seeks only to outbid the '11' in its fervour to exclude non-white third-country nationals from the EU.

per cent in the total population. Again this sharp difference was not found in any other EU country.

The net result of this failure to articulate any ethical reasons for being in Europe is that the British remain uneasy Europeans – uncertain of what good they are contributing to the common purpose. For the younger generation, there are signs of a creative European cultural syncretism – which might ultimately generate a 'new wave' at the level of the plastic, visual or performing arts and even in literary and intellectual life. But little of this capacity inheres in the older and wealthier generation, whose core identity remains locked in a problematic, antipathetic and largely unworthy interface with the European frontier.

The construction of 'the Alien'

The sixth and final frontier I consider is one which separates the British most firmly from the rest of humankind. I refer to the invention and sustenance of that chilling extraterrestrial category, 'the alien'. Unlike the five frontiers previously discussed (the Celtic, the Dominion, the Commonwealth, the Atlantic and the European), there is a much greater interest by the frontier guards in clarifying and defining the alien boundary: to move, in other words, from a fuzzy to a more unequivocal frontier.

Whereas the ambiguities along the edges of the first five frontiers have the advantage of allowing the manipulation of the identity-construct and the exercise of discretion by the frontier guards through personal privilege, loose understandings and favours, the hardening of the alien frontier is necessary to express any permanent sense of belonging to a British identity. It is also the frontier most vulnerable to politicisation by populist, racist and xenophobic elements.

Despite the interests of the frontier guards and the extreme political sensitivity of the alien frontier, precise boundary definitions have remained elusive. As Cunningham (1969: 3) suggested as early as 1897, it was not always clear who constituted an 'alien':

So many diverse tribes and stocks have contributed to the formation of the English nation, that it is not always easy to draw a line between the native and foreign elements. . . . It seems a little arbitrary to fix on any definite date and designate the immigrants of earlier times, component parts of the English race, while we speak of later arrivals as aliens.

Although at various times nativist movements have opposed Cunningham's point and sought to proclaim the homogeneity of the currently-constituted English nation, such a notion has always attracted its fair share of critics and satirists. Take, for example, this poem in the *Pall Mall Gazette* in 1909 (cited Landa 1911: 2):

The Paleolithic, Stone and Bronze Age races
The Celt, the Roman, Teutons not a few
Diverse in dialects and hair and faces –
The Fleming, Dutchman, Huguenot and Jew
'Tis hard to prove by means authoritative
Which is the alien and which the native.

That making a rigorous distinction between alien and native was difficult did not, of course, mean that it was not attempted in social and political practice. Who constitutes the self (the acceptable, the insider, the familial), and who the other (the stranger, the outsider, the alien) is the warp and woof of all British migration history and the basic ingredient of a British identity. How the British-alien frontier was shaped is discussed in Chapters 2–6 of this book.

Conclusion

It is time to draw the threads of my argument together. British identity shows a general pattern of fragmentation. Multiple axes of identification have meant that Irish, Scots, Welsh and English people, those from the white, black or brown Commonwealth, Americans, English-speakers, Europeans and even 'aliens' have had their lives intersect one with another in overlapping and complex circles of identity-construction and rejection. The shape and edges of British identity are thus historically changing, often vague and, to a degree, malleable – an aspect of the British identity I have called 'a fuzzy frontier'.

With the advent of postwar immigration from the black and Asian Commonwealth, it became more difficult for white Britons to territorialise their identity to the exclusion of 'the other'. Nationality and citizenship, despite various cunning bureaucratic and political contrivances, had to be conceded on a non-racial basis. It is notable that younger members of the ethnic minorities assertively describe themselves as 'black British' or 'Asian British'. Events in the dominions and the signing of the Treaty of Rome also rent a giant tear across the notion of an exclusively racially defined British people, at home and in the diaspora. At the same time, their attachment to a new European frontier left many Britons, particularly older Britons, in an uneasy state of 'not belonging'.

I have suggested that the important global role of the English language has an ego-sustaining function for the British and is tantalisingly redolent of their country's nineteenth-century world dominance. At the same time, the disjuncture between real and imagined power, creates a dangerous gap in the identity frontier's defences. This gap may well be closed by attitudes of extreme hostility and xenophobia to those who are deemed undesirable aliens, undeserving asylum-seekers or unassimilable religious and racial minorities. The historical experience of such groups in British history and current policies directed towards them, form the subject of the rest of this book.

CHAPTER 2

Expulsions and deportations: the practice of anthropemy

> *Anthropemy* (from the Greek *emein*, to vomit) consists of ejecting dangerous individuals from the social body.
> – Lévi-Strauss (1977: 508)

The right to control entry and demand departure is part of the very constitution of a nation-state – as major a source of legitimate state authority as the right to dominate the means of violence. My primary object in this chapter is to show how the targets of deportation and expulsion shifted historically. By describing who was ejected and when, I seek thereby to demonstrate how the frontier guards of the British national identity came to delineate then exclude the 'dangerous individuals' threatening the health of the body politic.

Early nationalism and Protestantism

When did the state's right to control entry and exit become established? Roche (1969: 13), the historian of the Immigration Service, argued that immigration control in England commenced with William the Conqueror who, in the wake of his successful invasion, set up castles along the south coast to prevent somebody else emulating what he had just done. The five key control points, the Cinque Ports, were at Hastings, Romney, Dover, Hythe and Sandwich: the process of passing through these ports gave birth to the word 'passport'.

The policing of the frontier became an important aspect of royal power to be executed by the monarch's most trustworthy vassals. William the Conqueror and Henry I were particularly preoccupied with excluding Papal delegates and with threats to their own power from rivals who had taken refuge abroad. The famous assassination at Canterbury of 'the Holy Blissful Martyr', Becket, by Henry's four knights only occurred because they were not successfully intercepted at Hythe. In the second year of Henry II's reign, all 'aliens' were abruptly banished on the grounds that 'they were considered to be becoming too numerous' (Roche 1969: 15).

The early thirteenth century showed the first signs of the shaping of an exclusive English identity. With the seizure of Normandy in 1204 by the French king, Philip Augustus, some of the English magnates were in the uncomfortable position of having to choose between two liege lords on either side of the Channel. The ex-Norman baronage were now sufficiently indigenised to see Normans as 'foreigners'. One illustration can be found in the attempted invasion of Dover by Louis the Dauphin. When this was threatened in 1216, the port's custodian, with the decidedly Gallic name of Hubert de Burgh, provided a ringing declaration of early nationalism: 'As long as I draw breath I will not surrender to French aliens this castle, which is the key in the lock of England' (Roche 1969: 17–18).

The notion of a 'French alien' was especially novel in that (though they had lost Normandy) Poitou still remained under the control of the English Crown and many officials and nobles of continental origin sought and found preferment in England under Henry III's rule (1216–72). For much of his reign, Henry was tolerant of continental merchants, moneylenders and foreign wool-workers. He afforded them protection so long as they made suitable contributions to the Crown. However, as Cunningham (1969: 70) cynically remarked, 'they were protected only to be plundered'. Even this conditional haven did not last. The final years of Henry's reign were marked by increasing hostility to three groups the Flemish, some of whom were granted a 'denizen' (resident alien) status, but most of whom were deported; the Caorsine 'usurers' who were expelled at the insistence of the Church; and the Jews.

Jews were particularly vulnerable to exclusion. They had long been victims to the 'blood-libel' (the notion that they used the blood of Christian children to make Passover ceremonial bread) and anti-Jewish riots were common in the twelfth century. Within two years of Edward I's accession (1239), Jews found guilty of usury had to wear a placard around their necks. That the nobles and the monarchs themselves had to turn to Jewish bankers to pursue their schemes and to get out of their scrapes was deemed intolerable. The king demanded constant arbitrary payments, and the forfeit of all the goods and chattels of a 'usurer' to the Crown on death – on the grounds that they followed a condemned occupation. The execration of usury did not prevent the king selling back a Jewish father's estate to his heir, thereby starting another cycle of expropriation. The depredations of the monarchy and nobility became so great that many prosperous Jews were driven into poverty. Then, in 1290, the entire resident Jewish population, some 15,660 people, were deported.[1] They were not allowed to return until 367 years later during the Cromwellian period. As Stenton (1965: 200) laconically commented, 'Edward I expelled the Jews in 1290 because the days of their usefulness were over.'

---

1   It might be worth noting the full statistical import of this event. The English population stood at that time at about 2 million; thus 0.8 per cent of the population was deported. Estimating the English population at 80 per cent of the UK total, a modern-day Edward would have to deport 377,600 people to reach the same percentage, an action that no contemporary British government could contemplate.

The Jewish role as the classical 'middleman minority' (as the sexist sociological term has it), was supplanted by the Lombards, the Hansards and the Flemish who fared little better at the hands of the rapacious Crown or mobs manipulated by City magnates who owed money to their creditors. In a particularly excruciating test of political correctness, members of the Flemish colony at Southwark were enjoined to pronounce the words 'Bread and Cheese' in the proper London pronunciation. Those who failed were summarily executed (Cunningham 1969: 77).

But deportations and expulsions were rare in the fourteenth and fifteenth centuries. The Lombards were protected by the Pope, the Black Death meant that Edward III needed to rebuild the population of England while, at the end of the period – when the unsettling Wars of the Roses had finally ended – a new era of international trade between England and Flanders had been opened up.

The liberalism of movement that followed was, however, short lived. The religious oppression and intolerance that started in the mid-sixteenth century over much of Europe soon ramified at the English Court and in the Privy Council. At the accession of Mary (1553), all 'strangers'[2] were commanded to leave the realm. These included Walloon weavers who professed a Calvinist faith and were returned to the Continent (Cunningham 1969: 146). Another example can be found in the Privy Council papers of 1562, which referred to the expulsion of an unfortunate 'Dutch heretic', one Hadrian Hamslede, who was described as 'being found obstinat in dyvers erronious opinions' (Dasent 1890: 127).

Although Elizabeth (1558–1603) allowed the return of the weavers expelled by Mary, she used the royal prerogative to expel other religious dissenters fearing, in particular, a pro-Catholic revival. For the same reason, she also restricted movement out of England by her own subjects – in case they might be schooled at the Catholic seminaries in the Netherlands, Rheims and Rome which were dedicated to training missionaries for the English field (Bindoff 1961: 235–6). In 1585 alone, fourteen Catholic priests were deported; some were suspected of preparing the ground for an invasion by Philip II. Three years later when the long-feared Spanish Armada finally materialised, Elizabeth again used her power to expel Jesuits and 'Spanish agents' (Roche 1969: 39).

In the seventeenth century, the power to deport seems to have been progressively conceded to the Privy Council, though the notion of a royal prerogative still survived.[3] The principal targets remained relig-

2 The category 'strangers' did not, presumably include the 'denizens' – privileged aliens who had been granted the right to live and conduct their business in England by royal agreement. See later discussion.
3 The barrister and legal expert in immigration law, Nicol (1981: 9–10), pointed out that, as recently as 1971, section 33(5) of the Immigration Act stated: 'This Act shall not be taken to supersede or impair any power exercised by Her Majesty in relation

ious dissenters, especially Jesuits. In 1618, 'by letters patent of commission', James I (James VI of Scotland) gave the power to six or more Privy Councillors 'to exile and bannish out of and from his Majesty's realmes of Englaund and Irelaund ... so manie jesuits, seminarie priests and other eccelesiasticall persons whatsoever made and ordayned accordinge to the order and rites of the Romish Church' (LCHMT 1930: 338).

The Lord Chancellor, Lord Treasurer, Lord Privy Seal and others set about their task with determination, the Acts of the Privy Council recording no less than 49 Jesuit priests so expelled in the 1620–21 session alone. The Privy Council also formalised the procedure. A deportation order issued in December 1620 was issued in the recognisably modern form of a warrant to constables and other officers. They were asked, in this instance (LCHMT 1929: 334), to apprehend

the person of Pierre Reynaud, a Frenchman, and convey him to the next constable or other like officer in the direct way towarde Dover, and so from constable to constable, untill he arrive there, and be delivered over into the hands of the maior of that towne, who we require ... to cause him to be imbarqued and transported by the next convenient passage into France.

From revolutionaries to the 'Alien Menace'

In his history of the Home Office, Troup (1925: 124) suggested that 'in the eighteenth century the right to exclude had fallen into abeyance'. None the less, an important legal landmark was initiated by the British government in reaction to the French Revolution. In 1793, Grenville's Aliens Act was passed, which gave parliamentary sanction for the expulsion of aliens for the first time. The Act provided, inter alia, for the transportation of an alien who returned after being expelled. If the alien were so imprudent as to return yet again, the Act allowed capital punishment.

The most prominent victim of Grenville's Act was the French politician and diplomat, Talleyrand, who had been elected President of the French Assembly in 1790. When the Revolution debouched into the Terror, he had swiftly fled to England. Talleyrand was deported to the USA in 1793, but argued in his memoirs that he was expelled so as to

to aliens by virtue of Her prerogative.' In practice, the royal prerogative seems not to have been exercised since Elizabeth I, though Nicol is wrong in saying that the last occasion was in 1575. As indicated earlier, Elizabeth signed deportation orders at least as late as 1588. Research by Kenneth Rose has also shown that during the Russian Revolution George V kept out Tsar Nicholas II and his family through the exercise of a sort of royal prerogative. They would probably have reached a safe exile in Britain if not for the King's opposition. He evidently was concerned that the unpopularity of the Tsar would rub off on him (*Observer*, 26 Aug. 1984).

show that the Aliens Act was no dead letter. Under Clause XVII of the Act, all principal secretaries of state were empowered to issue a deportation under specified conditions. This provision was strengthened in 1803 when expulsion was allowed on 'mere suspicion'; this sweeping power prevailed until 1836.

Lord Loughborough's speech in defence of the 1793 Act was instructive in alluding to the crisis that had faced Elizabeth in 1588 when the country was threatened by 'religious fanaticism'. Now, he opined, England was threatened by 'the fanaticism of infidelity'. This referred to the progress of French revolutionary ideas including 'atheism' and 'anarchism'. The Act contained a clear legal distinction between an alien and a denizen (privileged foreigner), its provisions not being applicable to 'foreign ambassadors' or to an 'Alien who shall have Letters Patent of Denization' (Roche 1969: 47, 53).

The 1793 Act was only rarely deployed and intermittently re-enacted (in 1816, 1826 and 1836). Indeed, the evaporation of the tensions that followed the defeat of Napoleon led Troup (1925: 125) to consider that the measures against aliens 'fell into desuetude'. However, powers of deportation were renewed in 1848 in readiness for another 'alien menace' from continental revolutionaries. The Removal of Aliens Act of 1848 gave the home secretary and the lord lieutenant of Ireland the right to expel foreigners if it was deemed that they threatened the 'preservation of the peace and tranquillity of the realm'. Nine years later, Palmerston insisted on the repeal of the 1848 Act on the liberal grounds that deporting aliens on this vague basis would lead to an abuse of power.

The relaxed attitude of the period 1815–90 came to an abrupt end with the influx of Russian and eastern European Jews. The discriminatory May Laws in Russia (1882) had precipitated the first big wave of migrants to the UK. Press and popular opinion was not slow to respond, albeit with contradictory representations of the newcomers. According to the *Manchester City News* (2 April 1887), 'Jews [were] advanced socialists who sympathise with the Paris Commune and Chicago martyrs.' On the other hand, English trade unionists and socialists frequently represented all Jews as wicked capitalists (S. Cohen 1987: 7).

A Royal Commission on Alien Immigration which reported in 1903 accepted the force of various popular accusations against the Jewish immigrants. For example, the Commission regarded it as an 'evil' that 'immigrants of the Jewish faith do not assimilate and intermarry with the native race' (cited Roche 1969: 66). Fierce controls were proposed. But when the Aliens Act of 1905 was passed in parliament the restrictionists did not have it all their own way. The Act limited the powers of expulsion granted to immigration officers (IOs) to the exclusion of 'undesirables'. These were defined as previous deportees, fugitive offenders, the mad and the destitute. Moreover, those refused admission had the right to appeal to an immigration board whose members were often surprisingly sympathetic.

Potential 'undesirables' were thought to be exclusively found among the steerage passengers. The restrictionists in the Home Office were unhappy – not at the stunning demonstration of class justice that allowed those who could afford cabin fares to escape examination, but at their limited powers to stop what they saw as mass immigration.

That noses were out of joint in the Home Office can be discerned in Troup's previously cited history of the department. The permanent under-secretary of state at the Home Office over the period 1908–22, Sir Edward Troup was probably the most important of the 'hidden frontier guards' in the first quarter of this century. He claimed the 1905 Aliens Act was disliked on the purely pragmatic grounds that it was difficult to administer, but it is clear that he and his immediate colleagues identified fully with the restrictionists. Competition from the 'aliens from eastern Europe', he asserted (1925: 143), 'lowered the wages in some of the unorganised trades to starvation point and their habits had a demoralising effect in the crowded areas in which they settled.'

As is so often the case, the civil servants tried to claw back in the exercise of administrative discretion what they were not granted by parliamentary sanction. Two groups highly vulnerable to arbitrary action by officialdom were foreign-born servants and sailors.

For over fifty years, there had been considerable confusion of authority between those administering the Merchant Shipping Act (1855), the local authorities administering vagrants' legislation and tnose with overlapping responsibilities in the Home Office and India Office. Significant numbers of servants and ayahs (nannies) had been brought back from India to England by wealthy colonial families, then abandoned. The India Office only recognised their responsibilities to indigent lascars (Indian seamen) and at the end of the nineteenth century donated some £200 per annum to the Strangers' House – which became charged with the repatriation of many destitute Asian, African and South Sea Island seamen (Visram 1986: 34–54).

Under the Merchant Shipping Act of 1894 an early form of privatisation was announced. Responsibility for destitute sailors was henceforward to be shifted from the India Office to a ship's master or owner, who could be fined if an African or Asian seaman was in receipt of public funds or found vagrant within six months of his discharge at a UK port (Gordon 1985: 6). By the turn of the century, the Home Office had, somewhat resentfully, become involved in the enforcement of the repatriation and expulsion of indigent sailors.[4]

---

4 The expulsion of the destitute did not only affect minorities, but orphaned and indigent British children too. Under various 'child migration schemes' the first batch was sent to Richmond, Virginia in 1618; the last group of 90 children left for Canada in 1967. A total of 150,000 children were exported to Canada, Australia,

Other minorities began to be identified as 'undesirables' and ways were found to exclude them outside the scope of the Aliens Act. For example, a group of German Gypsies who started to arrive in 1904 were treated with 'sharp antipathy', this time by the politicians as well as the Home Office, who contrived to circumscribe their movement through the Moveable Dwelling Bills. Holmes (1991: 18–19) records that 'a few hundred' were expelled during 1905/6.

While Indians, Africans and Gypsies were all victims of restrictionist attitudes, there is little doubt that the main targets of animosity just before the First World War were the Jews. The term 'alien' was the turn-of-the-century newspeak for 'Jew'. Chamberlain campaigned on an anti-alien platform, the anti-Semitic British Brother League was established, while the journal, *The Alien Immigrant*, thought it 'scarcely necessary to labour the point that the first generation of children of Russian Jews in the East End are only English by legal fiction' (cited Landa 1911: 137). The Jews also had no friend in court, as W. Haldane Porter, the chief inspector under the Aliens Act and 'the founding father of the Immigration Service' (Kaye and Charlton 1990: 6), was covertly associated with Major Evans Gordon, the Enoch Powell of his time, and one of the most vocal of the anti-alien agitators.

One commentator on the 'alien invasion' dropped all restraint and penned this verse offering the alternatives of departure or death:

Be he Russian, or Pole, Lithuanian or Jew
I care not, but take it for granted
That the island of Britain can readily do
With the notice: 'No aliens wanted'.
I would give them one chance – just one week to clear out
And if found in the land one hour later
Then – death without trial or fooling about
Whether Anarchist, banker or waiter.

A curious gentility surrounded these odious sentiments. They were published in *The People* in February 1909 over the nom de plume of 'a lady' and described by the columnist 'Mr Will Workman' as 'a rousing patriotic stanza'.

Wartime expulsions and the aftermath

Administrative discretion and popular agitation, however, had their

---

New Zealand, South Africa, Rhodesia/Zimbabwe and the Caribbean. This form of people-export is, however, better understood as part of the imperial plan, discussed in Chapter 1, to populate the colonies of settlement. Some 11 per cent of Canada's population is descended from orphaned and destitute British children (Bean and Melville 1989).

limitations. Sir Edward Troup was clearly a great deal happier with the logic of the military mind. In 1914, the Committee of Imperial Defence discussed the issue of aliens in Britain. The Aliens Act of that year – which placed rigid controls over the registration, movement and deportation of all aliens – was rushed through in a single day, 5 August. It was introduced in the House of Commons at 3.30 p.m. and gained the Royal Assent by 7 p.m. Troup (1925: 143, 152) had no doubts as to its efficacy and justification:

the base was laid for the effective control of aliens which was maintained throughout the war ... [before the war] ... all attempts on the part of the Home Office to exclude persons who had not identified themselves with English life and remained in sentiment really foreigners proved abortive [emphasis added].

Troup saw no difficulty in bureaucratically separating 'the real foreigners' from 'the English'; he ignored the rest of Britain. Modern historians (for example, Holmes 1988, 1991) have shown that it was not quite so easy in practice to segregate the sheep from the goats, due to the almost hysterical levels of Germanophobia that the outbreak of the First World War had generated. George V felt constrained to drop all German family titles and adopt the name 'Windsor'. German Knights of the Garter were struck off the roll, grocers with German names were accused of poisoning the public, while *The Times* ran a series of 'loyalty letters', in which German or German–Jewish public figures were enjoined to declare themselves. (Those who refused found themselves cold-shouldered.) Another revealing example, in the light of Britain's international reputation for the care of domestic animals (the RSPCA was founded as early as 1824), was that dachshunds were stoned in the streets of London. Spy stories also abounded. Once, the Immigration Service historian, Roche (1969: 87), breathlessly disclosed, the famous spy Mata Hari was discovered on a neutral ship in Falmouth and was 'sent to France'.

After the sinking of the *Lusitania* off the coast of Ireland in May 1915 with the loss of 1,201 lives, all restraints on the frontier guards of British identity were off. In the previous autumn, the repatriation of women, children, elderly men, invalid men of military age, ministers of religion and medical doctors of German origin had been initiated by the government. Henceforth, German-background women and men over military age were obliged to show why they should not be expelled – a stunning administrative diktat significantly reversing the traditional burden of proof. According to Holmes (1988: 96), over the period 1914–19, 28,744 aliens were repatriated, of whom 23,571 were Germans. Cesarani (1987: 5) offered even higher figures: 30,700 Germans, Austrians, Hungarians and Turks over the 1914–18 period, together with 7,000 Russians, probably all Jews.

Paralleling these expulsions and repatriations was the internment of more than 32,000 enemy aliens. Many of them ended up in the windy, muddy and far-from-waterproof Knockeloe camp on the Isle of Man. (As I discuss detentions separately, I will return to the issue of the internment of aliens in Chapter 4.)

The xenophobia of the war years no doubt helped in recruitment and in manufacturing a patriotic consensus in support of the increasingly costly, blood-drenched and futile war. But no amount of jingoism could keep pace with the losses at the front. In January 1916 the British government introduced conscription.

Conscription placed particular pressures on three minority groups: the Belgians, the Russian Poles and the Lithuanians. The Belgians on the whole took up an offer for repatriation worked out jointly between the Belgian and British governments. The Russian Poles, who were mainly Jewish, split three ways. Established Anglo–Jewry persuaded some of their coreligionists to show their gratitude to their country of refuge by enlisting. But many Russian aliens, a substantial number of whom had not taken out British nationality, saw no good reason to support Britain's anti-Semitic ally, the Tsar – whom they considered responsible for their enforced flight. A third group, with socialist sympathies, simply saw the war as a capitalist conspiracy which any self-respecting internationalist should denounce (Holmes 1988: 101–6).

The frontier guards in the Home Office and War Office pressed the issue: the Russians and Lithuanians either should serve in the British army or in the armies of their original citizenship.[5] The Lithuanians became wedged in an uncomfortably tight vice. The conscripts split into two bodies: in 1917, 700 joined the British army, while 1,100 returned to serve in Lithuania, then part of the Tsar's empire. With the Russian revolution came another turn of the screw. Only 300 of the Lithuanian returnees were permitted to come back to Britain, on the grounds that the remaining 700 could not prove they had fought on the side of the allies, or had not fought for the Bolsheviks. The small allowances made to their families in Britain were withdrawn by the Treasury and 600 dependants (all women and children) of the Lithuanian returnees were deported.

The aftermath of the extensive wartime expulsions and repatriations saw the frontier guards riding high. The ejection of 'enemy aliens'

---

5 Thus stated the Military Service (Allied Conventions) Act of August 1917. To this day, British passports carry a printed warning directed to dual nationals: 'If under the law of [another] country, they are liable for any obligation (such as military service), the fact that they are British nationals does not exempt them from it.' As countries of origin often make it difficult or impossible to renounce citizenship, in effect many British passport-holders still face the dilemma created in the 1917 Act and are not offered the full protection that citizenship in many other countries-of-adoption would imply. Any competent semiologist would also not miss the social distancing implied in the use of 'they' and 'them' rather than 'you' in the passport warning.

became an election pledge for Lloyd George in 1918 and some 19,000 Germans were repatriated by April of the following year. Some vintage mystagogy was produced by *The Times* and the *Morning Post.* The Jews were Bolsheviks and the Bolsheviks were bankrolled by the Germans. Thus an anti-alien position conveniently dished all three (Cesarani 1987: 7–8).

Given the fanning of popular sentiment, it was no surprise that the emergency wartime powers over aliens were largely retained in the Aliens Restrictions (Amendment) Act of 1919. An Order-in-Council in 1920 reserved the home secretary's right to deport someone if he considered it 'conducive to the public good', a phrase that still echoes through the corridors of the Home Office. Home Secretary Shortt also insisted on additional Clauses to exclude or deport aliens who encouraged sedition in the armed forces or promoted industrial unrest.

These Clauses reflected the general apprehension of the ruling élite immediately after the war. The Bolsheviks were triumphant in Russia and the rot looked like spreading to Germany. Anti-British riots had occurred in a number of colonies. The Chicago meat-packers were on strike and socialist political organisations were making great headway in the USA. And in Britain itself, suffragettes chained themselves to the railings of Buckingham Palace, a Soviet was briefly established in Glasgow and the first major race riots had broken out in Liverpool and Cardiff against a background of a police strike (May and Cohen 1972). Truly, hands must have wobbled in the gentlemen's clubs as they reached out to grab the port.

The frontier guards lashed out. Eighty 'Bolshevik sympathisers' were deported in May 1919. The Labour Member of Parliament (MP) for Whitechapel complained that the Home Office was sending out Russian Jews almost weekly. Excluding dependants, 31 were expelled in November 1920, 49 in December 1920, 58 in March 1921. Some of the 1917 conscripts who had elected to serve in the Russian Army illegally returned to Britain: 40 were found and deported, 29 others were sent to Brixton jail (Cesarani 1987: 7, 13).

As home secretary, Shortt's administrative powers included, but also transcended, the enforcement of a court's recommendation for deportation following conviction. This form of dual power (impossible in any country where a written constitution separates administrative and judicial powers) allowed the issue of a deportation order even when the court had not made such a recommendation or, indeed, had acquitted an alien defendant (Nicol 1981: 12). The home secretary saw no problem. He maintained that deportation need not be treated as a judicial issue, 'but rather as a matter of administration'. Deportation was not punishment for a particular offence, but 'administrative action taken on behalf of the public'.

During the 1920s and 1930s, the 1919 Act was extended on an annual basis, despite an attempt in 1927, thrown out in parliament, to have the powers accorded to the home secretary made permanent.

Reformers and pressure groups, notably the British Board of Deputies (the representative body of Jewry), managed to establish an independent Aliens Deportation Advisory Committee in 1930. The Home Office held to its old line of 'administrative discretion' in the cases of illegal entry and overstaying, but the home secretary agreed to refer all other cases to the Committee on the basis of a 'private understanding' and after 'radicals' like Harold Laski (a politics lecturer at the London School of Economics) were dropped from its membership. When the Committee had the temerity to question the home secretary's judgements in 33 cases, the Committee was quietly sidetracked, then discontinued.

That the Committee was batting on a sticky wicket can be deduced from the attitudes of the top civil servants at the Home Office. For example, in a departmental memo to the home secretary in 1924 (cited Cesarani 1987: 17), Troup's successor as permanent under-secretary of state at the Home Office, Sir John Pedder, explained why he systematically delayed looking at some classes of applications for 'far longer' than the statutory minimum time of five years' residence. This was because his experience suggested that

different races display very different qualities and capabilities for identifying themselves with this country. Speaking roughly, the Latin, Teuton and Scandinavian races, starting some of them, with a certain kinship with British races, [are] prompt and eager to identify themselves with the life and habits of this country and are easily assimilated. On the other hand, Slavs, Jews and other races from Central and Eastern parts of Europe stand in quite a different position. They do not want to be assimilated in the same way and do not readily identify themselves with this country. Even the British-born Jews, for instance, always speak of themselves as a 'community', separate to a considerable degree and different from the British people.

While Sir John wrestled with his comparative studies of the differential rate of assimilability of various 'races', another committee of the Home Office planned for future encounters with other alien beings. In the light of the negative Isle of Man experiences with internment during the 1914–18 conflict, the Committee of Imperial Defence concluded in 1923 that there was no point in depriving the enemy of its able-bodied men if it took a large number of British troops to look after them. It was thus agreed (with the exception of a limited provision for exactly 5,490 internees) that in any future conflict, expulsion would be far better than detention (Gillman and Gillman 1980: 23).

As the Second World War loomed this policy looked dangerously simplistic. Thirty thousand German–Jewish refugees had been admitted, while other Germans had put down roots, hoping to be naturalised. In 1938, the Home Office still clung to the 1923 ruling suggesting that all enemy aliens who had come to Britain after 1 January 1919 should be 'required to return to their own countries'. Clearly forcible repatriation of the Jews would be politically indefensible, so the Home Office, rather than abandon its expulsion plans, proposed a system of appeals against deportation. But what if these appeals were successful and the individuals concerned were still considered a security risk? Surely internment, the rejected policy, was bound to be reinstated?

In fact some repatriations were effected: 110 women and 8 children were sent back to Germany between December 1939 and January 1940. But as I shall show in Chapter 4, the policy and practice of detention and internment during the Second World War paralleled, then soon exceeded, the hopeless mire of the detention policy operated during the First World War.

Deportations after the Second World War

With respect to the state's powers of deportation, the Aliens Acts of 1905, 1914 and 1919 were supplemented by the British Nationality Act of 1948, the signing of the European Convention on Establishment, and the Immigration Acts of 1962, 1968 and 1971.

With the single exception of the European Convention, which gave rights to proposed deportees in certain categories to make representations to the courts, the effects of all this legislation were to extend the reasons for deportations and to widen the categories of people who could be expelled. In particular, the rights of Commonwealth citizens, especially black Commonwealth citizens, were gradually legally reduced to the status of aliens. The key developments (here I summarise Nicol 1981: 15–19) were these:

- Up until 1962 there were no statutory powers to inhibit entry or to deport Commonwealth citizens. (Like the inhabitants of the British Isles themselves, they were all the Crown's subjects.) In that year, the Commonwealth Immigrants Act allowed IOs to refuse admission to Commonwealth citizens and to remove them, provided they did so within 24 hours. For the first time also, the home secretary was allowed to deport Commonwealth citizens after a court conviction and recommendation for removal.
- In 1968, the Commonwealth Immigrants Act made an illegal Commonwealth entrant, if caught within 28 days, subject to 'administrative removal'.
- Under the Immigration Appeals Act of 1969, all overstayers and other immigrants who had broken a condition of their 'leave to enter' could be deported, without being prosecuted. (But they could now appeal to an administrative appeals system.)
- Under the Immigration Act of 1971, the immunity against deportation given to Commonwealth citizens who had been resident in the

UK for five years was watered down.[6] Like aliens, Commonwealth citizens could be deported for 'the public good'; the wife and children of a deportee could also be deported even if they were totally innocent of any wrongdoing; there was no time limit imposed on the home secretary to order a removal of an illegal entrant; finally, an illegal entrant who had been served with a removal order could only appeal to an adjudicator after having left the country.

The succession of measures was harsh by any standards, but the restrictions were made more odious by the barely concealed appeal to colour as a key differentiating category between those who were immune from deportation and those who were subject to this state power. In particular, the 1971 legislation gave a right of abode to 'patrials' (nearly all of whom were white) and denied that right to 'non-patrials' (nearly all of whom were black, brown or yellow).[7]

As many commentators (for example, Solomos 1989: 54–8; Gilroy 1987: 85–8) have pointed out, the moment in the post-1945 period that has come to symbolise the racialisation of the 'immigration issue' was Enoch Powell's infamous speech in Birmingham in April 1968. Gilroy has provided an incisive linguistic examination of this address which uncovers the messages behind the language and imagery used by Powell.

Let me just select some highlights of his analysis. Powell developed the theme of 'an alien wedge' which was damaging to British national culture. While the numbers in the alien wedge were important, even more pertinent were the character and effects of black settlement. Powell gloomily predicted, 'in fifteen or twenty years' time the black man will hold the whip hand over the white man.' As Gilroy commented, this image inverts the customary roles of master and slave, thereby accepting historical guilt, but immediately counteracts an acceptance of guilt with an appeal to fear.

Later in the speech, the masculine black remains (either in the form of 'charming wide-grinning piccaninnies' or 'negro workers') but the white is transformed into a vulnerable little old lady. She is taunted by the cry of 'racialist'[8] by the blacks, who also push excreta through her

---

6 The immunity fell away unless the individual concerned was ordinarily resident before 1 Jan. 1973, when the Act came into force, or unless he or she became the UK citizen through naturalisation or registration.

7 The legislation fell just short of an explicitly racial classification scheme by allowing the notion of 'patriality' to include marginal numbers on a non-racial basis. Thus patrials were those citizens of the UK and Colonies who had been ordinarily resident for five years or more, or acquired their citizenships through naturalisation or registration (a small number of non-white citizens were so qualified), as well as those whose birth, adoption, parenthood or grandparenthood made them citizens through descent (overwhelmingly a white category).

8 'They cannot speak English, but one word ["racialist"] they know.' Powell's well known pedantry is a dead give-away here. Even in 1968, it stretches all credulity to

letter box. Powell is distraught; he is 'filled with foreboding'. Like the ancient Roman he sees 'the River Tiber foaming with much blood'. Moreover, all of this is a 'preventable evil' visited upon the UK 'by our own volition and our own neglect'.

Much as I am tempted to pursue a fuller psychological and linguistic decoding of Powell's imagery, I must stick to my more narrow purpose. What effects did this curious speech and the enormous row it provoked, have on the question of deportations and removals?

First, and most important, it lent force to the gathering view that black Commonwealth citizens were as 'alien' as the foreigners and aliens of old. Instead of evoking the Empire and Commonwealth, or common military service against the Nazis, the differences between white Britons and non-white Commonwealth citizens were now stressed. Notice, for example, one frontier guard's (Roche 1969: 207) characterisation of Indian immigrants published the year after the 'rivers of blood' speech. Indians, he claimed, presented

a veritable shock, for here were people with whom the majority of the population had come in contact only as soldiers, students or politicians turning up in our midst with a way of life wholly different from our own, bewildered, gregarious, defensive, like those Russian Jews about whom our grandfathers' generation had complained so bitterly seventy years before.

'Not like us, more like them', that was the core of Powell's first message and Roche's echoed sentiment. If they were like them, they could be treated equally as badly. So, in short, Commonwealth citizens should have no special privileges.

This extended also to the East African Asians who as UK and Colonies passport-holders had the untrammelled right of entry. Many believed they had been promised protection by successive colonial secretaries should their situation in independent African countries become intolerable. Powell, however, angrily denounced these historic rights and denied any suggestion that Britain had any responsibilities. Suddenly, the East African Asians were India's responsibility, despite their UK citizenship. Notice below how the notion of 'belonging' was used by Powell to elide the force of international law and separate the 'them' from the 'us':

When the East African countries became independent there was no suggestion, let alone undertaking, in parliament or outside, that those inhabitants who remained citizens of the UK and Colonies would have the right of entry into this country . . . the practice of international law which requires a country to readmit or admit its own nationals applies in our case only to those who belong to the UK and not to other Commonwealth countries, whether classified as citizens of the UK and Colonies or not (Powell, cited Goulbourne

imagine that the verbally-inadequate 'piccaninnies' would 'chant' the linguistically proper but passé term 'racialist', rather than the more common epithet, 'racist'.

1991: 117).

In short, the first effect of Powell's intervention was to draw the frontiers of identity more tightly around the British Isles and to try to renounce any responsibilities inherited from empire.

Second, despite his phantasm of a foaming river of blood, like all successful populists, Powell did not project a message of complete fatalism. The 'evil' was 'preventable'. For his parliamentary supporters, the problem was how. The 1971 legislation probably went as far as it could in explicitly diminishing the former privileges of Commonwealth citizens. To play with 'Powellism' more openly was both unrespectable and possibly dangerous, with unpredictable outcomes in the politics of the streets and perhaps in open racial violence.

Table 2.1 *Alleged illegal entrants removed, 1973–86*

Year	Foreign	Commonwealth	Total
1973	35	44	79
1974	33	80	113
1975	76	78	154
1976	127	137	264
1977	184	312	496
1978	275	263	538
1979	330	255	585
1980	589	319	908
1981	357	283	640
1982	223	208	431
1983	179	195	374
1984	188	237	425
1985	n.a.	n.a.	528
1986	246	458	704

Source: Correspondence with the Home Office Research and Statistics Department (1992).

But Powell had touched a nerve of popular sentiment across party lines which sanctioned tougher action by the frontier guards. This is most dramatically evidenced in the use of the powers the home secretary was given (in practice exercised by IOs) to 'remove' alleged 'illegal entrants' by administrative fiat. Whereas the power to 'remove' was conditional and very rarely used in the case of Commonwealth citizens prior to the 1971 Act, once the Act had come into force (on 1 January 1973) the numbers of alleged illegal entrants removed from the Commonwealth were either comparable to, or exceeded, the number of 'alien' foreigners removed (Table 2.1). It is interesting to note that, after 1986, the distinction between foreigners and Commonwealth citizens was thought irrelevant by the Home Office statisticians. However, the total number of removals of those deemed illegal entrants rose steeply – from 1,044 (1987), 1,639 (1988), 1,820 (1989) to 1,976 (1990). The provisional figures for 1992 were 2,891, an increase of 36 times the number removed in Mrs Thatcher's first year of office.

In addition to the removal of alleged illegal entrants, successive home secretaries have also used powers of deportation against those who are deemed 'threats to national security'. For the most part the system works quietly and efficiently, with the deportees finding themselves in no position to appeal against a decision or stimulate adverse publicity. However, the decision to remove two articulate Americans and one resolute Jamaican woman provoked rather different outcomes.

The case of Hosenball and Agee

In 1977, the Labour home secretary Merlyn Rees decided to remove Philip Agee and Mark Hosenball on the grounds of national security. Agee, a former Central Intelligence Agency agent, had written a book called *Inside the Company*, exposing the work of the CIA in Cuba, the rest of the Caribbean and Europe. Although the book provided considerable discomfort to the US authorities, it apparently had little relevance to British security. Service loyalty across the Atlantic (and perhaps a feeling that the British secret services could regain some credit after the calamitous exposure of a number of highly placed Soviet spies in their midst) dictated that Agee be tossed to the Americans.

Hosenball's offences were that he had published the names of 60 CIA operatives and, in a piece co-authored with a British writer, suggested that Government Communications Headquarters in Cheltenham regularly spied on Britain's and the United States' allies.

Perhaps because they were both confident, articulate and indignant, with contacts and, in Hosenball's case, a professional attachment to the media, Hosenball and Agee were able to stir enough mud to see a bit of the bottom of the murky pool of intelligence operations. 'Three Wise Men' had been called in: a system instituted by Home Secretary Maudling in 1971 to allow some limited hearing of a disputed case. The 'hearing' took place in the United Services Club in Pall Mall before three frontier guards – Sir Derek Hilton (ex-intelligence), Sir Clifford Jarrett (formerly in the Home Office) and Sir Richard Hayward (a former trade union official). As Duncan Campbell (Guardian 28 Jan., 1991) remarked, the judicial aspect of this procedure was wholly deficient: 'the panel does not operate like a normal court; subjects of deportation are not told of the charges against them;

they are allowed no legal representation; the hearings are in secret; and at the end of them, the panel merely advises the home secretary who can ignore their advice'.

Hosenball and Agee were deported and remain prohibited immigrants.

The case of Joy Gardner

Joy Gardner was admitted to the UK from Jamaica in July 1987 on a visitor's visa and subsequently married a Briton (of Caribbean origins). As she had overstayed her visa and her marriage had only lasted one month, the Home Office took the view that she should be deported. In 1993 her solicitor provided 'compelling compassionate circumstances' to the home secretary asking for the deportation order to be revoked. Gardner had a five-year-old son born in Britain, she had been in the country for six years. Her mother, two sisters, one brother, three uncles, two aunts and various cousins also lived in the UK.

The plea fell on deaf ears and in July 1993 three officers from the Metropolitan Police's special deportation squad cut the chain on Gardner's door, then cuffed, taped and gagged her after a violent struggle. Paramedics from the London Ambulance Service were called when she had stopped breathing. Despite there being 'no vital signs of life' she was, grotesquely, placed on a life-support machine at the hospital.

About 1,200 members of the black community and their anti-racist supporters held a street march in protest and the ethnic minority newspapers were filled with angry stories, letters and cartoons depicting Joy Gardner's death. A number of commentators drew the link between the manacles used in the slave trade and the apparatus (unauthorised by senior police officers) deployed by the snatch squad. The broadsheet newspapers concurred (for example, *The Times,* 5 Aug. 1993) that only the intervention of the black London MP, Bernie Grant, and the immediate suspension of the special deportation unit by Metropolitan Police Commissioner Paul Condon, had prevented a serious outbreak of civil violence.

Deportations arising from Empire

One effect of Enoch Powell's contributions to the political debate in the UK was that he was able to link the issue of immigration to the question of race relations so intimately that in British political discourse the two are inseparable. Even those who were liberals on domestic race relations matters (Powell's followers were, of course, often openly racist), were none the less induced into accepting his political agenda by arguing that harmonious race relations in Britain depended on rapidly cutting down the numbers of non-whites admitted to the country.[9] Inevitably this meant chipping away at the ideological raison d'être for the Commonwealth, a consequence, as suggested in Chapter 1, that would have very far-reaching consequences for Britain's international relations. Was it just a fateful coincidence that the date of Britain's accession to the Treaty of Rome was the same day (1 Jan. 1973) that the Immigration Act of 1971 came into force?

Despite Powell's cruel renunciation of non-white Commonwealth citizens as 'not belonging', as part of 'the other', it was not going to prove quite so easy to escape the heritage of empire as Powell had hoped. The case of the admission of the East African Asians has already been mentioned, but with respect to my current theme of deportations, two other groups need separate discussion – the Cypriots, and the Vietnamese in British-governed Hong Kong.

Cypriots

Cyprus had become a British Crown Colony in 1925. Despite a four-year state of emergency (1955–59), the British were largely unable to stop the competing demands by the Greek Cypriots for enosis (union with Greece) and the Turkish demand for taxim (partition).

In 1974 some 10,000 Cypriots fled to the UK following the Greek Colonels' coup, the invasion of the island by Turkey and its subsequent division. The island was divided into two parts by the Attila line, with a displacement of over 160,000 Greek Cypriots (one-fifth of the total population) from the Turkish-dominated section of the island. The Turkish sector is nominally independent (but recognised by no one but the Turkish government), while the British government continues to occupy two sovereign bases in the Greek part of the island, at Akrotiri and Dhekelia.

The migration of Cypriots to the UK had always been governed by somewhat different rules from Commonwealth citizens, with whom they were sometimes confused. In fact, because Cyprus was still a Crown Colony until its very precarious independence was negotiated, Cypriots were subject to immigration control. After 1974, when the mass displacements of population occurred, Cypriots were admitted to the UK, not as convention refugees, but as colonial citizens 'with special concessions'. These special concessions were to apply only so long as the unsettled conditions on the island continued.

The denial of formal refugee status meant that the Cypriots were not protected by the Geneva Convention. Instead, their situation turned on the assessment by the Immigration and Nationality Department (IND) in the Home Office as to when it was prudent for them to return. In

---

9 The parallel conviction in France alluded more to the spatial distribution of immigrants within France and was described as a 'seuil de tolérance' (a threshold of tolerance). Again, this view was held by those declaring that they were not racists. (See Chapter 6.)

1979, after 8,000 had already returned to the island when their 'leaves to remain' had expired, the position of the remaining 2,000 was spelled out by the IND: 'Cypriots will be expected to return to Cyprus as soon as circumstances there allow. They are thus liable to the provisions relating to deportation and in appropriate cases deportation orders continue to be made' (cited CCWAG 1982: 13).

Despite the continuing division of the country, the presence of Turkish troops and the internal displacement of many, the IND insisted that the 2,000 who had decided it was unsafe for them to return, had to go. An effective campaign by the Cypriot Community Workers' Action Group and the Joint Council for the Welfare of Immigrants secured the status of 'indefinite leave to remain' for 600 individuals. A pioneering attempt at sanctuary undertaken by a Cypriot couple, Katherina and Vassillis Nicola described fully in Chapter 5, also gave dramatic publicity to the deportations. None the less, the Nicolas ultimately were deported as were numerous others. Rather than suffer the adverse legal consequences of having a deportation order served on them, many left under the threat of deportation.

The deportation of Vietnamese from Hong Kong

Under cover of darkness, at 5.09 a.m. on 12 December 1989, 51 Vietnamese (25 adults and 26 children) were deported from the British dependency of Hong Kong against their will. A chartered Cathay Pacific Tristar jet returned them to their homeland, Vietnam, with the agreement of the Vietnamese government. The UK government had become enmeshed in a second case of deportations deriving from its colonial responsibilities, one that has not proved so easy to manage as the case of the Cypriots.

For a start, the world's press were there. An immediate barrage of outrage and criticism was directed at the British government. The former European Commissioner, Stanley Clinton Davis, then Chairman of the British Refugee Council, compared the round up to 'the practices indulged in by tyrannies over the ages – the Nazis, the communists, South Africa'. President Bush condemned the element of compulsion. *Le Monde* (13 Dec. 1989) claimed that the careful British government phrase 'mandatory repatriation' fooled no one and that Britain was 'flouting fundamental humanitarian principles'. Gerald Kaufmann, the UK Labour Party's spokesperson on foreign affairs, called the deportations 'shameful'.

Many of the Vietnamese arriving before June 1988 were given admission to Hong Kong as a country of first asylum, with the expectation that most would move to other countries of settlement. When the USA, UK and Australia began to baulk at the increasing numbers, new arrivals were penned into grim detention camps, pending the outcome of a refugee determination procedure.

The international criticisms of the Hong Kong and UK governments were targeted on three issues: the initial mandatory repatriation, the conditions in the camps and the fairness of the screening process. In a report prepared for the Washington-based Indo–China Resource Action Center by a US Attorney-at-Law, Diller (1988) argued that without a guarantee of safety from Vietnam, the compulsory repatriations violated the duty to observe the principle of non-refoulement which prohibits the return of refugees or asylum-seekers to a country where their lives or welfare may be in danger. As to conditions in the camps, some were 'severely overcrowded and inadequate', the physical security of the inhabitants was threatened and, in one case, 'government prison officers beat, kicked and kneed approximately 100 Vietnamese at Hei Ling Chau for at least three to four hours on 19 July 1988' (p. ix). Diller also found that the screening procedures of 1,300 asylum-seekers were wholly inadequate. (There was no explanation of purpose, no legal assistance, an inadequate questionnaire, a poor-quality interpreter service and no record of the responses of the Vietnamese.) After September 1988, when the United Nations High Commission for Refugees (UNHCR) became involved, the screening procedures improved somewhat but, the report suggested, they still fell far short of international legal standards and the UK's obligations under the Refugee Convention and Protocol of 1951 and 1967.

An Amnesty International (AI) Memorandum (1990) confirmed the findings of the Diller report and called for an urgent halt to the policy of forcible repatriation. The AI delegation also extracted a damaging admission from an official at the Hong Kong Security Branch. When he was asked why the Immigration Ordinance was amended in 1982 to provide for the detention of asylum-seekers, 'he responded frankly that the motivation was "deterrence".' As the writers of the AI memorandum were quick to point out, deterrence is not a lawful reason to detain asylum-seekers.

Faced with this barrage of criticism, the UK government lashed out. The US attitude was regarded as particularly 'hypocritical' – a typical journalistic hype leaked from Downing Street contended that Mrs Thatcher was 'furious' with President Bush's breach of the 'special relationship'. Six weeks later, the foreign secretary formally asked for the USA to admit some of the Vietnamese in Hong Kong. Disingenuous advice from beckbench Conservative MPs suggested that 'the Commonwealth should help', seeing that it was always striking moral attitudes. However, the argument that 'others should help' fell on stony ground, as the refugee agencies and other governments were all too aware that the British government had admitted a disproportionately low share of the world's refugees (see Chapter 3). The attack on the USA was seen by Washington as unseemly as Britain had only taken 3 per cent (4,000) of the Vietnamese settled through Hong Kong, while the USA had accepted 50 per cent. The jibe at the Commonwealth was equally misguided as Canada had admitted 121,000 Vietnamese,

Australia 118,000 and Malaysia 21,000, compared with Britain's total of 19,000. (Even little New Zealand, with its host population of 3,371,000, managed a respectable 8,000.)

The Hong Kong and British governments also vigorously maintained that what they had done was legal. The British government 'let it be known' that a draft agreement had existed since July 1989 with the Vietnamese government to readmit its citizens. The deportations were thus represented as part of a bilateral agreement, not an arbitrary unilateral decision. Officials also rather implausibly claimed that no force was used on the grounds that the 'removals' were carried out by uniformed officers in accordance with international procedures for the refoulement of illegal entrants.

Was force used? Police had arrived at the camps in full riot gear (including batons, revolvers, helmets and shields). In anybody's language, this certainly constituted the threat of force. They arrived at 3 a.m. – the time, according to war manuals, when resistance is lowest. There was also a deliberate and elaborate attempt to keep the operation secret. The timing and character of the deportations suggest a reluctance to have the operation witnessed. If it were legal and to be non-violent, why should it not have taken place in the full light of day?

Despite their claims to reasonableness and legality, the Hong Kong and British governments were, in truth, reacting to two political exigencies in addition to the sheer pressure of numbers. First, the Beijing authorities had made it clear they would not favour large numbers of 'non-Chinese' in Hong Kong after 1997, when the colony reverts to China. Second, despite serious sectoral labour shortages in Hong Kong arising from emigration due to the uncertainties of '1997', the level of local antagonism directed at the boat people was considerable and voluble.

Voluntary repatriations conducted under the aegis of the UNHCR continued over the 1989–92 period with over 2,000 Vietnamese being returned to their country. However, the British and Hong Kong authorities, despite a temporary lull after the adverse publicity arising from the forcible repatriations in 1989, continued to press for the compulsory return of some 40,000 people in the camps. The authorities accept that only 11,221 asylum-seekers had a prima facie claim to refugee status. In 1991 the Hong Kong authorities tried compulsion again – this time sending 123 Vietnamese back. Sedated women and struggling boat people did not provide the convincing evidence of the 'conditions of order, safety and dignity' that Hong Kong's secretary for security avowed would mark all future deportations. In May 1992 another agreement with Vietnam, which involved cash-transfers to resettle repatriates was negotiated. The first flight under the Orderly Return Programme took place in June 1992. They continue, with less publicity, to this day.

The deportation of the Vietnamese boat people has raised difficult moral and practical dilemmas for the authorities in Hong Kong that are not easily solved. This is particularly the case if some legitimacy is conceded to the argument that the colonial power, Britain, has not absorbed its 'fair share' of refugees compared to other countries, or to the dependency itself. On the other hand, there is no reason why one should sanction the flagrantly xenophobic attitudes manifested by a number of Hong Kong Chinese. Local legislators have demanded that boats should be turned back at sea. One highly publicised comment by a Hong Kong woman described Vietnamese as 'filthy, lazy, disease-ridden thieves' while another young woman working for the Justice and Peace Commission received abusive calls for daring to stand up *for* the Vietnamese (*Guardian Weekly*, 10 Dec. 1989). Clearly a hardening of attitudes and a loss of empathy with asylum-seekers is not a monopoly confined to European countries.

The Conservative Party and deportations

As was shown in the deportation of Hosenball and Agee, a home secretary in a Labour government is just as prone to use his powers of deportation in the interests of 'national security' as is a Conservative home secretary. However, there is little doubt that there is a qualitative distinction in immigration matters between the two parties, one which turns on the Conservatives' more intimate association with the ideas that Powell's 1968 'rivers of blood' speech brought to the surface.

In her much-quoted television speech in February 1978, Mrs Thatcher linked herself firmly to that tradition. Referring to trends in New (the official code name for 'non-white') Commonwealth and Pakistani immigration, she said:

That is an awful lot, and I think it means that people are really rather afraid that this country might be swamped by people of a different culture. The British character has done so much for democracy, for law, and done so much throughout the world that if there is any fear that it might be swamped, then people are going to be rather hostile to those coming in.

This was precisely the message that a large part of the British electorate wanted to hear. Paradoxically, however, for a politician whose popularity lay in the claim that she always did what she promised, Mrs Thatcher was already making an anachronistic appeal. The immigration legislation of 1961 and 1971 had already throttled off all primary ('breadwinner') immigration from so-called New Commonwealth countries and the British-Caribbean population, including their descendants, was actually declining. All that was left, in respect of controlling the inflow, was making it as difficult as possible for Indian, Bangladeshi and Pakistani spouses and dependants to join their breadwinners in the UK. The Home Office, the British visa officials in Asia and the IOs at Heathrow obliged with a series of petty, vindictive and obstructionist measures.

Some of the unrequited hostility of Mrs Thatcher's supporters was slaked by these actions, while xenophobia directed against asylum-seekers (see Chapter 3) provided a second outlet. Finally, however, a series of highly-publicised deportation cases provided much symbolic satisfaction to the anti-foreigner and anti-black brigade. The increased use of deportations can in some measure also be seen as a sop to the Tory right who had demanded 'voluntary repatriation' at a noisy inter-vention at the Tory conference in October 1983. While the demand was resisted by the platform, the issue of voluntary repatriation was to surface from an unexpected source ten years later (see below).

How was anthropemy practised in the post-1979 period? It may be useful first to provide some quantitative data on deportations during the three Thatcher terms of office (1979–90) and under the first two years of the leadership of Mr Major, which commenced in November 1990 after her enforced resignation. The Home Office records those required to leave the UK in complex tables involving 29 substantive categories and a number of subcategories.

The three main categories are: (a) 'RLEs', i.e. those who are 'refused leave to enter' the UK; (b) 'illegal entrants', i.e. normally those who are seen as having practised 'deception' at the port of entry and are consequently 'removed'; and (c) 'deportees', i.e those who are served with a deportation order arising from a court judgement or following a post-entry administrative decision by the IND.

The numbers of RLEs are quite considerable and rose by over 2,000 in the first year of Mrs Thatcher's government (1979) to 18,904. This number dropped back to 12,234 in 1982 (about the same level as the mid-1970s), then started rapidly climbing again, to 17,925 in 1985 and 23,110 in 1986. The Home Office justified these large numbers of refusals by pointing out that they are a very small proportion of the growing number of passengers arriving at British ports of entry. While this observation is valid, there is a considerable amount of pinpointing of particular flights. This is shown by the high variation in the RLEs by nationality. The IND department reports are careful not to attribute too much significance to differential rates of refusal by nationality, but the department and the minister none the less justified the imposition of visas for certain countries from the mid-1980s using the somewhat questionable notion of a differential 'pressure to emigrate' from vari-ous countries.

The particular range of countries selected for new visa controls included a number of Commonwealth countries – thus further 'demot-ing' them to a generalised post-empire category of alien countries. The list also corresponded closely to the countries mentioned as showing high rates of RLEs, illegal entrants and deportees.[10] In short, what we

---

10 The UK imposed visa restrictions on Sri Lankans in 1985, then on Indians, Bangla-deshis, Ghanaians, Nigerians and Pakistanis. In 1989, visa restrictions were abruptly

may be observing is the classic social scientific error of a 'self-fulfil-ling prophecy': creating the outcome by holding a predetermined expectation.

Although Jamaicans have not yet been added to the list requiring visas, a Christmas holiday flight from Jamaica in December 1993 was targeted by IOs who were, apparently concerned that 'Yardies' (Jamaican drug dealers) were posing as relatives of British-Caribbean residents. Over half the 323 passengers were detained, a riot was threatened at the detention centre at Campsfield House in Kidlington and adverse publicity associated with the Christmas spirit rattled the Home Office. Its spokesperson ingenuously sought to disarm criticism by stating that '*only* 407 Jamaicans had been detained in the previous year.' As the indignant relative of one of the passengers complained: 'They behaved as if every Jamaican was a Yardie. They might as well say every Italian is in the Mafia and every Irishman is in the IRA.' The *Daily Telegraph* (28 Dec. 1993) thought the episode 'a race relations fiasco'.

By contrast, the high rates of RLEs from the USA and Sweden, which showed up despite the relatively slack targeting of flights from these countries, were simply discounted on the grounds that 'such refusals are unlikely to reflect any general pressure to emigrate from the USA or Sweden' (IND 1984: 17). This argument is probably disin-genuous, as it would have been politically and economically impossi-ble to impose visas on the USA, if for no other reason than that the tourist trade would have collapsed. On the other hand, morally such an imposition would have conformed to the international law of tit-for-tat for, until recently, UK citizens had to have visas to enter the USA. Instead, government policy went in the opposite direction. In 1987, after noticing a 25 per cent drop in North American visitors, the secre-tary of state for employment proposed to ease immigration controls on US citizens by allowing pre-entry clearance on the US side (*Indepen-dent*, 28 July 1987).

When we consider the categories and many subcategories of 'illegal entrants' and 'deportees', the bureaucratic distinctions become finer, in so far as they refer not to the final outcome (people being required to leave) but to the means and the legal and administrative route that was used to reach that objective. Some people are even referred to as having 'departed voluntarily' though the word 'voluntarily' has to be taken with a pinch of salt. Those falling foul of the immigration authorities are confronted with the possibilities of detention, an elabo-

---

imposed on Turkish nationals, at a time when substantial numbers of Kurds were claiming asylum. Uganda was added in May 1991. At that date nationals of 99 countries needed visas. Compare this list to this IND's (1984: 18, 19) statement: 'The countries which feature prominently on lists of refusals, illegal entrants and deportations are Pakistan, Ghana and Turkey; while Bangladesh, India and Nigeria are prominent in two of the three lists.' (Sri Lanka was recorded as eighth on the list of illegal entrants.)

rate legal process, or being formally served with a deportation order – with a consequent likelihood of being never able to return to the UK.

Table 2.2 *Removals and Deportations under the Conservative Governments, 1979–92*

1979	1,382	1986	1,880
1980	1,872	1987	2,700
1981	946	1988	2,961
1982	863	1989	4,500
1983	1,365	1990	4,330
1984	1,545	1991	5,600
1985	1,665	1992	6,100

Sources: Home Office Statistical Bulletins (various years); reports of the IND, Home Office (various years); correspondence with the Home Office.

Table 2.2 records those removed from the UK under the enforcement powers of the Immigration Act of 1971 as illegal entrants, as deportees, or as 'voluntary' or 'supervised' deportees.

A cursory examination of the statistics shows that there has been a massively increasing propensity to use the powers of removal and deportation since 1979, particularly in the period 1989–92. This increased activity should be primarily interpreted as a way of keeping the Powellites and Euro-sceptics quiet. Despite a less forceful manner than his predecessor, Prime Minister Major is apparently intent on showing those who think that closer European union might involve the loss of national control over immigration matters that this is not a danger.

The quantitative data, however, tell only a part of the story. As pertinent as the figures themselves were four more qualitative changes in the practice of anthropemy: first, an increased propensity to deport and detain asylum-seekers requesting refuge in the UK (see Chapters 3 and 4); second, a greater determination in the Home Office to see through highly publicised and often controversial cases 'to the end'; third, an attempt to restrict the right of MPs to intervene in deportation cases; finally, the passing of additional legislation tightening the powers of deportation even further. I will examine the last three tendencies in turn.

Increased determination of the Home Office

The proliferating use of deportation orders by the immigration authorities triggered determined opposition by the Church, by newly formed pressure groups, by left-wing fringe parties and amongst friends and neighbours of those threatened. These protests mainly took the form of a sanctuary and anti-deportation 'movement' (if that is not too grand a term), discussed fully in Chapter 5. Here let me provide just one illustrative example, carefully chosen on the one hand not to provoke automatic sympathy with the victims but, on the other hand, to demonstrate the increased hardening of attitudes at the Home Office.

First some background. In the 1980s roughly one-third of deportation orders followed a drugs conviction. The courts have the power to recommend deportation, and in anything from one-third to one-half of drugs-related cases they did so. Almost invariably the Home Office complies with a court recommendation, but even where the court does not suggest deportation, the Home Office can still proceed with a deportation order.

This is what happened in the case of Andy Anderson and Farida Ali, whose campaign against deportation was taken up by the Greater Manchester Immigration Aid Unit. According to a pamphlet from the campaigners (AFA–DC n.d.), Anderson arrived in the UK from Jamaica in 1976 and was given permanent residence in 1978. He married a British citizen and had two children born in the UK. All his family were in the country. In 1987 the couple were convicted for the possession and supply of cannabis. Farida Ali (his spouse) was given a twelve-month sentence, her husband – who had one previous conviction for supplying – was imprisoned for four years. In September 1988, while in prison, he was served with a Home Office notice that his presence in the UK 'was not conducive to the public good'. His appeal was rejected at an Immigration Tribunal (with one out of three members, who happened to be black, strongly dissenting) and by the High Court.

In this case the trial judge had not ordered deportation, but the home secretary decided to deport, despite very favourable reports from the prison governor, the prison education officer, the probation officer, the prison chaplain and even an IO sent to interview Ms Ali. The campaigners argued that the mass of positive evidence was ignored because Anderson was black and a Rastafarian. The relevant minister at the Home Office, Peter Lloyd, refused to withdraw the deportation order, but offered to pay the fares for Ms Ali and the children to join him in Jamaica! As the campaigners contended, it was extraordinary that the government of the day was prepared to pay a British citizen to go into exile. Andy Anderson was ultimately deported.

Although it is more than likely that a convicted drug dealer does not constitute most people's idea of a solid citizen, this case illustrates several general features. First, any residual notion that Commonwealth origin provided a privileged status was firmly disabused. Second, the hidden frontier guards at the Home Office considered their own assessment of the case for deportation superior to the advice of prison officers, care workers close to the individual and even to the court itself. Third, in their determination to proceed with deportation, the fates of three British-born citizens (the wife and two children) counted for little.

The restriction of MPs' rights

Members of Parliament have a right (indeed a responsibility) to represent their constituents in immigration matters where they, or a constituent's relative or friend have fallen foul of the immigration authorities. The principal forms of intervention available to MPs are two: first, the 'stop' procedure, initiated in the 1960s, whereby a removal direction is delayed pending representation by a MP and the further consideration given to the case by the relevant minister of state at the Home Office. Second, MPs can ask the minister to allow a person entry 'outside the immigration rules', a power of administrative discretion allowed in the 1971 Immigration Acts. Taking these forms of representation together, Table 2.3 indicates the number of representations made over the period 1979–87.

There is no doubt that many of these representations were conscientious responses to genuine cases of distress at the ports of entry. On the other hand, it has to be accepted that some MPs became well known as sympathetic to deportation cases and often pursued cases even where there was no obvious constituency connection. Again, the power to ask for a 'stop', particularly if a number of members made this request, delayed matters for long enough for an ordinary visitor – perhaps without the necessary visa – to see their families.

Table 2.3 *Representations by MPs on immigration cases*

1979	10,395	1984	13,164
1980	10,029	1985	16,024
1981	8,945	1986	17,511
1982	9,931	1987	11,842
1983	11,456		

Source: Morgado (1989: 9) citing a parliamentary reply to Mr Jeremy Corbyn MP, 12 April 1988.

By July 1983, the minister of state at the Home Office, David Waddington, had had enough. He wrote to all MPs stating that he would only consider the first representation and that this should be made by a MP with a constituency interest. Then in May 1985, he initiated a brief experiment which only lasted two weeks, requesting that MPs should intervene in port-of-entry cases within 24 hours. With the assistance of the Tamil Refugee Action Group and the United Kingdom Immigration Advisory Service, the MPs swung into action to beat the deadline, only to find the Home Office was not able to respond as quickly. The experiment was abandoned (Morgado 1989: 14).

Rattled by this fiasco and the continuing flow of correspondence, in October 1985 Waddington accused MPs of 'abusing their right to make representations' and during the course of 1986 he issued four successive sets of 'guidelines' with which he asked MPs to comply. He failed in his attempt to get the chief IOs at the ports of entry, rather than his own office, to be responsible for giving reasons for refusal. But he succeeded in halting the grant of an automatic 'stop' in cases where visas had been required and where there was 'a clear attempt to seek entry through clearly bogus application for asylum'. The minister's mailbag was lighter by nearly 6,000 letters (see Table 2.3) in the year following this new ruling. He also was able to press the ruling that removal would be deferred only by twelve days if an MP intervened. Subsequently this period was reduced to eight days.

Further immigration legislation

As I have already explained in Chapter 1, the Nationality Act of 1981 was not so much an immigration act as a way of reconciling (and multiplying) definitions of nationality to conform to the evolution of immigration law and practice – in particular, the determination of who had the ultimate right of abode in the UK. With respect to my current concern with deportations, it is worth drawing attention to the difficult (though thankfully rare) situation that after the Act can result for those who are deported without having gained a *jus soli status*, a citizenship derived from their birthplace.

On such case concerned a London-born baby, Sidrah Syed, who happened to be born just four months after the implementation of the 1981 Act on 1 January 1983. His father, Shahid Syed, had come to the UK as a student in 1975 and worked for British Gas as an accountant after graduation. When his work permit was not renewed in 1983, he, his wife and baby Sidrah were faced with deportation to Pakistan, a country that Sidrah had no formal right to enter. Though the Home Office ultimately retreated, in essence the 1981 Act had created a stateless minor.

Seven years later, the Conservative government passed the Immigration Act of 1988. Lord McNair in the House of Lords lambasted this legislation as 'another mean-minded, screw-tightening, loophole-closing concoction imbued with the implicit assumption that almost everybody who seeks to enter this demi-paradise of ours has some ulterior, sinister, and very probably criminal motive and the sooner we get rid of him the better.'

In truth, the justification for another round of national legislation did seem rather thin. The government could not detect widespread abuse of the system or the influx of large additional numbers demanding entry. (According to the Home Office's own figures, 1986 was 'the lowest calendar year since Commonwealth citizens first became subject to control in 1962'.) So it appears that, once again, the legislation was directed to the ideological right who, like the hydra-headed Cerberus of classical times, needed continual supplies of honey cake to quieten them. One small example which reinforces this interpretation is the abrupt insistence in the Act that polygamous wives should no longer have the right of abode in the UK. This is both a demonstration of cultural arrogance and an illustration of the mean-mindedness Lord McNair referred to, as there were only about 25 such claims each year.

On the other hand, with respect to deportation the 1988 Act did contain some real teeth. Clause 4 severely limited the availability and scope of appeals for all those without UK citizenship and also constrained the right to appeal against deportation for those seeking refugee status. In the case of an overstayer who had been in the UK for less than seven years, no appeal would be allowed. In effect, the government appeared to be viewing the courts as getting in the way of the running of a smooth immigration control system and as interfering in the minister's discretionary powers. This impression was strongly reinforced by the speech of Mr Timothy Renton in the House of Commons who referred to the courts as a 'thicket within which the immigrant [sic] is well protected. He goes from one appeal to the next while the years drag on, at the end, after eight or nine years it is almost inevitable that he will be given leave to remain in Britain.'

The Act was also interpreted by the home secretary as having allowed changes at the administrative level, so that deportation orders could be made by IOs at the inspector level (instead of by staff at the IND). Under the 'supervised departure' power accorded to them, IOs were allowed to offer the alleged offender a speedy exit, rather than waiting 14 days in jail for all the formalities to be completed. Some 70 per cent of deportees in 1989 took this option.

Three immediate effects of the increased power granted to the IOs were visible. First, the number of deportations went up dramatically in 1989. Second, the police got involved to a much greater extent on the grounds that, as a Home Office spokesperson claimed: 'It is useful for immigration officers to have police along for their expertise. They attend in an advisory capacity' (*Standard*, 29 Nov. 1989). Joint raids by the police and immigration service also increased. One, on British Petroleum's headquarters in London, turned up 39 allegedly illegal cleaners, who were served with deportation orders.

Finally, a number of cases appeared where IOs exercised their newly assigned powers with such indecent haste that they deported British citizens. One instance concerned the unfortunate Mr Koyobe Alese, a 25-year-old British citizen, born and educated in Britain and whose parents live in northwest London. Stopped for a driving offence, he gave a false name which the police could not find on their computers.

They tipped off IOs who refused to believe him even after he had given his correct name. Distressed and bemused, he found himself at Lagos airport the next day (*Independent*, 29 April 1989).

These high-handed actions by IOs showed a scandalous disregard by the Home Office for the decision of Lord Justice Woolf in the High Court on 21 February 1990 that the home secretary had no right to delegate the power to issue deportation orders to IOs and that consequently 500 deportation orders were legally invalid. Individual IOs and the Home Office itself appeared to ignore this decision even though their own lawyers – in a confidential memo leaked to a newspaper in April 1989 – had anticipated the judgement.

Voluntary repatriation

As was mentioned earlier, a vociferous demand for 'voluntary repatriation' made at the Tory Party conference in 1983 was strongly resisted by David Waddington, the Home Office minister responsible for immigration: 'The government is not in the business of telling people who have made their lives here, who perhaps have even become British citizens: You are unwelcome. Here is some money. Clear off!' (*Financial Times*, 14 Oct. 1983).

But behind this public posture distancing the leadership from what was seen as an embarrassing Powellite legacy, there had in fact existed modest government support for at least two repatriation schemes. One, the Homeward Bound Fund run by a West Indian voluntary agency, had been endorsed by a previous home secretary, William Whitelaw, who thought the 'vast majority' of West Indians might be interested (*Guardian Weekly*, 29 Nov. 1981).

The second, an unpublicised scheme run by the grandly titled International Social Service of Great Britain from as early as 1971 on behalf of the Home Office, provided government money for fares, baggage and other incidental expenses for immigrants who wanted to be voluntarily repatriated (*The Times*, 20 Jan. 1984). The numbers involved are small – 32 people in 1990/1, 57 in 1991/2 and 38 in 1992/3, but the administrator of the scheme, David Harrison, had 'no qualms if the numbers of applicants increase – so long as I can get the resources required' (*Weekly Journal*, 24 Oct. 1993).

Mr Harrison's bureaucratic backwater was suddenly turned into a tempest by a proposal by the black MP, Bernie Grant, in October 1993 that black people should be given the option of a state-assisted return to their countries of origin. Many black organisations, the Labour Party and anti-racist groups immediately condemned Grant's proposal, arguing that he was resurrecting, even if inadvertently, Enoch Powell's 1968 objective. Grant himself immediately began to back-pedal. His proposal was for a 'conditional return' for those fed up with racism; he linked his remarks with his prior support for a 'reparations programme' to compensate Africans on the continent and in the diaspora for the slave trade.

Despite much indignation on the left and amongst British-born blacks, it is notable that many older people of Caribbean origin took a more relaxed view of Grant's statement. Many of the generation who had arrived in the 1950s had reached or were about to reach retirement and those with good occupational and state pensions had already begun returning in significant numbers to the Caribbean (roughly one fifth of the Caribbean population and their descendants had been lost over the 1970s and 1980s). In a letter to the *Independent* (7 Oct. 1993), one dissenting black activist with a strong record of anti-racist activity in local government, Linda Bellos, also sought to justify Grant's comments:

Perhaps because of Bernie's boldness there will be a serious discussion about the attitudes and actions that make so many British citizens feel so unwelcome in Britain. He has voiced the concerns of a significant section of the African and Caribbean community, but it is an indictment of British society.

Conclusion

Who, historically, have the British authorities made so unwelcome as to 'vomit them out', ejecting them from the body politic? As I have skipped through the centuries, the cast list has grown quite bloated. Former French allies, Jews, Lombards, Hansards, Flemings, Calvinists, Catholics, Spanish agents, continental revolutionaries, Indian seafarers and servants, Jews (again), Germans, Gypsies, Bolsheviks, black Commonwealth citizens, American radicals, illegal entrants, overstayers, drugs dealers; finally, a black Briton who had committed a driving offence – all these have been deported by executive authority, judicial recommendation or administrative decision.

The very diversity of the deportees' backgrounds questions any mono-focused characterisation of the motivations of the state and its agents. At various times their fears were structured by appeals to national security, economic competition, religious uniformity, ideological rigidity, cultural distinctiveness and racial purity. Yet behind this diversity there is also a common thread of insularity and fear of 'foreigners'. Hubert de Burgh's refusal to surrender Dover to the 'French aliens' in 1216 is not so different from Enoch Powell's classification of black Commonwealth citizens as 'an alien wedge' more than 500 years later.

But who becomes the alien, who 'the other', who has to be distrusted, despised and deported, remains historically and politically contingent. The victims of a nasty version of the old game of 'pass the parcel' are those who appropriate to themselves the task of defining the 'self', and in so doing identify those they most need to exclude and repulse.

Before the last war all manner of people fell victim to this horrid game. From the 1950s to the 1980s the victims have primarily been black and brown people from the Commonwealth. Unfortunately, they are still subject to the most disgraceful forms of racial discrimination within Britain, which I in no way wish to discount or minimise. However, it became apparent in the 1980s and 1990s that another alien menace is being constructed by the frontier guards. These are the 'undeserving asylum-seekers', from the Middle East, Turkey, Asia, eastern Europe or the New Commonwealth. Colour is now less relevant. Wherever they come from, these are not 'genuine refugees' but disguised 'economic migrants', we are told. The history, fate and uncertain future of asylum-seekers and refugees form the subject of my next chapter.

CHAPTER 3

Asylum: the shrinking circle of generosity

> Remove the chains of oppression and the yoke of injustice, and let the oppressed go free. Share your food with the hungry poor and open your homes to the homeless. . . . If you put an end to oppression, to every gesture of contempt and to every evil work; if you give food to the hungry and satisfy those who are in need, then the darkness around you will turn to the brightness of noon.
>
> — *New English Bible*, Isaiah, 58: 6–10

The biblical injunction to open your homes to the homeless symbolises the generous and humane motives that are often thought to underlie the offer of asylum. While I have no wish to deprecate the power of altruism, a more careful examination of the circumstances in which asylum is normally granted suggests that state interest or ethnic solidarity, rather than the milk of human kindness, are more often at the root of a generous policy. I detail the history and recent changes to asylum practices and policies in the UK. Finally, I examine the agents who implement asylum policies, the press media that seek to influence public attitudes and the international, domestic and diplomatic pressures that have led to increasingly restrictive policies.

Granting asylum: general reasons

States have withheld or permitted asylum in a variety of circumstances. However, four important considerations have normally obtained.

First, the states concerned wished to display their moral superiority or political legitimacy *vis-à-vis* other countries with which they were in diplomatic or actual conflict. Sometimes this public posture was enshrined in constitutional form, as in the Preamble to the 1793 French Constitution. This proclaims: 'Anyone persecuted because of his action for Freedom has a right to asylum in the territories of the Republic.' Article 16 of the post-1945 West German constitution – which was fundamentally amended in May 1993 (see Chapter 6) – also included generous provisions for asylum. In each case, these provisions were not simply of historic interest, for they provided the constitutional basis for how individual applications for refugee status were processed.

Even where constitutional enactment does not obtain, declarations of political preference are provided in immigration laws or in statements by the leading politicians of particular countries. Thus, before 1980, the *definition* of a refugee in the USA was someone 'fleeing from communism, or fleeing from a communist-dominated country'. The openly political aspect of refugee status was starkly revealed in the period of the Cold War, in that Western countries – notably the USA – welcomed those from 'behind the iron curtain', but were very sceptical of the claims of those seeking asylum from other countries.

The differential treatment in the 1980s of those leaving Cuba for the USA compared to those leaving Haiti is another case in point – though political freedoms under the personal autocracy of the Duvaliers could hardly be said to be greater than the freedoms obtaining under Castro (R. Cohen 1987: 148–56). After a military coup against an elected president in 1991, many Haitians once again took to their boats to flee the political chaos on the island.

In addition to political considerations, the second general consideration that influenced the conferring of refugee status was the use-value that could be obtained by the receiving state of the skills and resources possessed by the refugees. Again, some early and more recent examples will illustrate the point.

In 1228, Henry III attempted to induce the whole university community to move from Paris to England, after scholars there had rioted. He claimed to want to lead the university 'back to true liberty' but, more cynically, was also aware of the knowledge, power, prestige and revenue the scholars brought with them (Speier 1969: 87). The combination of cocking a snook at Catholicism and deploying the useful skills of the Huguenots also accounts for their general welcome in England. As a former immigration officer and historian of the UK Immigration Service enthused, 'of all the refugee waves which have washed ashore on these islands, one of the most beneficial and widely welcomed by the native population was the Huguenots, with their intelligence, steadfastness, culture and love of liberty' (Roche 1969: 36–7).

Though few people of goodwill would wish to deny small numbers of itinerant intellectuals or religious dissenters the prospect of asylum, the principle of use-value can on occasions lead to the granting of asylum status to wholly obnoxious and undeserving individuals, such as the Nazi scientists who were recruited by US laboratories and agencies to further the defence and space programmes initiated by the US government after the Second World War.

Of course not all scientific refugees to the USA were Nazis; many others had shown their undoubted value to their country of asylum by making fundamental or benign discoveries in science and engineering. Up to 1982, US Nobel prize winners in physics numbered 52, 20 of whom were non-native born, while of the 61 winners in physiology and medicine, 24 were foreign-born. Although the data do not distinguish refugees from other foreign-born scholars, the figures presented by period and place of birth suggest that many foreign-born prize winners were refugees from Nazism or Fascism (Lerner and Roy 1984: 254–5). The notable contribution of refugees to the UK can also be gauged by Lord Ashby's remarks on BBC radio in July 1977. He referred to 53 (1 in 14) of the Fellows of the Royal Society, 28 Fellows of the British Academy and 15 Nobel prize winners being refugees from Nazi Germany or their descendants (cited BRC 1987).

The third reason why states may be inclined to confer asylum status is related to demographic or nationalist pressures. In the case of France after the First World War – when two out of every ten young men had been killed and a further three disabled – demographers, economists and politicians expressed serious concern about the level of French industrial activity, indeed about whether the country could survive as a 'great power', without an increase in the population. As a consequence of this concern, France became the largest net recipient of refugees and migrants after the USA in the interwar period. A similar motive arose in the case of Germany, which again took large numbers of 'white' Russians after 1917.

The fourth form of asylum commonly recognised is when 'the kith and kin' of the majority of a state's population runs into trouble abroad and has to be repatriated. The Germans have perhaps been the most inept colonisers in this respect. They had to repatriate their kinsfolk from their African colonies after the First World War (a small group remains in Namibia) and have also managed to 'leave behind' some 1.6 million ethnic Germans spread across Poland, Romania, Czecho-slovakia, Yugoslavia and Hungary (in that order of magnitude) together with some 1.7 million ethnic Germans in the former Soviet Union. With the collapse of communism, much of this diaspora is demanding repatriation, the ethnically based 'law of return' in the German constitution acting as a permissive factor. Similarly, the French had to evacuate large numbers of settlers from Indo–China and Algeria, while the Portuguese absorbed 600,000 settlers from their colonies in Africa over the period 1975–77 (some 18 per cent of the total population of Portugal).

In addition to those with a direct ancestral link to the colonising country concerned, local or mixed-race civil servants, supporting merchant groups or affiliated military allies were absorbed by the former colonial powers. Loyal functionaries from the Dutch East Indies were returned to Holland in 1945, Harkis (Arab Christians supporting the French) from Algeria came to France, while *assimilados* from Mozam-bique and Angola were given rights of abode in Portugal. Often the process of integration of such groups is highly fraught. Those supporting the continuation of the French presence in Algeria, for example, resorted to terrorism, subverted a considerable proportion of the army and came within an inch of assassinating President de Gaulle, whom they saw as having betrayed them. As loyal supporters of the colonisers, the Harkis in France also militantly espoused their difference from Muslim Arabs.

The four previously mentioned criteria (political accolades, use-value, demographic reasons and ethnic solidarity with communities and their supporters abroad) also sometimes work in combination. Joly (1993), for example, argued that domestic and foreign policy considerations jointly define how the 'national interest' is construed in immigration matters. Contested interpretations of the national interest can, further, allow ethnic factors to emerge as a significant variable in asylum decisions.

Decisions based on political and economic factors were gradually supplemented, though never supplanted, by the evolution of international law, which somewhat limited the previously arbitrary powers of the signatory states to withhold asylum. In 1951 this development led to the signing of a Convention by a number of countries stating that the right of asylum would be granted to those 'who had a reasonable expectation of losing their life, property or liberty if returned to their country of origin'. The 1967 Protocol Relating to the Status of Refugees was signed by nearly 100 countries; it permitted, for the first time, the use of humanitarian judgements and an individual's claims to be taken in conjunction with the state's predominant role in granting asylum status.

Refugee history

It is often asserted and widely believed that Britain has an exemplary record of offering hospitality to those fleeing from political and religious persecution. Indeed, the very word 'refugee' was first used to describe the French Huguenots who fled to England from Catholic intolerance as a result of the revocation of the Edict of Nantes. The belief in the UK's open-hearted history also derives from the granting of asylum to conservatives fleeing the French Revolution. (The lofty superiority of English Royalism to French Jacobinism is romanticised in the novels by Baroness Orczy describing the exploits of the 'Scarlet Pimpernel'.)

Again, the admission of nineteenth-century socialists and revolutionaries fleeing the European counter-revolutions of the years following 1848 is well known. The case of Karl Marx is one often evoked as a demonstration of English insouciance in the face of the strange doings of the foreigners in their midst. The story is told, for example, of a porter working for the British Museum, where Marx drafted his masterpiece, *Das Kapital*. When asked if he knew the great man, he confessed he did indeed know the German gentleman who came there every day for over a decade. But he had suddenly stopped coming and had not been heard of since.

The porter's ignorance symbolises Britain's insular location which had left it relatively immune from the swirls of ideas and populations in nineteenth-century Europe. The small numbers of socialist, radical and nationalist dissenters escaping from the continent could be absorbed with little fuss. Only in the three decades before the First World War did the number of European migrants and refugees become significant. Britain received some 120,000 Jews from eastern Europe and this influx led to the first formalisation of asylum policy (Marrus 1985: 36–7).

In the Aliens Act of 1905 limits were set to unwanted immigrants and, as shown in Chapter 2, deportations became increasingly common. However, a distinction was still drawn between immigrants and political refugees. No one would be refused admission to Britain, 'who proves that he is seeking admission to this country solely to avoid prosecution or punishment on religious or political grounds, or for an offence of a political character, or persecution involving danger of imprisonment or danger to life and limb' (cited Marrus 1985: 37).[1]

In the interwar period refugees from the Soviet Union, Fascist Italy, Franco's Spain and Nazi Germany all washed up on British shores, though the numbers involved were generally small. After the fall of Archangel to the Red Army in February 1920, anti-Bolshevik Russians started arriving in the UK. Anna Pavlova established her ballet school in Hampstead, but the cultural attractions of Berlin and Paris were more alluring and, after onward migration to the USA and other parts of Europe, the Russian émigré population in the UK soon dropped well below its peak of 15,000.

Similarly, the number of exiles attracted to the UK from interwar Italy and Spain was modest. Relatives of Claudio Treves, a founder of the Italian Socialist Party, came to Britain to form the Italian League for the Rights of Man, an anti-Fascist movement. Again, 'several hundred' Italian Jews fled to Britain in 1939 when Mussolini passed a number of race laws to placate Hitler (Gillman and Gillman 1980: 148). Despite the friendships wrought during the valiant service of a

---

1 The distinction between immigrants and refugees remains a controversial one. In a sense, most migration is compelled, if only by force of economic circumstance. However, it may be possible to hold that a refugee is fleeing from much *more* compelling, immediate, and life-threatening circumstances – a civil or international war, famine, a natural disaster or an imminent political threat involving torture, imprisonment or other forms of persecution. After 1951, the Geneva Convention laid a greater stress on the element of persecution and since that time the expression 'Convention refugee' has been used to make clear that the individual concerned qualifies under the terms of that Convention. The expression 'asylum-seeker' has been used (in this book and more generally) to refer to those who request, but who have not yet obtained, Convention refugee, or a similar, status. Pressure groups and many asylum-seekers themselves are forced to recognise the host state's exclusive right to confer the formal status of 'refugee'. None the less the informal, but legally erroneous, appellation 'refugee' – rather than 'asylum-seeker' – is popularly used to describe those who have fled their homes to seek safety elsewhere.

good number of British socialists and communists in the International Brigade, Republican exiles from Spain went largely to Spanish-speaking America.

Only in the case of those fleeing from the Nazis did the numbers arriving in Britain reach a total comparable with other destinations. The refugees of the 1930s arrived mainly from Germany, Austria and Czechoslovakia. Most were Jews, but many were not and it is important to remember too that a good number were Jews only in the sense that the Nazis decreed (by descent, and sometimes remote descent). German Jewry had always been among the most assimilated in Europe and many Jews had no religious convictions. Holmes (1988: 118–19) estimates that of the 360–370,000 Jews who left the Greater Reich (Germany, Austria, Bohemia and Pomerania) between 1933–39, 50,000 came to Britain, 53,000 left for Palestine and 57,000 went to the United States; the rest scattered to numerous other countries.

The cohort of German Jews that came to Britain has been intensively studied (for instance, Sherman 1973; Berghahn 1984) and a number have supplied their own reminiscences of their journeys and reception. As a group they contained a remarkable array of talent – in the arts, in history, philosophy and the social and natural sciences. Taken together with the prewar Austrian and Polish émigrés, they became the dominant figures in British intellectual life. Perry Anderson (1992: 48–104), in his incisive essay on the 'Components of the National Culture', went so far as to suggest that the pre-eminent influence of these often fearful, conservative figures in so many disciplines had a 'chloroforming effect' on the development of both an English Marxism and a critical sociology.

The continentals, he maintained, served to reinforce and validate conservative and backward thinking. Anderson's view can be challenged on the grounds that his Cambridge-focused spectacles have missed intellectual developments in the Celtic fringe and in the English provinces, but what is indisputable is that the refugee intellectuals on the left generally found a more congenial setting and more receptive audience for their views in the USA rather than the UK.[2]

In the stress on distinguished intellectuals and Nobel prize winners, a feature of the group that has often been missed is that many of the prewar refugees were industrialists who took advantage of 'special

---

2   As Hoch (1985) shows, *all* the refugees, of whatever political disposition, had a difficult time getting their claims to eminence recognised. The British Medical Council rejected German qualifications while the Association of University Teachers passed a resolution in May 1933 that any facilities granted to refugee academics should be 'temporary'. As late as May 1938, the Association of Scientific Workers refused to encourage 'the admission of foreign scientists unless there are definite and specific openings for them'. The principal academic refugee aid organisation, the Society for the Protection of Science and Learning, noted in 1946 that of the 2,561 scholars they had helped since 1933, only 601 were still living in the UK. Most had moved on to the USA.

area' grants by the government to lift Britain out of the depression. One estimate, made in 1947, contended that the refugees of the previous sixteen years had established over 1,000 firms, giving employment to 250,000 people, several times more than their own number (Holmes 1988: 127–8). Moreover, as Hoch (1985) notes, the businesses promoted included the newer science-based industries like photography, electronics, radio and television, the last being extensively developed by German refugee engineers.

Refugees after 1945

During the 1939–45 war itself, Belgians, French and other Europeans, about 10,000 of whom were Jews, fled from the advancing Nazi forces (Holmes 1988: 162–3). Toward the end of the war about 200,000 Poles and other east Europeans, who had sought refuge from Nazi occupation in the UK, now asked to stay rather than be placed under the hegemony of the Soviet bloc.

The British authorities both accepted those who would not or could not return to their countries of origin and in addition recruited some 80–90,000 'displaced persons' (DPs) from the camps in the British zones in Austria and Germany. Neither group fitted exactly into conventional immigration definitions. The Poles (who numbered 115,000 with their families) had fought for the Allies and were felt to deserve postwar sanctuary. They were formed into the Polish Resettlement Corps. The DPs were given a brand-new name, the European Voluntary Workers (EVWs) though, as Kay and Miles (1992) have demonstrated, whether they were volunteers, labour migrants or refugees was far from certain.

The emptying of the DP camps conformed to two political impulses and one more overriding economic imperative. The postwar refugee agencies and the UN were pressuring the occupying powers to solve the costly and embarrassing problem of leaving over one million people in the camps who refused to be repatriated. The second political impulse was that many DPs were firmly anti-Soviet, a posture that now conformed to Britain's position at the opening of the Cold War. Finally, there was an economic imperative in that Britain was desperately short of the labour needed to regenerate industrial production.

In the crucial debate in the House of Commons in February 1947, the Home Office frontier guards' objection that the DPs would not be repatriable was loudly dismissed. The Conservative MP for Solihull insisted that Britain needed 'an infusion of vigorous new blood'. The DPs were described as 'ideal immigrants', 'first class people, who if let into this country, would be a great benefit to our stock' and people 'with a love of freedom' (Kay and Miles 1992: 53–4). To the objection that there might be public hostility, the impassioned MPs argued that it was up to the government to 'remove this wretched prejudice'.

The EVWs were admitted in a sequence conforming to a rough-and-ready ethnic and gender hierarchy, with Baltic women near the top of the tree. Through the poetically titled Balt Cygnet Scheme women were recruited for work in the TB sanatoria. Other Latvians, Estonians and Lithuanians, together with Polish-Ukrainians, Yugoslavs, Hungarians, Greeks, Czechs, Volkdeutsche and Sudetens followed. The hierarchy included quite a number of those who had fought for the Nazis, including 8,500 Ukrainians in the Waffen SS 'Galizien' Division. Many had volunteered to serve the Nazis and some had massacred Jews while in Ukrainian police and militia units (Cesarani 1992: 14).[3] On the other hand, the recruiters refused additional Polish men – there were thought to be enough already – and most definitely stopped short at the prospect of enrolling Jews, only 3,000 of whom were allowed to enter Britain. Despite the pictures of the concentration camps, despite the holocaust, old prejudices ran deep. Moreover, the attacks by the Jewish terrorists on the British army in Palestine served to offset any sympathy for the principal victims of the Nazi atrocities.

The admission of the EVWs was the last large group of 'refugees' to enter Britain and, as already suggested, they were refugees in a rather special sense. The Cold War still produced the occasional defecting dancer, sportsperson or intellectual who could be used to demonstrate the UK's moral preeminence over Stalinism (which, in truth, was not that difficult to show). But the British government's enthusiasm for waging the Cold War never reached the levels of fervour found in the USA and the policy toward accepting anti-communist refugees was normally reactive, not proactive.

Inside the Soviet bloc, the denunciation of Stalinism at the twentieth congress of the Soviet Communist Party in 1956 triggered a national uprising in Hungary led by radical students and workers. Its brutal crushing dispersed many thousands of dissidents, 15,000 of whom were admitted to Britain. Twelve years later, when the 'Prague Spring' again proved a premature challenge to the tenaciously entrenched Communist bosses, some 5,000 Czechs arrived in the UK after the Soviet invasion of their country.

From the mid-1970s the largest groups of refugees have come under special programmes as 'quota' or 'programme' refugees. About 3,000 Chileans, most of whom were political activists, arrived after Allende's government was overthrown in 1973. Approximately 18,000 Vietnamese, some of them 'boat people' picked up by British merchant or naval ships, others via Hong Kong, have also settled in Britain.

---

3 Early in 1987, these admissions of Nazi immigrants were suddenly and embarrassingly to resurface, after representations to the Home Office by the Soviet Union for the extradition of 34 alleged war criminals. Research by Scottish Television and the Simon Wiesenthal Centre turned up a further 17 British residents who could be so described.

In addition to the small quota refugee programmes, asylum-seekers often identify themselves at the port of entry. Their claims, where not immediately discounted, are then passed to the Immigration and Nationality Department (IND) at the Home Office. Post-entry applications for asylum or extensions of their 'leaves to remain' also arise in the case of nationals who have been visiting, studying or working in the UK who can argue that they are unable to return because of the conditions obtaining in their home countries. Iranian, Polish, Iraqi, Somali and Kurdish visitors and students have been notable beneficiaries of favourable decisions by the IND in recent post-entry cases.

While it would be churlish to undervalue the numerous and praiseworthy examples of the opening of British homes to the homeless, Britain's shrinking circle of generosity towards refugees in recent years, compared with other countries, can be all too adequately statistically demonstrated. In the period 1984–86, for example, the UK had processed 13,300 asylum-seekers' claims compared with West Germany's 208,000 and France's 71,300. Measured in terms of numbers per million of the host population, Sweden was top of a European table of ten countries with 4,975 applicants per million. The UK was last, with 240 applicants per million UK residents (Joly and Cohen 1989: 11).

Quota refugees: the Chileans and Vietnamese

Although they involved small numbers, the quota refugees presented some important innovations in UK refugee policy. The Chilean programme started in the wake of the repression that followed the military's assassination of the legitimately elected President Allende. This was given widespread coverage in the British press. The detention and torture of British citizens in Chile, in particular Dr Sheila Cassidy, also attracted opprobrium to the government of General Pinochet. The fact that the Labour Party was in office with ministers such as Judith Hart (at Overseas Development) and Alex Lyon (at the Home Office) in sympathy with the broad aims of the Allende government, lent additional credence to the claim by Chileans fleeing the regime that they were political refugees.

Even then the government moved cautiously. It set up investigating committees to examine the strength of the claims of refugees who had found their way to Argentina and other Latin American countries, before they were allowed admission to the UK. The programme for the admission of 3,000 Chilean refugees was agreed with other governments and implemented with the help of voluntary agencies such as the World University Service.

In the case of the Vietnamese, the first 645 admitted were boat people picked up on the high seas by British merchant ships answering

SOS calls. Initially, there was considerable public sympathy for the plight of the boat people, but this soon soured as the numbers increased. By 1979, Britain was under strong UN pressure to take its share of the Vietnamese arriving in Hong Kong (see Chapter 2). At first the UK government agreed to 10,000, but this climbed to about 18,000 when an extended definition of family reunion was permitted.

Again the Home Office sought the help of voluntary agencies, this time consciously opting for a policy of dispersal away from the capital city. (The Netherlands and Sweden had pioneered such an approach.) The Joint Committee for Refugees from Vietnam (JCRV) acted as a co-ordinating body, while agencies like Refugee Action, the British Refugee Council (which later also took over the JCRV's role) and the Ockenden Venture were given responsibility for resettlement in the different regions.

A detailed study of the resettlement process in Birmingham (Joly 1989) throws light on a number of the problems encountered. The Home Office 'front-loaded' the financial support for the programme too much, so that when later difficulties emerged there was nothing in the kitty; English language acquisition was spotty; the Vietnamese tended to regroup into more viable groups and defy the intentions of the dispersal policy; the southern Catholic Vietnamese found it easier to integrate than the northern Buddhists; the agencies found it difficult to co-ordinate their efforts rather than compete for funds. While concurring with many of these critical judgements, the Home Office's valuable internal study (Jones 1982: 52) concluded that, 'the general feeling of the people directly involved in the running of the programme was one of support. Dispersal, despite its various shortcomings, was felt to have been an asset from a practical point of view.'

Notwithstanding the real difficulties encountered, the Chilean and Vietnamese examples illustrate that the UK government and voluntary agencies are able to respond positively when there is a broad sympathy for the case of the refugees, where the programme is organised and controlled, where the numbers are known and limited and where arrangements for reception and resettlement have been made.

Repatriates and 'Loyalists'

Britain's emigration history is distinguished by the near-universally successful establishment of its colonies of settlement abroad. The British diasporas in Australia, New Zealand, the USA and Canada have all constituted themselves into stable and prosperous states. This contrasts sharply with the diasporas of a number of other expansionist powers – the repatriation of unsuccessful German, French and Portuguese diasporas and their supporters has already been mentioned.

Although they have not generally been understood in these terms, the East African Asians who were allowed to settle in Britain are an analogous case to the loyalist groups of other colonial powers. As independence approached in East Africa, nationalist leaders were able to insist on the requirement that non-Africans should decide for themselves whether they wished to remain as British nationals or become Kenyans, Ugandans or Tanganyikans. As Goulbourne (1991: 108) suggests, it is a testament to Nyerere's leadership that about half the Asians threw their lot in with Tanzania. On the other hand, there were dramatic expulsions of British Asians from Kenya in 1966 and even more frightening attacks on Asians in Uganda over the period 1971–73. Some 30,000 British Asians were finally expelled from Uganda by President Amin: most came to Britain.

A second group of loyal servants of the Crown likely to arrive in significant numbers is from Hong Kong. Since 1981, the government has tried to throttle this potential flow. Before that date, Hong Kong had the formal status of a British colony, though in reality it was a territory leased from China until 1997. In 1981, the UK altered Hong Kong's status (along with some other territories) to that of a 'dependent territory' – the crucial difference in immigration terms being that a citizen of UK dependency carries an inferior British passport which does not allow the automatic right of entry, settlement and work in the UK. Although at the time it was vehemently denied that the British Nationality Act was drafted predominantly with Hong Kong in mind, there is no doubt that this was indeed the main purpose of the legislation.

While the Act provided reassurance for the Tory right wing that they would not be 'flooded' with indigent people from Hong Kong fleeing from the consequences of the return of the territory to Beijing in 1997, the high-handed redefinition of the nationality laws undoubtedly had some deleterious effects on UK interests. With some pique directed at their former protectors, most wealthy Hong Kong entrepreneurs have centred their emigration plans on Canada, the USA and Australia (so denying to Britain the very epitomes of the enterprise culture that the government of the day so admired and lauded).[4]

The destabilising effects of the Nationality Act on the dependency were so great that even the 'old swamper', Mrs Thatcher, was constrained to allow a 'safeguard' plan permitting 50,000 Hong Kong 'loyal' civil servants and key decision-makers (and their families) the ultimate right to settle in the UK. The covert manner in which the select list has been compiled (in conformity with British traditions of

4 The guru of the monetarist right, the Chicago economist Milton Friedman, based his enthusiastic defence of free-market capitalism and the enterprise culture on the example of Hong Kong. Some would argue he misunderstood what he saw, in that one of the primary factors of production in Hong Kong is land, which is, in effect, nationalised as Crown Land. At any event, the Reagan – Thatcher ideological axis was predicated on what was *assumed* to be the Hong Kong paradigm.

closed government) has caused much bitterness in Hong Kong, but has probably served its primary purpose of anchoring the administration until 1997. The concession was also the occasion of a public fall-out between Mrs Thatcher and her hitherto devoted ally, Norman Tebbit, who acknowledged no obligation from empire, no honour due from those who profited from it and even no case on the pragmatic principle that an unstable Hong Kong would destabilise the British economy itself.

The final group that needs consideration here are repatriates 'proper' from southern Africa who may arrive in significant numbers in the 1990s. Under the patrial Clauses of the 1971 immigration legislation, anyone with one British parent or grandparent has a right of abode along with their spouse and children under eighteen. For many white Zimbabweans who were so qualified, the Mugabe regime proved less threatening to the white minority than some had feared. But by the early 1990s, the honeymoon period seemed to be drawing to a close. Farmers with large landholdings were faced with the prospect of compulsory purchase so as to provide something for the numerous landless and poverty-stricken Africans. There was a severe drought, inflation was running at 35 per cent and the regime itself appeared increasingly unpopular and vulnerable. The non-convertibility of the Zimbabwean dollar acts as a disincentive to potential repatriates, but it is likely that several thousand will return to the UK during the course of the 1990s.

The number of patrials in South Africa itself is considerable – perhaps as many as 800,000 adults and their dependants could qualify. In addition, British immigration law has always allowed 'persons of independent means' to enter the UK. Though the sum is large, despite difficulties in exporting Rands, it might be within the range of some thousands of non-patrial South African whites.

The first statistically significant signs of restiveness were seen in 1985, when net migration from South Africa to the UK rose threefold to 7,000. In the next year the number of whites leaving South Africa exceeded the number entering for the first time in many years. In April 1993, after the feared unrest following the assassination in South Africa of the prominent African National Congress leader, Chris Hani, local removals companies reported unprecedented business.

It is difficult to interpret the salience of these indicators with certainty. Some of the inflow from South Africa to the UK may be of recent British migrants who have decided to return to their homes because of the political and economic uncertainties in South Africa. Of the long-resident whites leaving South Africa, only about one-third appear to be coming to the UK – there are richer pickings to be had in Australia and Canada. Despite these ambiguities in interpreting the data, we can surmise that the course of progressive political change in South Africa is bound to be contentious and somewhat bloody. Amongst the whites, it may be that only the Afrikaners and those committed to the necessity of change will have the stomach to stay. Those who have access to British passports and the patrial right to return may well take advantage of the repatriation option.

From refugee to 'economic migrant'

Contemporary British refugee policy is predicated not so much on any plans for future quota refugees nor on any calculations that can be made in respect of the return of repatriates and loyalists. Rather, policy is largely framed as a reaction to the arrivals at the port of entry claiming asylum and the post-entry admissions who claim that conditions in their home countries have altered so adversely that they cannot safely return. For such groups, especially those without the influence of an established co-ethnic indigenous group lobbying on their behalf, British refugee policy has become increasingly hostile.

Between 1979, when the figures first began to be kept in this form and 1986, some 28,029 applications for asylum were processed (Table 3.1). The period is not only a useful statistical bench mark, it also was characterised by the start of the 'Thatcher years' and concluded by the adoption of major restrictions against asylum-seekers, first by the imposition of visa requirements on certain countries and second, by the Carriers Liability Act.

Table 3.1 *Main countries of origin of asylum-seekers, 1979–86*

	1979	1980	1981	1982	1983	1984	1985	1986	Total
Iran	797	1,421	1,547	2,280	1,862	1,310	1,126	865	11,208
Sri Lanka	1	18	12	16	380	548	2306	1009	4,290
Ghana	122	29	13	407	689	337	175	174	1,946
Iraq	65	149	14	271	298	348	350	237	1,732
Poland	42	55	92	494	127	109	71	57	1,047
Ethiopia	189	97	90	90	126	135	209	178	1,114
Uganda	38	28	99	66	199	165	203	162	960
Sub-total	1254	1797	1867	3624	3681	2952	4440	2682	22,297
Others	309	530	558	599	615	917	1004	1200	5732
Total	**1563**	**2327**	**2425**	**4223**	**4296**	**3869**	**5444**	**3882**	**28,029**

Source: Home Office Statistical Bulletins. Correspondence with the Home Office (IND).

It is important to interpret these figures carefully. The increasing absolute number of applicants, which peaked in 1985, provided the key justification for Home Secretary Douglas Hurd to argue in favour of visa controls for selected countries (imposed mainly in 1985–86). He also proclaimed his conviction that the asylum applicants coming to Britain were not true political refugees, but 'disguised economic migrants' from poor countries. Despite the continual repetition of this description by Hurd and other politicians, his argument is crucially flawed in three respects:

- First, the home secretary took no notice of the clear evidence that the number of indisputably genuine refugees worldwide had increased dramatically since 1975, perhaps by about ten million people, due mainly to civil wars, regional conflict and ethnic violence (Zolberg *et al.* 1989). It is therefore not the slightest bit surprising that Britain – like virtually every other stable nation, including many in Africa, Asia, the Middle East and Latin America – received an increased number of applicants.
- The second error in the home secretary's reasoning can be discerned from the *outcomes* of the applications themselves. Some 70 per cent of the 1979–86 applicants were either granted full refugee status, or were given 'exceptional leave to remain' (ELR), implying that their cases could not be rejected outright. This pattern of recognition is not greatly out of line with earlier decades, as the Home Office reports themselves stress. Unless Mr Hurd was suggesting that he had suddenly acquired a whole lot of 'softies' in the IND – for which proposition he gave no hint – the increased numbers simply reflected the fact that there were a whole lot more genuine refugees around.
- The final refutation of Mr Hurd's viewpoint is that the pattern of applicants does not suggest a generalised movement from all poor countries, but a *periodic* movement from *some* poor countries, a movement which correlates strongly with political disturbances in those countries. The argument can be replicated for all the countries listed in Table 3.1, but is most evident in the case of Sri Lanka. Prior to 1982, there were hardly any applicants from that country; from 1982, when Sinhalese–Tamil communal violence commenced and massive government repression was instituted, the numbers suddenly shot up.

Visas, the Carriers Liability Act and 58 Tamils

The construction of a new stigmatised group, the 'disguised economic migrant', was necessary to the deconstruction of the morally untouchable category of the 'deserving political refugee'. The frontier guards were, in other words, more anxious to show that they were responsive to popular and right-wing demands for restricting all 'immigration', than they were to conform to the letter and spirit of the International Conventions signed by successive British governments.

That the frontier guards were not fundamentally interested in the exercise of separating 'genuine' from 'spurious' refugees is shown by their determined attempts to prevent all asylum-seekers from reaching Britain in the first place. This was done first by imposing visa requirements on so-called 'pressure to migrate' or 'refugee-producing' countries, notions derived from the sort of data presented in Table 3.1 above. The UK repeatedly implemented visa requirements when refugee claims increased: for Sri Lankans in 1985, then for Indians, Bangladeshis, Ghanaians, Nigerians and Pakistanis. In 1989, visa restrictions were abruptly made mandatory for Turkish nationals, at a time when substantial numbers of Kurds were claiming asylum. Uganda was added in May 1991, making a total of 99 countries whose nationals henceforth needed visas to enter the UK.

The imposition of visa restrictions created a high hurdle even for family visitors from the Indian subcontinent where documentation, for such simple matters as a birth certificate, is scarce or non-existent. In the case of refugees, the acquisition of the new visas required the running of a double hazard. Now refugees were required to carry a passport obtained from the very authorities who might be persecuting them. As to a visa, a visit to an accessible British embassy may well be interpreted as an act of dissent in itself. Suppose further that a British embassy was under observation by government agents or surrounded by security forces? In that event, applying for a visa may give the authorities the opportunity to brand a refugee a subversive; collecting it may invite arrest or detention. In such circumstances and contrary to the government's view, the possession of a valid passport and visa is more likely to indicate that the claim to asylum is invalid rather than the reverse. As the Refugee Council (1991: 13) claimed:

Asylum seekers have been presented as bogus because their travel documents sometimes are. The truth ... is quite the opposite. It is precisely the persecuted who are most likely to need to use false documents. The Act simply criminalises without distinction. The official insistence that genuine refugees are not affected is unconvincing.

In the event, the new round of visa restrictions slowed, but did not significantly reduce the numbers requesting asylum, so within two years a second legislative barricade was built to keep out these troublesome 'disguised economic migrants' – the Immigration (Carriers Liability) Act of 1987. This compels airlines and shipping companies to check that their passengers bound for the UK carry apparently valid travel documents. The employees of the carriers have, in effect, been turned into extension workers for the immigration service.

Though they are not required to judge the legality of the documents presented to them, carriers' employees may be placed in a highly iniquitous and unenviable situation, perhaps deciding between an applicant's prospects of life or death. As some counter staff have disavowed this unenviable role the airlines and shipping companies have found themselves liable to heavy fines. (It is indeed not quite clear why, say, a Nigerian clerk working for Nigerian Airways in Lagos should act as an unpaid assistant of the British Immigration Service.) In the first 12 months after the Act came into force, 4,366 demands were served on carriers, amounting to some £4.8m. The fines were later doubled to £2,000 a passenger and, by 1990, the bills to carriers (which included accommodation costs while claims were being processed) had mounted to £24m.

The case of 58 Tamils

The immediate occasion for the introduction of the Carriers Liability Act was the arrival of 64 Tamil asylum-seekers in February 1987 without valid travel documents. The Tamils had the gall not only to arrive with a mixture of forged and valid passports and without visas, they also immediately asked for refugee status.

The legal issue posed was whether the non-possession of documents or the possession of forged or invalid documents was sufficient reason for the Home Office to detain the Tamils pending deportation. The minister in charge of immigration at the Home Office at the time, David Waddington, strongly upheld the view of IOs that 58 of the 64 Tamils were involved in 'an organised attempt by racketeers to secure admission by fraudulent means' and that the absence or forging of documents indicated that the Tamils were attempting 'to seek entry through clearly bogus applications for asylum' (*Guardian*, 18 Feb. 1987). He agreed with the IOs' decision to deport them.

In making this comment the minister was presumably relying on the 1976 Court of Appeal and 1980 House of Lords judgements which placed a good deal of power in the hands of the IO who could deem an entrant illegal if the officer 'reasonably suspected' that an entrant told lies or 'failed to disclose a material fact'.[5] However, the minister's insistence on the possession of valid travel documents in the case of those claiming to be *refugees* seems to have been made in ignorance of Article 31(1) of the 1951 Geneva Convention, signed by Britain. This states that:

---

5   In a 1980 judgement, the House of Lords imposed a 'duty of candour' on the entrant. Their entry would be treated as illegal, their lordships argued, if they failed to volunteer information which they knew, or ought to have known, was relevant to their entitlement to enter. As discussed later, this judgement was not, however, to remain uncontested.

the contracting states shall not impose penalties, on account of their illegal entry or presence, on refugees who, coming directly from a territory where their life and freedom was threatened ... enter or are present in their territories without authorisation, provided they present themselves without delay to the authorities and show good cause for their illegal entry or presence.

The conditions established in Article 31 were met by the 58 Tamil asylum-seekers. It was, of course, open to the minister to challenge whether conditions in Sri Lanka were such as to 'threaten life and freedom' and he indeed asserted that he did not believe this to be the case after a visit to that country. His espousal of the views of the Sri Lankan government was, however, inconsistent with the grant, for the four years up to 5 March 1987, of ELR status to 2,551 Sri Lankans and refugee status to a further 40 – over half the total of 4,360 applicants over that period. As if fate had decided to embarrass the minister even further, shortly after his return to the UK, major incidents of bombing and violence in the Sri Lankan civil war were widely reported in the international press.

As to the deportation of the 58 Tamils, the government soon found itself in a legal morass largely of its own making. In 1985, in response to a House of Commons home affairs committee report which recommended the granting of appeal rights for asylum-seekers refused entry, the government had replied that this was 'unnecessary' as the refugees could make representations to MPs, apply for a judicial review or be given access to the United Kingdom Immigration Advisory Service (UKIAS).[6] The government made particular play with the argument that the referral procedure to UKIAS provided a 'broader safeguard' than a formal appeal system. However, as I have shown in Chapter 2, the system of MPs' representations had been undermined and neither judicial review nor referral to UKIAS had in fact taken place in the case of the Tamils.

---

6 Some background is necessary here. UKIAS is principally funded by the Home Office and operates in a rather low-key way from an anonymous building near Waterloo Bridge in London. Despite being supported by the Home Office, the counsellors and lawyers working for the service slowly built up a reputation for independence and competence, together with a satisfied client base. In 1991, the government suddenly sought to give UKIAS *sole* responsibility for the representation of asylum-seeker cases. This immediately antagonised the numerous other agencies offering support to refugees and undercut the fundamental principle of an accused person being allowed to seek independent and self-selected legal advice. A number of barristers and solicitors with expertise in the field had scored notable legal victories against the Home Office and this announcement therefore looked very much like the government trying to side-step the possibility of critical judicial decision. As it happens, the UKIAS itself did not welcome the role so abruptly assigned to it – as the government's proposal would have undermined its carefully built reputation for independence. Over the period 1991–2, the managing committee of UKIAS fractured into opposing and supporting groups. The government finally backed away from the hornets' nest it had stirred.

On Thursday 17 February 1987, as the 58 Tamils were about to be deported, they enacted an eye catching and dramatic protest by stripping down to their Persil-white Y-fronts in a departure lounge at Heathrow. Whoever among them had inspired this extraordinary demonstration must have had a touch of genius in intuiting the deep embarrassment that their near-nakedness would cause. The bobbies looked confused and red-faced, the flashbulbs popped, the TV cameras rolled. By undressing, the Tamils had effected a symbolic jujitsu throw that left the government's action looking bereft – naked, so to speak, of all morality.

On the same day as the strip protest, Mr Justice McCowan ordered a halt to the deportation of the '58' on the grounds that they had no opportunity to present their cases. One week later the Tamils won the right to a judicial review, after a compelling presentation of their claim by Nicholas Blake, QC. The Home Office at first announced that it would challenge the High Court's ruling, then on 2 March, it suddenly backed down. The cases of the 58 Tamils would, after all, be referred to UKIAS. Rather than face an open judicial review, Mr Hurd had selected the less public option. The Tamils' solicitor, David Burgess, taunted the government by suggesting that it backed away from court action where they could be judged independently. Government, he asserted, had retreated into a privileged situation where they rewrote the rules they did not like.

But if the frontier guards had been bloodied, they were not bowed. Less than 24 hours after Mr Hurd had ducked a judicial review for the '58', he disowned the label 'liberal' with which the far right had tagged him and announced his intention to introduce the Carriers Liability Bill. The timing of his announcement and the provisions of the Act leave little room for any interpretation other than that the government was determined to stop asylum-seekers having their cases considered internally or heard publicly.

Despite the government's move, it had not quite wriggled free of the Tamils' capacity for a surprise counter-throw. Over the next six months (March–October 1987) some of the '58' had their cases for refugee status recognised (thus demonstrating the error of the original blanket decision), some were detained pending further consideration and some were deported or scheduled for deportation. Six of the last group took their case to the Court of Appeal and, in a historic judgement in October 1987, won their case. The case turned on the meaning of the crucial expression in the 1951 Geneva Convention suggesting that a refugee has to have 'a well-founded fear' of persecution. Master of the Rolls, Sir John Donaldson, held that the six Tamils had to prove 'actual fear' and a good reason for that fear. Fear was clearly a subjective state and a fear that was shown to be misconceived was not, he thought, excluded from consideration.

Douglas Hurd, the home secretary, reacted furiously to the judgement:

There are many parts of the world where there is a lot of trouble, a lot of fighting. I really don't think we can get into the position where anybody who would prefer to live here than in those parts of the world can turn up here and say: 'Look, I am a refugee, I have this genuine fear of persecution', and no one is able to test objectively whether that is well-founded or not (*Independent*, 15 October, 1987).

Three months later, after an appeal by the home secretary, the Law Lords reversed Sir John's decision and supported the view that the decision to deport the six Tamils was 'reasonable'. The power to exclude had reverted to the *status quo ante*. The frontier guards were back in the saddle.

Agents and agencies

I argued earlier that whatever the formal position in respect of Britain's signature on the international conventions on refugees, the attitudes and practices of real agents and agencies – be they government ministers, Home Office officials, politicians, newspaper editors or IOs – have a great deal of influence on the final determination of refugee status. I want to focus here particularly on two of these agencies – first, the IOs and the organisation to which most belong, the Immigration Service Union (ISU) and second, the popular press. Both have a great deal of informal power, the IOs in having to make the initial decision whether to 'refuse leave to enter' – thereby discarding any potential claim before it has been made, the tabloid press in creating the popular iconography and received images of the new 'strangers' – the asylum-seekers.

Immigration Officers and the Immigration Service Union

The initial perception by officialdom of those seeking asylum is likely to be informed by a number of interrelated precognitions, several of which may be contrary to the letter or spirit either of the relevant international agreements or even domestic legislation. These views may include the following elements:

- IOs being particularly concerned to exclude those who do not qualify for admission as immigrants, visitors or students. Since the 1930s wave, Britain has taken very few refugees, but has admitted (before firmly closing the door on) a significant number of immigrants. This may have lead to a natural presumption that asylum-seekers are intending immigrants under another guise.
- The politicians being under some pressure to honour electoral promises and to respect the force of public opinion to stop *any* 'immigration'.

- The IOs, politicians and press being equally unable to deal with a relatively novel situation of rapid population movements facilitated by quick international transport and brought on by civil war, natural disaster and other hazards in many parts of the world with which they are totally, or virtually totally, unfamiliar.

These background factors provide some indication of the likely reception and treatment given to those who arrive at the ports of entry, particularly those who arrive without notice, or those without a significant co-ethnic or pressure group in the UK acting on their behalf.

In 1986 it surfaced for the first time that the ISU had acted not merely as a somewhat surly gatekeeper and enforcer of parliament's wishes, but as an active lobby group in its own right. According to apparently reliable reports (*New Statesman and Society*, 10 Oct. 1986; *Guardian*, 8 Sept. 1986) the decision to impose visas in 1986 was not discussed with the Commonwealth countries concerned and was made against the advice of the Foreign Office, whose staff would have to issue the visas. Nor was any consideration given to the impact of the restrictions on race relations in the UK. Instead, the ISU itself seems to have orchestrated a campaign for more staff, for visas and for a general toughening-up of policy. The union also appears to have put David Waddington up to attacking MPs for abusing their rights of representation in immigration cases (see Chapter 2). According to the internal ISU membership circular No. 56 (1985):

It was accepted (by the assistant under-secretary of state) that the ISU approach to the minister [Waddington] and his subsequent statements in the House of Commons had initiated the necessary debate on the problems caused by uncontrolled representation by MPs. . . . The ISU delegation undertook to supply a list of the types of case *which the union considered* as having no proper place in the system of MPs' representations [emphasis added].

The 'chaotic conditions' at Heathrow that the ISU alluded to in defence of their objectives seem partly to have been manufactured by the IOs themselves, then presented to sympathetic members of the press, particularly in the *Daily Express*, in support of their arguments. That the ISU got its own way is shown by the fact that a senior official in the IND was convinced that it would take at least two years before the issue of visas could be agreed and decided. Instead, Home Secretary Hurd responded to the ISU lobby within weeks. On 15 October the *Independent* described the ISU as 'virtually running Heathrow'.

So what are the origins of this powerful body? Traditionally the IOs were organised by the Society of Civil and Public Servants (SCPS), but the IOs were always uncomfortable in that union and early signs of restiveness were visible. For example, on 23 August 1979, the Immigration Branch Secretary of the SCPS wrote to the *Guardian* defending the deportation of four children who had been refused entry to join their family in the UK. The branch also strongly objected to the SCPS calling out members of the Passport Office on strike, to the union's anti-apartheid position, to the support of the union for a Commission for Racial Equality investigation into immigration control and finally, to the call at the SCPS conference in 1981 for the repeal of the Immigration Act of 1971.

The last issue was the proverbial straw that broke the camel's back. The branch split away to form the ISU. The new union was recognised within the year by the Home Office, who also provided generous help in allowing members time off for union work and free use of the telephones. By contrast, the TUC refused to allow the new body to affiliate, while the ISU is also banned from the Council of Civil Service Unions. Despite the friendly recognition accorded by the Home Office, the ISU backed its 1988–89 pay claim with an explicit attack on the 'obsolete Lunar House bureaucracy', referring to the building in Croydon where the IND was housed. According to the ISU, the 'bureaucrats' at Lunar House refused leave to 'only' 9,800 people and 'the effectiveness of this figure is further diminished by the fact that many, if not the majority, will still be in the UK ... pursuing their appeal rights' (GMIAU 1990).

The ISU was ultimately unsuccessful in deflecting the Commission for Racial Equality from carrying out its statutory right to conduct an investigation into immigration control procedures. The resultant report (CRE 1985) highlighted many ways of improving the process and was strongly critical of the discriminatory practices they found.

Though largely resistant to the criticism, what has finally 'got through' to the Immigration Service is that it is politic to employ suitable members of the ethnic minorities in 'frontline' positions: it is now common to see non-white staff at the airport entry-points. On the other hand, there have been persistent (but, as far as I know, unproven) rumours in the anti-racist movement that National Front members have been encouraged to join the Immigration Service and have done so in significant numbers.

The documentation for the 1988–89 pay claim also provides open evidence of one example of the ISU blatantly ignoring the critical CRE report. In the wake of the sudden imposition of visas, IOs were sent to Dhaka (Bangladesh) to act as temporary entry clearance officers. According to the ISU's own document, 'settlement cases are decided on the basis of one issue, one deferral and one refusal for every three interviews conducted'. If this was true, they might as well throw dice as go through the farce of interviewing visa applicants.

The popular press

A full analysis of the role of the popular press in constructing prevailing images of the visitor, the immigrant, the stranger and the asylum-seeker is properly the subject of a separate study. All I can do here is provide a quick impression of the tabloids' coverage of two of these groups, visitors and asylum-seekers.

Two predominant tendencies emerge. First, the popular newspapers normally conflate visitors, students, immigrants and asylum-seekers into one undifferentiated category, 'immigrants' – itself a barely disguised code word for 'blacks'. Second, the tabloids make only the most token gestures to 'fair coverage' – the characteristic diet supplied to their readers consists of exposés of 'illegal immigration rackets', ignorant attacks on the courts if they appear to be favouring an asylum-seeker's case and an uncritical acceptance of the views of the frontier guards.

The ISU were particularly successful in effecting sympathetic links with two newspapers, the *Daily Mail* and the *Daily Express*, both papers with well established Powellite views. The *Express* was invited by the ISU to see immigration control at work in mid-1986. The paper responded with an 'exclusive report' headed '*Express* dossier on the illegal arrivals who find a back door into Britain' (18 July 1986).

The papers were successfully used to advance the ISU's demand for visa controls which the papers then vigorously defended. David Rose's reports in the *Guardian* in October 1986 provided a useful counterweight to the coverage in the *Sun*, the *Daily Mail* and the *Daily Express* when the effects of the sudden imposition of visa restrictions were seen. Rose was sent to live and work with the entry clearance officers in Bangladesh. He found tedious queues for visas (around 12,000 long), endless waits, demoralised and inadequate secretarial backup for staff and judgements made on no more rational a ground than whether an applicant looked 'shifty' or not.

Hundreds of Asian visitors trapped in a Kafkaesque nightmare chose to avoid this humiliating process and apply for an entry visa on arrival – which, before the passing of the Carriers Liability Act, they were perfectly entitled to do. The consequent chaos at Heathrow, with swirls of shouting and distressed people, many spending a night on the floor awaiting an interview, was read in two completely different ways. For the *Guardian* editorial-writer (16 Oct. 1986)

The scenes of chaos, misery and frustration at Heathrow airport these past three days shame us all. They are not the way a civilised nation should behave. They represent either official incompetence on the grand scale, or the callous indifference of explicit racism. And just possibly both. . . . The squalid spectacle at Heathrow is the apotheosis of a squalid policy. . . . the blame moves to the ministerial desk of Mr David Waddington. The policy is a cruel shambles. The right thing to do is to resign.

By contrast, the tabloids followed the logic of their long-running campaign in defence of visas. This started in July 1986 with a two-page spread in the *Express* claiming that 'hundreds' of 'illegal immigrants' were slipping into the UK pretending to be visitors – and then absconding. This story fell short of an absolute lie in that exactly 222 out of some 452,000 visitors from the 'new-visa countries' (Ghana, Nigeria, Bangladesh, Pakistan and India) had become overstayers in 1985, and 20 of those had been arrested. So by the merest whisker of three overstayers, the expression 'hundreds' was accurate.

As for the distressed crowds at Heathrow, this did not trouble the tabloids in the slightest. On the contrary, they went on the offensive. Amongst the 'porkies' presented was the *Mail*'s story supported by a 'Mac' cartoon, then parroted in the others, that taxpayers would have to pick up 'posh' hotel bills for arriving Indians waiting for their interviews by IOs. As it was the British government who had imposed visas at short notice and with inadequate staff (in Asia or at Heathrow) to process applications, there was every reason why the state *should* have paid. Actually, the bills were charged to the airlines, who in turn could legally charge the passengers.

For its part, the *Sun* (15 Oct. 1986) carried a massive front-page headline, 'The Liars', claiming that the visitors *must* be deceitful immigrants on the bizarre grounds that they wanted to go to places like Bradford and Slough (where, of course, many Indian family visits would normally take place). 'Heathrow was under siege today after a mass invasion of *illegal immigrants* trying to beat the deadline for getting into Britain', the paper further proclaimed. The headline in the *Daily Mail* on the same day read '*Immigrants* Paralyse Heathrow'. If the 1985 absconder figures are used as an index of who was a visitor and who an illegal immigrant these two newspapers had offensively maligned 99.95 per cent of the people who had been so badly treated at Heathrow, not to mention the hundreds of British Asian friends and relatives who had invited them for a visit.

The tabloids' treatment of asylum-seekers characteristically varied hardly at all from their treatment of the Indian visitors. They welcomed the predictable announcement by the home secretary made at the Tory Party conference in October 1991 that new measures would be introduced to restrict 'bogus asylum-seekers'. By 1991, it had become customary to provide at least one sop to the party's 'anti-immigration' lobby at each conference. The usual accusation that most asylum-seekers were fraudulent was again repeated from the platform. 'Millions' were trying to leave eastern Europe, Africa and Asia. While the government would maintain 'the proud tradition' of welcoming those with a well-founded fear of persecution, 'we simply cannot provide a home for those who only want to live in a richer country. Such people are economic migrants' (*Independent*, 10 Oct. 1991).

The home secretary also took the opportunity to attack his Labour shadow, Roy Hattersley, for his supposed 'open gate' policy. The attempt by the pro-Tory popular press to smear Labour with this charge and the Tories' ideological conflation of asylum-seekers with illegal (and non-white!) 'immigrants' was well illustrated by the ever-obliging 'Mac' in his cartoon in the *Daily Mail* (4 Oct. 1991). In the sketch, Hattersley stands on the beach at Brighton gesturing to rowing boats, liners, sampans, parachutes and planes filled with people of different nationalities. 'No, no, later – we're not in yet', he says. Caricatured Sikhs and Chinese feature prominently, Europeans apparently not at all – again underlining the unwillingness of the tabloids to move beyond their fixation with illegal and non-white 'immigrants'.

The personal attack on Hattersley was thought opportune as for months before the election Labour had looked like a possible winner. By April 1992, when the prospect of a Labour government looked serious, the Tories pulled out 'the race card' for real. The home secretary argued that the Labour Party and the Liberal Democrats were offering a 'deadly political cocktail' of 'slack immigration controls and proportional representation ... I have warned for many months about this rising tide. Last year 45,000 people came to Britain and applied for refugee status. Three-quarters of applicants failed the test. Many were bogus. They were economic migrants abusing refugee status.' He also cynically used the fear of continental fascism: 'I am determined that what we have seen in Germany and France will not happen here' (*Express* 7 April 1992). The editorial that accompanied this report opined that: 'The opposition of the Labour Party and the Liberal Democrats to the [proposed] asylum bill is short-sighted, irresponsible and cynical (Labour owes its hold on many inner city seats to its immigrant following)'.

In the event, the election campaign itself interrupted the passage of a new asylum bill and the Tories were again returned. It is doubtful that the debate on asylum shifted many voters' allegiances, but it served, with other fears about the economy, higher taxation and unemployment, to consolidate the Tory vote behind Mr Major.

Mr Major, 'safe havens' and the 1993 Asylum Act

The internal shift of power within the Tory party did not signal any major shift of line on asylum, as was made apparent by Britain's new prime minister, John Major, at the European summit in Luxembourg in late June 1991. There, the supposed soft alternative to Mrs Thatcher, warned against the 'rising tide' of immigrants and asylum-seekers to Europe: 'We must not be wide open to all-comers just because Rome, Paris and London are more attractive than Bombay or Algiers' (*Independent*, 29 June 1991).

Safe havens

There has, however, been one important new initiative taken by Mr Major, which arose in the wake of a new flow of problematic asylum-seekers, the Kurds, after the outbreak of the Gulf War. Most of the Kurds claiming asylum in the UK were from Turkey, others were from Iraq or Iran. Some of the Kurdish asylum-seekers had begun to show disturbing signs of a mulish determination not to be sent back to their countries of origin. As early as May 1987, a mother and her 18-year-old child slashed their wrists rather than be bundled on a plane by IOs and employees of a private security firm (*Guardian*, 18 May 1987). In October 1989, in an incident that was hushed up, two Kurds in the Harmondsworth detention centre, near Heathrow, shut themselves in a room and set themselves alight, after being told they would be denied asylum. One died, the other was seriously burnt. Rather than face adverse publicity arising from similar incidents, Kurds who had been detained for months began to be released.

As war with Iraq loomed, it became more and more difficult to bear down on the Kurds, particularly since many of them, like the Alevi Kurds of Turkey, claimed to be escaping from fundamentalist Muslims and other anti-Western elements – precisely the 'enemy' in the Gulf War. The prospect of turning demands for an independent Kurdistan into a fifth force against Saddam Hussain also dictated that Kurdish asylum-seekers had to be treated with more sympathy by the British authorities.

Saddam's suppression of the rebellions in northern (and southern) Iraq saw the mass flight of 2 million Kurds and Shias towards Turkey and Iran. Anxious for a good press, Western leaders were abashed at their abandonment of the Kurdish rebellions, the visible suffering of Kurds in their pathetic trek to the north and the harsh treatment of them by the West's ally, Turkey. 'Operation Provide Comfort' was launched to give support to the Kurdish refugees. By April 1991, with the most intense part of the war over, Operation Provide Comfort was superseded by assistance given to encourage the mass return of Kurds from Turkey (and Shias from Iran). As van Hear (1991: 18) recalls:

> Their return took place in a context of tenuous security brought about by the establishment by Western military forces of a controversial 'safe haven' for the Kurdish population in northern Iraq; the conclusion between the government of Iraq and the UN of a 'memorandum of understanding' governing humanitarian assistance and the beginnings of UN intervention; the resurgence of Kurdish guerrilla groups and their control of substantial swathes of territory.

This particular story is remarkable enough in its own right, in that the mass exodus and mass return of the Kurds had taken place on a historically unprecedented scale and in an unusually compressed period. But the Kurdish experience also provided something of a model of future initiatives by Western leaders in response to the mass displacements of populations.

Prime Minister Major himself took credit for the Kurdish 'safe haven' scheme (though President Bush also filed a claim for copyright). Clearly at least part of the logic was that rather than deal with Kurdish refugees to the UK whose claims would have been difficult to deny, the British government went as far in recognising an independent Kurdistan as it could (something the Foreign Office had fiercely resisted for over a century). The advantage of this posture was that it became possible to argue that as Kurds now had their own country it was not necessary to grant them asylum in the UK.

That this tendency towards precipitous recognition of irredentist and nationalist movements is becoming a more general feature of Western diplomacy can be seen too in events in the ex-Soviet Union and ex-Yugoslavia. Once again, from late July 1992, the notion of a 'safe haven' has been wheeled out, this time in relation to Bosnians fleeing from Serbian forces and in respect of the Muslim enclaves.

Whereas Germany agreed to take 200,000 refugees from former Yugoslavia (and Hungary, Austria and Sweden between 45,000 and 50,000 each), the UK initially refused to accept more than 1,300 war victims. In announcing the government's disinclination to accept any principle of quotas for western Europe, Lady Chalker declared that she thought it cruel to accept large numbers of former Yugoslavians to a country where they had few fellow nationals. Instead, food corridors would be opened up and 'safe havens' established for the Bosnians.[7]

As the butchery and 'ethnic cleansing' continued in former Yugoslavia, western governments, especially the Clinton administration, came under increased pressure to 'do something', though it was not apparent, even to gung-ho generals, what they could do. Ultimately NATO is likely to blunder toward a military intervention for symbolic purposes or in pursuit of the establishment of what may well turn out to be highly unsafe havens. However nebulous and uncertain such policies are, they are thought preferable by western leaders to facing up to the possibility of accepting large numbers of refugees.

The 1993 Asylum Act

Delayed by the 1992 General Election, the Asylum and Immigration Appeals Bill, first announced earlier that year, was debated in the

---

7   It might be worth remarking that this sort of solution to a refugee crisis is not quite so innovative as is currently believed. The Palestinian camps, especially the Gaza Strip, established after the formation of the state of Israel in 1948, are a close, and not that comforting, precedent of a 'safe haven' policy. A much less exact, but suggestive, analogy is the Bantustan policy of the South African government during the period of classical apartheid. Rather than face mass migration from the 'have-not' areas to the 'have-all' areas, there are desperate attempts made to shore up self-governing zones of hastily fabricated ethnicities and nationalities – thus the Bantustans, Kurdistans, and what now may be deemed the 'Croatiastans', 'Bosniastans', etc. of this world.

House of Commons on 2 November 1992. The essential aim of the new legislation was to deal with the burgeoning number of applicants, the difficulties of arriving at firm decisions, the long delays in processing claims and the large number of applicants who were granted exceptional leave to remain in Britain while their cases were processed (see Table 3.2).

The Asylum Bill, the home secretary averred, was designed to eliminate bottlenecks in decision-making through a rigid application of new, streamlined procedures. The main provisions of the bill were:

- A new right of appeal for asylum-seekers against an IO's decision to refuse entry. (But this right was immediately undermined by the insistence that an appeal had to be lodged in 48 hours, with a hearing, in most cases, within five days.)
- Asylum-seekers and their children were to be fingerprinted. (This provision effectively criminalised people who were simply asking for refuge.)
- Asylum-seekers' rights to housing were withdrawn. (This was in response to lobbying by some London boroughs that they could not fulfil their obligations to house people arriving in their areas.)

Table 3.2 *Applications for Asylum to the UK, Decisions and Percentages, 1986–1991*

	1986	1987	1988	1989	1990	1991
No. of Applications	4266	4256	3998	1640	22000	44840
No. of Decisions	2983	2432	2702	6955	4015	4685
Grants of asylum	348	266	628	2210	900	420
Grants of asylum (%)	12	11	23	32	22	9
Exceptional leave	2102	1531	1578	3860	2400	1860
Exceptional leave (%)	70	73	58	55	60	40
Refusals	533	635	496	890	710	2410
Refusals (%)	18	26	18	13	18	51

Source: Home Office Statistical Bulletin Issue 12/92, 24 June 1992.

- Draft regulations accompanying the bill suggested that failure immediately to apply for political asylum on arrival, 'failure to make prompt and full disclosure of material factors' and the destruction of travel documents *en route* would be held against the applicant.

(This put enormous discretionary power in the hands of unaccountable officials.)

- The government used the occasion of the Asylum Bill to abolish rights of appeal against an IO's decision in the case of visitors and students. (This further exacerbated the compulsive British habit of treating all non-British people arriving at a port of entry as an undifferentiated 'Other'.)[8]

That there was a rapid increase in the numbers of asylum-seekers is evident from the data in Table 3.2. What was not so evident was why a new law was needed. As the 1991 figures indicate, existing legislation already permitted the Home Office to restrict the absolute numbers of grants of asylum and increase the percentage of refusals from 18 per cent in 1986 to 51 per cent by 1991.

It is a poor reflection of the state of British popular opinion that the government's persistence with the Asylum Bill was not effectively opposed either in the country or in the Commons. It was left to the unelected House of Lords to show some old-fashioned humanitarian concern. In its debates on 4 and 11 March 1993, an amendment to the bill asking that special grants be given to housing authorities adversely affected by the housing needs of asylum-seekers was narrowly defeated. A wider margin of defeat greeted a passionate plea to leave the appellate rights of visitors, which had existed for 21 years, intact.

Two members of the House movingly evoked their personal experiences. Lord Jakobovits, the former Chief Rabbi, recalled his own refugee history: 'finding shelter here from Nazi persecution some 56 years ago, I am naturally concerned that others in similar circumstances of oppression should share my good fortune.' For his part, the black peer, Lord Pitt of Hampstead, told of having to furnish a letter of invitation to his Trinidadian grandchildren to ensure that they could get an entry certificate to visit him. The subsequent exchange between the minister of state at the Home Office (Earl Ferrers) and Lord McIntosh (*Hansard*, 11 March 1993 col. 1166–7) was instructive:

McIntosh: Of course if my noble friend writes a letter on House of Lords notepaper saying that his grandchildren are his grandchildren and should be admitted, they will be admitted. But if his name was Patel and not Pitt and if he did not have access to the House of Lords notepaper and the letter came from Hackney instead of Hampstead, the grandchildren might have considerably greater difficulty in obtaining admission to this country . . . .

---

8 In 1991, out of 8,010 immigration appeals decided against entry refusal for visitors and students, 1,495 (1 in 5.4) were successful, showing that many decisions had been arbitrary and wrong. As was shown earlier in this chapter, visitors from New Commonwealth countries trying to keep in touch with their families in the UK are often victims to misinformed press comment and prejudiced decisions at the airports. None had claimed asylum and their situation is markedly different from that of the asylum-seeker.

Ferrers: My Lords I interrupt the noble Lord because he is being most ungenerous to those who work the immigration system when he suggests that those who send their letters on House of Lords notepaper take precedence over those who send letters on ordinary notepaper. The noble Lord should know the system works better than that.

McIntosh: My Lords, if the Minister believes that, quite frankly he will believe anything.

But passion and conviction on behalf of a more generous asylum policy was consistently voted down. The only concession given was to accept a periodic review, by an independent person, of a sample of cases where entry clearance had been refused. The frontier guards had won.

Conclusion

I have argued in this chapter that the grant of asylum is often less predicated on the assertion of the humanitarian impulse, than on reasons of state and ethnic solidarity. However, it is important not to be too cynical. Governments *can* be abashed by public concern for the fate of refugees. The global village is brought to our living rooms through television and the reactions to disturbing images of the suffering caused by mass displacements can be galvanised by concerned citizens in an attempt to persuade a government to provide humanitarian assistance. The force of international law and public opinion (such as in the case of the Vietnamese in Hong Kong or in the Bosnian crisis) can also act to constrain too harsh a policy by the government. Sympathetic pressure groups, MPs, competent lawyers and eminent judges may also disturb the frontier guards' monopolistic claims to control the fate of asylum-seekers.

Sir John Donaldson's judgement concerning the nature of a 'well-founded fear' was especially unnerving to the home secretary and he was not slow to retaliate. The almost unbridled power given to the home secretary by the Law Lords in December 1987 (which reversed Donaldson's decision) was ultimately to go to the head of the new home secretary, Kenneth Baker. When a deportation order issued to a teacher from Zaire had been successfully challenged in the courts, Mr Baker allowed the deportation to continue. The Appeal Court retaliated by finding him in contempt of court, the first government minister ever to be found guilty on this charge. An interesting constitutional issue then arose as to whether a minister, acting in the Queen's name, could legally be held in contempt. The minister immediately announced he would appeal. Moreover, he saw no ethical issue in using the taxpayers' money in pursuing his defence!

At first sight the sheer arrogance of this stance (quite forgetting the fate of the teacher who had been sent back to face Mobutu's murderous regime) was a quite stunning display of braggadocio. But it conformed to the old legal bias that, whatever the letter of the international conventions, a good deal of power is left in the hands of the state's agents to confer or withhold refugee status.

Essentially, the frontier guards have responded to humanitarian demands by shifting the frontiers of identity outside of the British Isles. By demanding visas from over 100 countries, the first line of defence has become the British embassy or consulate. By passing the Carriers Liability Act, the second line of defence has been neatly privatised and displaced to the airline companies. By recognising fledgling states like Kurdistan, Bosnia or Croatia, attempting thereby to create 'safe havens' *in situ*, the government can treat the victims of civil war, ethnic violence and international conflict as foreign nationals rather than political refugees. Finally, by forcing through the 1993 Asylum and Immigration Appeals Act, government sent a signal to its right-wing backbenchers, its voters and its European partners, that 'immigration' matters were still firmly under the control of Whitehall.

All four strategies seek to keep asylum-seekers as far away from British shores as possible, while Britain's 'honourable tradition' of giving refuge is simultaneously used as a convenient fig leaf to mask the exclusionist policy. However, as I have shown in this chapter, successive UK governments have never been overwhelming in their generosity and rarely been generous without other motives. The current government is seeking to displace and externalise the issue of judging the applications of asylum-seekers rather than face up to the need for judicious, open and fair consideration of their claims.

CHAPTER 4

The detention of aliens
and asylum-seekers

> The prison form antedates its systematic use in the penal sys-
> tem. It had already been constituted outside the legal apparatus
> when, throughout the social body, procedures were being
> elaborated for distributing individuals, fixing them in space,
> classifying them . . . forming around them an apparatus of ob-
> servation, registration and recording, constituting on them a
> body of knowledge that is accumulated and centralised.
> — Foucault (1979: 231)

In this chapter I focus on the detention of aliens and asylum-seekers, a
phenomenon that may seem to some to be almost a contradiction in
terms. Social convention in many societies has frequently dictated that
a stranger with no hostile intent, or in a condition of distress, should be
met with hospitality rather than with the prospect of incarceration. In a
number of societies (those of the Arabian peninsula being the best
known), even sworn enemies are granted protection and treated with
respect and courtesy in the confines of a host's own home.

Yet, since the effective policing of Britain's frontiers, the detention
(and often the subsequent deportation) of unwanted strangers has been
common. Again, outside the ranks of the immigration agencies, the
Home Office and specialist researchers, few people are aware of the
large number of people routinely held by the immigration authorities.
However, a good deal of public interest and concern was aroused by
the scenes of 64 Tamil asylum-seekers demonstrating at Heathrow airport against being summarily removed in February 1987 (see Chapter
3), and by the lease of a car ferry, anchored off Harwich, to accommodate asylum-seekers whose fate had yet to be determined by the Home
Office. I investigated conditions on the *Earl William* ferry myself and
its bizarre fate is reported below.

I concentrate below on the wartime internments, the detentions
flowing from a terrorist threat and the detentions arising from the enforcement of the modern immigration acts. The last group has two
components – the Immigration Act Detainees (IADs), who are regarded as illegal entrants or as people who have violated their conditions
of entry, and a smaller (but symbolically significant) group of asylum-
seekers, who are detained pending investigation of their claims.

Wartime detentions[1]

In an earlier chapter, I described how the outbreak of the First World War was marked by an outbreak of Germanophobia in Britain. In harness with anti-German sentiment was a newspaper-fanned campaign of 'spy fever', which was much accelerated in 1915 by the sinking of the *Lusitania*, a Cunard passenger liner, with great loss of life. (The atmosphere of spy fever is well captured in John Buchan's novel *The 39 Steps*. Despite the highly implausible plot and crude caricatures of foreigners, the book was made into two successful movies.)

The public outrage at the sinking of the *Lusitania* gave retrospective public legitimacy to a clandestine counter-spy organisation that had become institutionalised in the War Office in 1909 under the direction of Vernon Kell. Known as the Special Intelligence Department, it was to become much better known under its later acronym, MI5 (Military Intelligence 5).

On 4 August 1914, the day before Britain was officially at war, the police picked up twenty 'known German spies' who had been shadowed by Kell's department. Four days later a conference of senior officials was held at the War Office. Our old friend and frontier guard *extraordinaire* Sir Edward Troup (see Chapter 2), was there to record the decision to intern 'only those aliens who were regarded by the police as dangerous, or likely to become dangerous'. Two hundred suspects were picked up. Less than a month later, the policy of interning only those hitherto kept under observation was abandoned and a stunning order was given to all chief constables – to intern all Germans of military age, between seventeen and fifty-five years old.

The order was difficult to execute partly because the Aliens Registration Act was barely a month old and nobody knew exactly how many would be caught in this net: estimates varied between 20–25,000. Nine days after the order went out, the War Office pleaded with the Home Office to stop arresting Germans – there were insufficient places to hold them. Thereafter, the rate of imprisonment fluctuated according to the fortunes of war, the level of public panic and the amount of available detention-space.

Showing their renowned capacity for improvisation, the British authorities had sought to increase the detention-space available by requisitioning the Olympia Exhibition Halls (which housed 1,500 men), several clapped-out liners moored in the Thames, a disused jute factory, an abbey in Hampshire and a skating rink. Security was often ludicrous (some German sailors from the abbey got roaring drunk at the local pub) and genuine prisoners-of-war were mixed up with long-standing residents of German origin. A dramatic solution to the increasing number of detainees was needed. This was to be found in

---

1 The material on the period of the two World Wars in this section relies strongly on Gillman and Gillman's comprehensive account (1980).

the construction of a massive concentration camp[2] at Knockaloe on the Isle of Man.

There were problems right from the start. The contractors did not finish in time and many more internees were sent than could decently be accommodated. When a demonstration against overcrowding took place, reservists guarding the camp panicked and killed five internees. The food was erratic, the camp was sited on a muddy wasteland, the huts rotted, the winters were bitter and sanitation comprised emptying buckets once or twice a day. Visiting Swiss and American inspectors denounced conditions in the camp.

In an attempt at buck-passing the Home Office complained angrily to the Isle of Man authorities. The secretary of state for war, Lord Kitchener, perhaps mindful of his experiences with the concentration camps in South Africa, demanded that Knockaloe be emptied of those who were not evident security risks. About 2,700 internees were released after signing an undertaking not to do anything prejudicial to the British war effort. However, this pragmatic solution to the problem of overcrowding soon gave way to a hard line after further war losses. The camp was eventually expanded to take 24,000 prisoners – mostly Germans, but also Austro–Hungarians, Turks, Africans and a few others. The war ended in November 1918, but by the following February there were still 16,000 interned at Knockaloe: the arrangements for repatriation were agonisingly slow. The camp was finally closed in September 1919.

The Second World War

Given the complications of running Knockaloe, it was perhaps not surprising that the Home Office desperately tried to keep out of the whole business of operating camps as the Second World War approached. The Home Office preferred deportation to detention (see Chapter 2) and if camps had to come, the department endeavoured to restrict its role to the arrest of enemy aliens, conveying them to the point of internment and supervising their ultimate release – with the detention itself being the concern of the War Office.

---

2 Given its later association with the Nazis, few now realise that the modern concentration camp was a British invention. It was patented first during the Anglo–Boer War (1899–1902) when women and children who were keeping the farms going were herded into camps to prevent the Boer *kommandos* (guerrillas) living off the land. In the early 1960s, when I quaffed a few beers in the *platteland* of northern Transvaal, it was still common to meet old people who were convinced that the British deliberately poisoned the camp food and used germ warfare to kill off the internees. Without these dirty tactics, it was firmly believed, the Boers would have won the war. This folk memory seems to have originated from the poor knowledge of public hygiene on the part of camp commanders, guards and internees alike and the apparently innocent introduction of tinned meat from Chicago factories where angry strikers had sabotaged the product.

UNIVERSITY COLLEGE LIBRARY SWANSEA

It was not going to prove so easy for the Home Office to get off the hook. At the outbreak of war in 1939, it was estimated that there were 28,500 male enemy aliens (including refugees), with places for only 18,000 internees. Rather than opting for wholesale internment on the Knockaloe model, two 'moderates' at the Home Office, Sir Alexander Maxwell (the permanent under-secretary) and Sir Samuel Hoare (the home secretary) chose a more complex scheme for protecting the British from the enemy aliens in their midst. If war broke out, chief constables and immigration officers (IOs) were instructed to 'encourage' aliens to leave. Only those on a specially prepared list (sent to chief constables in a sealed envelope) were to be arrested.

The list had been compiled by Vernon Kell, now a general but still heading MI5, the post he had occupied since 1909. Kell was generous in his definition of potential subversives. His version of Foucault's 'central body of knowledge' was a gigantic card index containing the names of German businessmen, resident Germans with Nazi sympathies and foreign journalists. But as the Soviet Union was also regarded as a likely enemy, Kell also listed British nationals thought to have Comintern sympathies, including hunger marchers, pacifists and those who had signed petitions opposing book censorship. Those enemy aliens not on the list and who had not voluntarily departed were, under the Maxwell-Hoare scheme, to be screened through a system of tribunals.

The operation of the tribunal system again followed the logic suggested by Foucault in the quote that opens this chapter. Not all who appeared before the 120 tribunals were interned, but the tribunals none the less constituted the means whereby 'throughout the social body, procedures were being elaborated for distributing individuals, fixing them in space, classifying them ... forming around them an apparatus of observation, registration and recording. ...'. The tribunals, comprising local worthies like barristers and JPs (the 'self'), had to place enemy aliens ('the other'), into three categories:

- 'A' – to be interned;
- 'B' – not to be interned but subject to restrictions;
- 'C' – to remain at liberty.

There were, the Home Office surmised, three types of enemy alien: (i) refugees who had been subject to oppression on racial, religious and political grounds (they should be classified 'C'); (ii) those who had lived in the UK and who had 'definitely thrown in their lot with this country' (if they could produce confirming evidence, they too should be placed in category 'C'); (iii) Germans and Austrians who could be expected to help their *own* countries (who should be put into category 'A').

With an inimitable capacity for compromise, muddle and muddled compromise, the tribunals produced regionally inconsistent classifications (Croydon and Manchester overwhelmingly favoured 'C' categorisation while almost everyone appearing in Reigate and Leeds was given the intermediate category 'B'). One former German academic of my acquaintance was categorised 'A' because he was living on the south coast and was thought to be in a position to aid an invading army. It was hinted that he would be classified 'C' if he agreed to live and work in the Midlands. He found his Berlin and Frankfurt doctorates not much help in making chocolates in Cadbury's Bournville factory in Birmingham.

The numbers placed in the 'B' category started as high as 50 per cent of the total (Lafitte 1940), rendering the whole exercise somewhat nugatory. Maxwell issued new guidelines greatly enlarging the category of 'refugee', such that when the final count was made, 64,200 of the 73,800 cases considered were classified 'C'.

Whereas the number interned through the tribunal system in the UK was relatively small, the Empire and Commonwealth loyally (and somewhat more excessively) followed British practice. India imprisoned all Germans over sixteen, Tanganyika and the Straits Settlements followed suit. In South Africa, where Boer memories stretched back to the Anglo–Boer War, the decision to enter the war on the British side was reached against fierce opposition and many of the prominent leaders of the Afrikaner nationalist movement were incarcerated for fear of a revolt.

Some of the Germans restricted in the colonies or captured at sea were traded for British nationals caught and imprisoned behind the German lines. The Americans who acted as intermediaries, found themselves somewhat embarrassed that the British government had initiated the internment of German nationals while the Nazis could legitimately argue that they were simply following suit.

The number of tribunal detainees might have stuck at its relatively low level, had not the Allied war effort come grievously unstuck during the Narvik operation in Norway in the spring of 1940. A well dug-in German force held firm against a much larger number of French and British troops, who showed themselves to be poorly trained and led. The press, led by an editorial in the *Yorkshire Post* (16 April 1940), blamed a new enemy, 'the Fifth Column', for the *débâcle*.[3] The Norwegian Fifth Column, the press hysterically proclaimed, was paralleled

---

3 The Gillmans (1980: 73–80) maintain that the expression 'Fifth Column' had its origins in the Spanish Civil War when the general commanding Franco's forces boasted that he not only had four columns marching on Republican-held Madrid, a fifth column of supporters was also in the city. The success of the Germans in Norway was attributed to a Fifth Column by the British press, who soon after turned their fire on the supposed Fifth Column in Britain. The *Sunday Dispatch* (14 April 1940) referred to Britain's Fifth Column as 'made up of Fascists, Communists, peace fanatics and alien refugees in league with Berlin and Moscow'. This theme was echoed by reports or editorials in the *Daily Mail, Daily Express, Daily Telegraph* and *The Times*.

by one operating in Britain.

The cacophony from the press together with the real threat of an imminent German invasion meant that the new home secretary, Anderson, was not strong enough to oppose a demand first to intern about 5,000 aliens living on the southeast coast, then all category 'B' aliens (another 3,000). After Dunkirk, the small but energetic Swinton Committee set up by MI5 effectively superseded the Home Office's carefully drawn policies on screening and internment and ordered the arrest of any category 'C' aliens, where there were 'grounds for doubting the reliability of the individual'. In effect, the only definite 'Cs' that remained were non-suspect German, Austrian and Italian women, the sick and infirm (Holmes 1988: 188).

On 10 June 1940, Mussolini entered the war on the Axis side, effectively delivering the fate of some 19,000 Italians living in the UK to the hands of the MI5 committee. About 1,500 had been identified on a list of Fascio living in Britain. The list was unreliable and the police overreacted – picking up naturalised British subjects of Italian origin, even an Italian Jew awarded an OBE for his work with the Ministry of Munitions. Some 629 were deported on the SS *Monarch of Bermuda*, while 4,300 others were confined, often in dreadful conditions.

To this group were added some 22,000 Germans previously categorised as 'C', who were interned following the new get-tough policy. Through the policies of the authoritarian frontier guards in MI5 and the overreaction by the media, the Home Office found itself back just where it was anxious not to be – in the muddy quagmire of Knockaloe and the First World War detentions.

That the tide turned away from mass imprisonment was due largely to a horrific episode at sea on 2 July 1940. The authorities had decided to deport up to 8,000 aliens to Canada and Australia for internment there. One of the liners used, the *Andorra Star*, was attacked by a U-boat and sunk at sea with the loss of 175 German and 486 Italian lives. Suddenly, the policy was under question. Were these aliens truly Fascists or Nazis? Was the policy too undiscriminating? Could 'Luigi' or 'Antonio' who ran a café round the corner truly be threats to state security?

Even inside the ivory towers of the Foreign and Home Offices some disturbing news of excesses began to filter through. For example, the Gillmans (1980: 215–23) tell the story of one Merlin Scott, then a young soldier doing guard duty at the Liverpool docks, who wrote a letter home describing how the Italian survivors from the *Andorra Star* had been met in Liverpool. Rather than being hospitalised, they had been treated with contempt. Their possessions were looted and they were prodded at bayonet point to the jeers of a crowd to *another* ship about to commence the transatlantic crossing to Canada. Fortunately, Scott's father, an under-secretary of state at the Foreign Office, showed his son's letter to his incredulous superiors. When the description turned out to be accurate, angry internal memoranda (cited

Gillman and Gillman 1980: 217) circulated denouncing Swinton's MI5 committee as having 'adopted a rule of thumb that any person of foreign nationality is to be presumed (almost, it would seem, irrebuttably presumed) to be hostile, while any person of British nationality is presumed to be loyal. This amounts to a confession of failure, for this department [MI5] exists for no other purpose than the examination and judgement of individual cases.'

With the evidence of overreach, the receding threat of invasion and the ending of the long, demoralising series of defeats at the hands of the Axis powers, a more liberal posture became possible. The camps gradually emptied: by August 1941 the number released had grown to 17,745. Only the diehards, the POWs and suspects with substantive evidence against them remained in the camps at the end of the war.

The Gulf War

The next notable wartime detentions occurred in January 1991, with the outbreak of the Gulf War, when some 70 Palestinians and Iraqis were detained and deported and 88 others were detained on the order of the home secretary, Kenneth Baker. There were immediate protests at the extent and indiscriminate nature of the pick-up. Significantly, on this occasion the Foreign Office broke ranks with the Home Office (as well as with MI5 which, as usual, had provided the pick-up list). One anonymous senior diplomat, who was clearly reflecting the Foreign Office's view, was quoted (*Independent*, 6 Feb. 1992) as follows:

It is damaging Britain's reputation against the background that we need to win the peace as well as the war. This country has extensive interests in the Arab world, and has a reputation as a place where people from the Middle East are welcome. The last thing Britain needs in this crisis is to be seen as an Arab-hater. [The Home Office had disregarded the Foreign Office's objections] . . . because the Foreign Office is always being accused of consisting of a bunch of Arab-lovers anyway.

Piecing together the bits of information from a few released detainees and newspaper reports it appears that the MI5 targets were selected partly from a list initially provided from the Iraqi embassy itself. The list comprised postgraduate students studying engineering and science at British universities such as Manchester, Bradford, Keele, Cardiff and Liverpool. The security authorities seem to have reasoned that as they were subject to the Iraqi military draft, their skills could prove useful to Saddam Hussein.

A few who were arrested were genuine supporters of the Baathist Party; others probably had joined it for opportunist reasons like obtaining a scholarship to study abroad. Some of the detainees were either distant (see the case of Mr al-Saleh below) or close relatives of members of known terrorist groups. In this category, for example, was

'Mr B', a computer engineer from south London, who was the terrorist leader Abu Nidal's nephew. He protested loudly that he had not seen his uncle since he was a child.

The clumsiest error was the arrest and detention of Abbas Shiblak, a Palestinian writer and journalist who had lived in the UK for sixteen years and had spoken out against Saddam Hussein's expansionist dreams. Friends in the media, neighbours, well-known writers, organisations like Pen, Amnesty International and the National Council for Civil Liberties all turned on the government. Notable support also came from the *Jewish Chronicle*, which commissioned an open letter from Simon Louvish, a Jewish novelist and a friend of Shiblak. Louvish recounted his impressions after the successful campaign to free his friend (*Independent*, 13 Feb. 1991):

The whole two-week episode had been like a third-rate thriller invented by some secret service agent based on unnamed but obviously dubious sources. What lay behind it all? I can only speculate. The hounding of innocent people because of some distant kinship, the targeting of a known Palestinian moderate for reasons hidden in the fog of state security, all this is grist to the mill of secret agent paranoia.

I have become aware of some interesting, and worrying facts. First is that the security services obviously have not got the foggiest idea of what they are doing on the issue. That means we are all exposed to the random dice of real terror. Second, the secret state is like a cowardly crocodile. It can snap you in half with one bite, but it hides in the shadows because it's scared of your opinion.

Despite the release of a number of victims whose detention was clearly based on erroneous information, the Home Office persisted in detaining 49 Arab nationals at immigration detention centres and a further 35 people at the Rollestone army camp on Salisbury Plain. While there were undoubtedly at least two senior Iraqi officers properly held as 'enemy aliens', the majority at Rollestone were army reservist students. As Anne Owers of the JCWI contended, it was rather implausible to imply that these reservists (who had, like all young males in Iraq, to do military service) were akin to soldiers under arms captured behind enemy lines. A number of detainees were subsequently released by the three-person Home Office advisory panel.

The final ironic comment on the Gulf War detainees should perhaps be that of Amnesty International, who issued a statement on the British detentions in late February 1991: 'While human rights violations in Kuwait and Iraq were being exploited as propaganda, others were being committed in the name of national security.'

Detention under the Prevention of Terrorism Act

In Chapter 1, I have already discussed the paltry attempts by the politicians to press a peaceable solution to the Northern Ireland question prior to Christmas 1993. By 1975, the security situation in the fuzzy frontier of Northern Ireland had deteriorated so far that civil liberties were suspended and draconian powers of arrest and detention under the Prevention of Terrorism Act (PTA) commenced. The numbers detained are shown in Table 4.1.

Table 4.1 *PTA detentions in Britain and Northern Ireland*

Year	1	2	3	4
1977	853	162	29	123
1978	622	155	23	144
1979	857	162	240	126
1980	537	222	126	186
1981	274	495	56	401
1982	220	828	37	639
1983	191	1,175	45	728
1984	159	908	22	533
1985	193	938	54	557
1986	147	1,309	37	483
1987	184	1,459	32	451
1988	61	805	16	248
Total	4,298	8,618	717	4,619

Notes: (1) Number detained in Britain; (2) number detained in Northern Ireland; (3) number of extensions granted after the initial 48-hour period in Britain; (4) number of similar extensions, Northern Ireland.

Source: *Guardian* (30 Nov. 1989) citing Home Office and Northern Ireland Office Statistics.

After the first twelve years of its operation, the PTA had netted 12,916 detainees all of whom were without access to normal civil liberties. If we take Northern Ireland's population as a base, the relative numbers detained begin seriously to rival traditionally despised authoritarian states like apartheid South Africa or South Korea. This odious comparison must, however, not be taken too far. The PTA has to be renewed each year in Parliament, there have been two major judicial reviews of the working of the Act and, most importantly, after the first 48 hours a detainee can be visited by a solicitor who can apply for a writ of *habeas corpus*.

On the other hand, David Hearst (*Guardian*, 30 Nov. 1989) has pointed out, and the table indeed reveals, that extensions after the first 48 hours appear to be freely granted. There have also been many challenges to the reliability of the confessions presented by detainees after an extended period of detention, which suggests some degree of torture or coercion. Moreover, the large number of detainees listed do *not* include those stopped at the ports of entry for random checks and detained for less than an hour. The Chief Inspector of Constabulary counted nearly 60,000 of these 'mini-detentions' on Irish security grounds in 1986 alone.

Immigration detentions

There are many early examples of the detention of aliens dating from the commencement of British immigration control at the Cinque Ports (see Chapter 2). But the codification of immigration detention procedures only occurred in the Aliens Act of 1920. This provided for those refused leave to enter to be detained at any place nominated by the secretary of state. In 1921, because there were no detention facilities at Tilbury and Gravesend, Brixton prison was approved, thus initiating the totally unsuitable practice of using ordinary prisons for immigration detainees. Bristol, Winchester and Cardiff prisons were added a few years later; by 1930 all police stations and fifteen prisons had been approved as immigration detention centres.

Following the passing of the 1971 Immigration Act, there were no less than eight different circumstances in which immigration detentions could occur (Shutter 1992: 195–6). These are:

* People arriving in the UK who are detained while their application for entry or asylum is being considered.
* Suspected immigration offenders who are held by the police while waiting for the immigration service to interview them.
* People charged with an immigration offence who are detained pending a court appearance or the Home Office's administrative action.
* People who are held in detention after a court order for deportation, even where no custodial sentence was ordered. (As mentioned in Chapter 2, the Home Office can decide to deport even where the court does *not* recommend such action.)
* A similar category held in detention following a deportation order issued by an IO or the Home Office.
* People who have been recommended for imprisonment *and* deportation, who will normally be detained in an airport detention centre or prison after their term of imprisonment is over and while arrangements are made for their deportation.
* Appellants against a deportation order who may be detained by the

Home Office or the immigration service while they wait for their appeal to be heard.

* Alleged illegal entrants who are detained pending removal or the further consideration of their cases.

Understanding the sometimes subtle differences between these forms of detention is important in legal terms, because the categories carry with them different possibilities for representation, appeal and intervention by a sympathetic lawyer. However, for my more limited purposes, the diverse kinds of detention allowed under the Immigration Act of 1971 can be reduced to two principal forms: (a) those who are detained *on entry*, pending a decision to admit, to vary the conditions of admission, to allow 'exceptional leave to remain', to remove or to deport and (b) those who are detained *after entry* and who are held to have violated the terms of their permitted entry. The most common violation is staying beyond the period stamped in the passport (thus the expression 'overstayer'): other violations are working when not permitted to do so or being convicted of a crime. These two main forms of detention gain further discussion below.

Comparative legal regimes

Before accepting the British frontier guards' unquestioned right to detain asylum-seekers under the detention provisions of the Immigration Act of 1971 as if this law has achieved Mosaic status, it is instructive to make reference to the issue of detention in international and comparative law.

The UN Charter is often seen as the starting point for human rights law. For example, Article 3 establishes the right to life, liberty and security of person; Article 5 to freedom from torture or cruelty; Article 9 to freedom from arbitrary arrest, detention or exile; and Article 14 to the right to seek asylum.

European law on the detention of aliens has been effected particularly through the application of the European Convention of Human Rights. Article 5(1) of the Convention states in part that 'No one shall be deprived of his liberty save in [specified] cases and in accordance with a procedure prescribed by law.' The specified cases refer to *detention under the criminal law and procedure* (normally suspicion of crime); *detention as a measure of social protection or control* (which refers to the compliance with a court order, detention of 'social misfits' and minors) and finally, *administrative detention* (which is the procedure often evoked by the UK frontier guards in the cases of immigration detainees). But though the European Convention permits administrative detention as a means of effecting deportation, in the legal testing and application of the Convention several important provisos have developed to limit the state's power. These include:

- Such detention must not be unduly prolonged, as where it can no longer lead to deportation in the reasonably near future (District Court [Amtsgericht] Köln, 10 March 1965 cited Fawcett 1969: 449).
- While detention for the purposes of deportation can legitimately be made by administrative decision, 'the inability of the detainee to challenge the lawfulness of his detention before a court would be inconsistent with Article 5(4)' (*ibid.*).
- It is possible, though no application in these terms has yet succeeded, that there may be an obligation on contracting states to ensure that no individual suffers treatment forbidden by Article 3 (for example, torture, inhumane punishment) at the hands of a third party.
- Dutch law has now established beyond dispute that a court may find a detention order unlawful in the case of *détournement de pouvoir* or *abus de pouvoir*.
- Another passage in the Convention, Article 5(2), states that 'everyone who is arrested shall be informed promptly, in a language which he understands, of the reason for his arrest and any charge against him'.

US law is even more protective of the individual about to be deported where 'the alien will only normally be arrested where this is in the public interest or if he is likely to abscond. The order to show cause must state the grounds upon which the *prima facie* case of deportability is based, in such a way as to enable the alien to meet the allegations against him. Although attempts to introduce the full requirements of the judicial process have generally failed, the statute does provide for the minimum rights essential to a fair hearing' (Goodwin-Gill 1978: 266). In 1925, Justice Anderson of the US District Court for the District of Massachusetts (cited Grahl-Madsen 1972: 431) made the most compelling statement regarding the detention of non-criminal aliens:

The right to arrest and hold or imprison an alien is nothing but a necessary incident of the right to exclude or deport. There is no power in this court or in any other tribunal in this country to hold indefinitely any sane citizen or alien in imprisonment, except as a punishment for crime. Slavery was abolished by the Thirteenth Amendment. It is elementary that deportation or exclusion proceedings are not punishment for crime.

Other cases from Brazil, Estonia, Belgium, France, Argentina, Canada and Germany, though less strident than the US judgement, tend to the enunciation of two similar principles – i.e. there should be no taint of criminality attached to immigration detainees and there should be a definite limit to the length of detention necessary to process the claim for asylum (*ibid.*: 431–5).

Even this superficial review of international law shows that there is no legal support for statements by the Home Office that the non-possession of documents or the possession of forged or invalid documents was sufficient reason to detain passengers pending deportation.

Second, in most of the forms of immigration detention allowed in the UK and listed above, there is often an absence of the right for detainees to dispute the lawfulness of their detention. This absence is inconsistent with Article 5(4) of the 1951 Convention. The known difficulties of interpreting the genuineness of a claim to asylum suggest that the right of representation and appeal for those refused asylum should be unfettered or at least greatly enhanced if the UK is to conform to international law.

Third, in other cases where rights of appeal against detention and subsequent deportation are allowed, these are only permitted *after* the detainee/deportee has left the UK. This form of appeal is largely meaningless[4] and probably violates established rights both in international *and* English law.

Appeal after detention and deportation infringes European law in respect of the entitlement to 'a fair and public hearing', a right which supersedes, so the European Commission of Human Rights argues, the right of a state to control the entry and exit of foreigners.[5] As for English law, historically anyone – alien, subject or citizen – was free to apply for a writ of *habeas corpus* calling on those who are effecting the detention to explain why it is justified by law.[6] The PTA and the 1971 Immigration Act are serious assaults on this hard-won right.

In short, immigration law and practice in the UK transgress a number of long-held legal principles in both comparative and domestic

---

4 Consider these figures. Of the 720 deportees who appealed from abroad against their removal over the period 1973–82, only four were successful (A-DWG 1985: 30). Though a mulish logician could argue that only four had merit, it would seem more likely this low figure has something to do with the inability of the appellant to conduct a cross-examination, call relevant witnesses and otherwise exercise normal legal rights. The very mildest criticism of the system is that justice is not seen to be done.
5 For the legal beagles, the European Commission's interpretation draws on Art. 6, Par. 1, of the European Human Rights Convention following an application by the Swedish government (Grahl-Madsen 1972: 276).
6 The unrestricted right to apply for a writ of *habeas corpus* in a detention case was given by Lord Denning in 1962 in the case of Dr Soblen, despite the fact that the Court ruled that 'he never lawfully set foot in this country' (Grahl-Madsen 1972: 341–2). This curious case has provided much joy to academic lawyers over the years. Soblen jumped bail and fled to Israel after he was convicted in the USA of espionage. He was deported from Israel at the request of the US authorities but mutilated himself at Heathrow while in transit. He was detained in hospital and subsequently deported to the USA, though a number of lawyers continue to think this was a legally flawed decision (see Thornberry 1963).

law which protect the individual from the abuse of power, arbitrary arrest and detention by a Leviathan state.

Immigration Act detainees: on-entry

The IO derives his unusual powers to detain (or remove) an entrant principally from a section in the Immigration Act of 1971 which states that: 'Where an illegal entrant is not given leave to enter or remain in the UK, an immigration officer may give such directions in respect of him (as if he had been refused leave)'. Temporary detention – at the moment of challenge – is then confirmed by the issue of an IS 81 Form and an interview in secondary examination areas (SEAs).

Surprisingly large numbers are detained in these SEAs. In 1981, d'Orey (1984: 9–11) estimated as many as 20,000 people were detained at Heathrow and perhaps 3,000 in Dover and Folkstone. Because the statistical information is incomplete it is impossible to give a current figure. However if we surmise the number temporarily detained in SEAs has moved up roughly in proportion to the total passenger arrivals, by 1994 this would mean about 50,000 detentions in SEAs.

Because the SEA detainees are those refused leave to enter when they were deemed obviously unqualified, their situation, indeed their existence, was barely reported, even by concerned voluntary agencies. SEA detainees may be held temporarily for some hours, detained overnight or, exceptionally, given temporary admission. They are rarely, if ever, given leave to enter.

Those who are deemed 'illegal entrants' enter the strange half world of the immigration detention centres at Harmondsworth and the Queen's Building (at Heathrow), the Beehive (at Gatwick) and the airport and port detention centres at Manchester, Birmingham and the Channel ports. A variety of other destinations can also be selected. For example, the Ashford and Risley remand centres (the former with a 'deport block' holding 117 prisoners) and any one of the 120 prisons in Britain are used to hold immigration prisoners for longer than over-night or temporary detention. The most important of the conventional prisons holding immigration detainees is Haslar prison, Gosport, Hampshire.

The majority of women are housed either in Harmondsworth or Holloway. Other facilities were added at Latchmere House in Rich-mond in the 1980s. For a while, the disused ferry the *Earl William*, anchored off Harwich, was used as a detention centre for asylum-seek-ers. In November 1991, the Home Office declared that it was preparing another 300 immigration detention places, ominously stating that they were 'to be used for the detention of asylum-seekers' (Shutter 1992: 197). In November 1993, the new facility Campsfield House at

Kidlington near Oxford, artlessly described in the news broadcasts as a 'refugee prison', was opened.

What perhaps will never be known is whether, among those refused leave to enter and held for short periods are some individuals with a good case for entry or those whose claim for asylum is casually dismissed or disbelieved by an IO. Given the pressures of numbers and the precognitions of many members of the Immigration Service Union, one can only surmise that it could happen that individuals with good cases may be held in temporary detention, then returned to their countries of origin or put on to onward flights without their cases ever having been referred to a responsible agency or heard by the courts.

The provisions of the Immigration Act of 1971 came into effect in 1973 and this date can therefore provide a useful base year to start the citation of statistical data on non-SEA detainees. Figure 4.1 below shows the rapidly accelerating rate of those detained as illegal entrants, the number having multiplied nearly thirty-five times over the nineteen years covered.

Immigration Act detainees: after-entry

It is pure speculation as to how many of those claiming asylum at the port of entry are simply shunted in and out of the SEAs or deemed to be 'illegal entrants'. In the case of asylum-seekers, they should be issued with Form IS 91, implying referral to a voluntary agency, normally UKIAS,[7] and a more lengthy detention pending the evaluation of the strength of their claims.

Although an increasing proportion of asylum-seekers are detained 'on entry', it is also the case that 'after-entry' asylum-seekers may be detained. Two common circumstances normally obtain. The first is when an 'genuine' asylum-seeker, out of fear, ignorance or even perhaps calculation, gains admittance as (say) a visitor, then later seeks to press a case for asylum. The second is when circumstances in a home country alter adversely, forcing those who were admitted as (say) students to argue that it is no longer safe for them to return home.

---

7 While the Home Office has no legal obligation to refer asylum cases to UKIAS, in practice it normally did so until the late 1980s. In March 1983, Mr Waddington argued that there was a 'strong case for formulating arrangements for the notification of asylum cases to an agency. ... The refugee unit at the Home Office will in future give formal notification to the UKIAS refugee counsellors of all cases when no other agency or Honourable Member has previously intervened and a negative decision has been proposed.' Unfortunately, rather than signal the formulation of a general principle, this very sensible proposal seems to have stemmed from the minister's reaction to the ire of some Tory back-benchers, furious that a Romanian was sent back 'behind the Iron Curtain'. (*Guardian*, 4 March 1987). The minister abandoned his own suggestion in the case of most Tamil asylum-seekers. More recently, the disputed role of the UKIAS has created considerable confusion over the issue of referral.

The Home Office has been particularly resistant to giving credibility to either of these two possibilities. Indeed there is often a strong tendency to try to place after-entry asylum-seekers into the same general category of those who have illegally entered the country. The same logic is frequently applied to overstayers or those who have violated the terms of their entry. Here too it is in the interest of the immigration service to treat the overstayer or violator as an illegal entrant. Sue Shutter (1992: 192) explains how, in practice, the crucial difference between remaining in the UK illegally and being an illegal entrant, is elided:

Figure 4.1: Number of Alleged Illegal Entrants Detained in Custody, 1973-1991

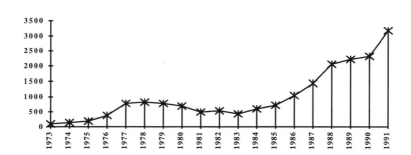

Sources: Control of Immigration Statistics (1973–93); Home Office Statistical Bulletins; Correspondence with the Research and Statistics Division, Home Office

Note: Data for 1973–79 include illegal entrants granted temporary release.

For example, if a man who was given entry as a visitor is subsequently found working, it is likely that he will be questioned by IOs about his original intentions when he first came to the UK – had he really intended just a visit? had he always wanted to work here? did he know before he came that he would work? had he always intended to stay longer than he said? If .e answer to any of these questions is 'yes', IOs may allege that he had concealed his true intention . . . [and that] entry was gained by deception.

As Shutter indicates, many overstayers or violators are questioned by IOs shortly after arrest or after having been in a police station for some hours; they have often not received legal advice and do not know the reasoning behind the IO's pointed questioning. If the IO is able to elicit a damaging admission to any of the probes (bearing in mind linguistic ambiguities that might arise in the cases of non-English-speakers), the trap has been sprung. The full force of the administrative powers of detention granted under the Immigration Act of 1971 can then be applied.

From 1986 onward, a number of non-governmental agencies concerned with issues of immigration and refugee reception – the United Kingdom Immigration Advisory Service (UKIAS), the Joint Council for the Welfare of Immigrants (JCWI), the British Refugee Council (BRC) and the local office of the United Nations High Commission for Refugees (UNHCR) – all expressed their concern at the increasing numbers of asylum-seekers detained, the longer periods involved and the conditions under which the detainees were held.

Were such representations the unduly alarmist special pleadings of lobbyists? The agencies' concerns were given startling judicial support on 22 March 1987 when a coroner's jury found that the suicide of a Ugandan asylum-seeker, Ahmed Katangole, in Pentonville prison showed 'official indifference and lack of care'. Inquest, an organisation monitoring the work of coroners' courts, immediately demanded that the verdict should lead to a 'monumental shake-up in the way immigrants and political refugees ... [are] treated'. It subsequently emerged that Katangole had attempted suicide before and that, had the examining psychiatrist been consulted, she would have strongly advised against the move to Pentonville. According to the JCWI, there were at least half-a-dozen suicide attempts by asylum-seeker detainees during the same year.

In a joint paper (PRT/JCWI 1984) issued by the JCWI and the Prison Reform Trust (PRT) the authors argued that:

... the workings of administrative detention under the Immigration Act [show] the dangers of injustice and abuse to be found in an executive discretion that can, and does, operate outside, and even in contradiction to, the recommendations of the courts. It is a discretion almost totally unfettered by independent scrutiny and which lies beyond the safeguards of liberty found in the Bail Act.

The UKIAS also displayed its relative independence from the Home Office, despite receiving an annual grant from that department, by expressing its concern with the manner in which the claims of after-entry refugees were being treated. In their evidence submitted to the Parliamentary Sub-Committee on Race Relations and Immigration in September 1984, the UKIAS drew attention to four issues:

- the totally inadequate and inappropriate appeal rights for refugees whereby rights of appeal are based on immigration status at the time of application;
- the non-disclosure of reasons for refusal where no right of appeal exists;
- the lengthy delays in processing applications;
- the treatment as illegal entrants of increasing numbers of asylum-seekers who have entered the UK as visitors and subsequently claimed asylum.

What the Home Office was virtually impervious to is an argument that turns on human fallibility and impulse. Could a student simply have spotted a good job or visitor inadvertently overstay? Of course, neither of these circumstances would justify somebody not applying to the Home Office for a reconsideration of their entry status, but the immigration service and Home Office characteristically regard an oversight or a change in plans as a cause for suspicion, thereby allowing them to exercise their maximum powers of detention and removal.

The cases of asylum-seekers who do not wish to return because of changed circumstances at home are conceded more often by the Home Office, though only after strong positive signals have been given at the political level. For example, Iranian students who did not wish to return after the fall of the Shah, Britain's ally, were the biggest single category of asylum-seekers from 1979 to 1984 (BRC 1987: 25). Similarly, a bulge of after-entry applicants from Iraq arose during the Gulf War, Saddam Hussein's opponents in the UK taking the opportunity to press their claims for asylum. In these cases, the exigencies of foreign policy and international alliances can turn the 'other' into an ally of the 'self', even if a complete transmutation is impossible.

Detention conditions and privatisation

The strange fate of the Earl William

New detention facilities providing 120 places for asylum-seekers were acquired by the Home Office in May 1987 aboard the *Earl William* car ferry, anchored in Harwich. I visited this facility in June 1987. At the time there were only two dozen detainees on board; by mid-July the numbers had risen to 70 (including some women). Although the ferry's full capacity was 252, an officer in charge of the facility assured me that it was unlikely to house more than 120 detainees. With some insensitivity, the ferry was opened by the Home Office for its new business in May 1987, shortly after the Zeebrugge ferry disaster.

The detainees were mainly Tamils, but there were also six Iranians and five Afghani nationals. They were confined to the ferry, but excluded from their cabins during the day. The cafeteria food was adequate to good, the lounge areas clean, a small shop had been set up on board and a doctor held a regular surgery. If dental attention was required, the detainees would be taken under guard to a dentist in the town. A tiny deck area had been roped off for a rough-and-ready mosque; table tennis was available on a greasy and gloomy car deck. No adequate exercise facilities were provided; the detainees were not even allowed to walk in the easily secured dockside area.

The facility's main problem was that it gave the general impression of being under siege from the surrounding town. Adverse comments in the local press about the ferry's health and sanitary arrangements were probably no more than thinly veiled expressions of xenophobia. Local residents, who had suddenly become enthusiastic defenders of the dubious glories of Harwich's marine environment, had initiated legal proceedings to stop the use of the ferry as a detention centre. Three street demonstrations, apparently inspired mainly from outside the town, also mobilised extreme right-wing opposition to the use of the ferry. The townsfolk tended to regard the detainees as criminals and many saw the ferry's 'offshore' location as an indication that the detainees were 'not really in Britain'. The ferry also took on the air of a hospital ship, with the associated ideas of contagion and disease.

Against this background of uneasy hostility from the town, the IOs and cleaners and the Securicor guards seemed conscious of the need to reassure the detainees that they were in safe and non-prejudiced hands. However, one of the detainees spontaneously expressed angry hostility to the Securicor guards and an equally robust preference for being guarded by normal prison officers (who, he asserted, knew the difference between criminals and the asylum-seekers 'who shouldn't be in prison'). He thought the Securicor guards inexperienced and untrained (some indeed had been seconded from such mundane tasks as guarding warehouses), unsympathetic and inclined to view the detainees in criminal terms. How far this view was shared is impossible to tell, but an experienced immigration counsellor believed it to be common.

While I personally found no evidence of brutality or conscious racism on the part of the Securicor guards,[8] their indifference to the personality and identity of their charges was indicated by the frequent message over the booming, indistinct and irritating Tannoy system, 'Tamil to the phone, please', 'Afghans (sic) to the phone', etc., quite ignoring that a particular person had been identified by the caller. Curiously, similar behaviour was recorded by Green (1990: 7) at the Harmondsworth detention centre three years later, only in that case the refrain was, 'Ghanaians to the phone', or 'Somalians to the phone'.

The aberrant telephone manner of the guards on the *Earl William* was clearly resented by the detainees and added to unease created by the expressed antipathy of the townsfolk and the eerie atmosphere on board. The ferry was certainly an inappropriate environment to secure

---

8 However, other visitors like Dean Nelson (*New Society*, 3 July 1987) reported being surrounded by angry asylum-seekers. 'They treat us like shit ... they use bad words, they call us fucking Tamils,' said one young Tamil. 'They' were the Securicor guards. A nineteen-year-old Punjabi said: 'We don't like it here. It is oily and dirty, and every day makes us sick. At Foston Hall [another detention centre] all the officers were kind, but here they treat us like prisoners.' After a hunger-strike had started (see above) one detainee complained to the *Sunday Times* (9 August 1987): 'the guards have become ruder and harsher in their treatment of us since we started the fast. They have no respect for us as prisoners. We do not feel that they are treating us as human beings.' A reporter from the *Scotsman* (4 August 1987) was told by Securicor guards that the detainees he wished to interview 'did not wish to be disturbed', yet when he finally got aboard the *Earl William,* he found that they had not been consulted.

individuals who needed sympathetic attention to their needs in a caring, therapeutic environment.

The ferry's use as a detention centre was constantly opposed in campaigns run by the refugee agencies and, in August 1987, 45 Tamils on board started a fast in protest at their continuing detention. Five of the hunger-strikers subsequently jumped ship. The home secretary, Douglas Hurd, immediately accepted an apparent offer by the protesters to go home – he would gladly provide free air tickets. It subsequently turned out that the strikers were saying that they *ultimately* wished to go home as and when political conditions had changed in Sri Lanka – a position totally consistent with their claim to be political refugees.

Hurd had egg on his face from his precipitous offer. The continuing use of the ferry was clearly causing more embarrassment than it was worth. But its fate was finally sealed by what the leader of the Tamil Action Group, Sinnapur Maharasingham, called 'the furious hand of nature'. There did, indeed, seem to be some message given from on-high. The tumultuous and memorable storm that struck southern England on 15–16 October 1987 left Harwich totally without electricity and holed the *Earl William* after it had burst from its moorings and run aground on a sandbank. The complaints of seasickness and queasiness on board gave way to sheer terror.

So abashed were the Home Office officials at the apparently divine reprimand that the ferry was immediately abandoned. Moreover, 35 Tamil asylum-seekers were released to their friends and relatives pending an investigation of their asylum claims, rather than being transferred to another detention centre.

Privatising detention

What I had thought at the time to be a minor ideological eccentricity in the use of a private security firm on the *Earl William* turned out to be merely part of an escalating policy to privatise immigration detention. In its latest manifestation, the security firm Group 4 was given the responsibility to run the new asylum-seeker prison at Campsfield House opened in November 1993. (The privatisation of the prison service itself had commenced one year earlier.)

Within a few months, Group 4's regime at Campsfield House was under attack by the asylum-seekers themselves. On 8 March 1994 demonstrations and hunger strikes began. By 17 March protests had spread to 10 detention centres and prisons in different parts of the country with at least 213 out of the 720 asylum-seekers refusing food. Some refused liquids. The asylum-seekers from Africa, Asia and South America vigorously condemned the 'inhumane conditions' and 'psychological torture' meted out by the Group 4 guards. One doctor in the employ of the company was rumoured to have resigned in disgust

(*Independent*, 17 March 1994). The Labour Party called for an enquiry.

Some eight security companies are involved in a range of tasks including guarding and escorting immigration detainees, safeguarding buildings and supervising cash-in-transit. The main contracts were placed with Property Guards Ltd, Security Express Ltd, Securicor, Group 4 and Total Security Ltd. One factor that seems to have influenced the Home Office in its decision to contract-out some of its detention facilities is the question of cost – the extremely low wages and long shifts worked by guards in the private security services gave them the edge in price.

Despite the assurance by the Home Office to the House of Commons Expenditure Committee that 'the employment of Securicor personnel is subject to the observance of strict rules for the humane treatment of "inmates",' a hard-hitting report[9] suggests that there are at least five grounds for concern as to the suitability of private contractors for this kind of work:

- First, contrary to the Home Office assertions, there have been many complaints about the attitudes and behaviour of the personnel employed by private firms.
- Second, the training given to them is risible. Group 4 Security, which provides the best training and has the lion's share of the Home Office's business, gives a five-day course to its employees including modules in: dealing with people, vigilance, protection of premises, patrolling, fire prevention control, health and safety, crime and criminal law, reporting and security restriction. The Immigration Service training unit of the Home Office provides a few additional seminars on race relations, coping with aggression, dealing with absconders and ethnic dietary needs. As Green (1990: 13) remarks, 'it is difficult to imagine that the effect of a one hour session on race relations will be at all significant in countering racism in the immigration service detention centres.'
- Third, the private security firms are largely unlicensed and unregulated with highly ambiguous powers to arrest, search or restrain detainees. They often exercise such powers as if they had legal sanction, but in law their powers do not greatly exceed that of an ordinary citizen.
- Fourth, given the irregular hours and poor pay, there is a massive

---

9 I rely here on Penny Green's (1990) report for the Howard League for Penal Reform. As the League argued: 'Many persons reading this report will be convinced that the management of these [immigration] detention facilities should be directly undertaken within the public sector and that the involvement of commercial security companies should cease.' The League was also justifiably concerned that the privatising of the immigration detention centres was but a prelude to a wider contracting-out of the prison service. In August 1992, the first large prison contract managed by private enterprise was announced. Appropriately enough, it was for Strangeways prison.

turnover of staff in the private companies. Despite the public commitment to training many personnel do not even go through the five-day course. Their backgrounds and suitability are not investigated; instead recruiters largely rely on self-declaration. It is thus quite possible to surmise that ill-educated, prejudiced members of extreme right-wing parties would have little difficulty securing employment with private security firms.

- Fifth, Home Office supervision of the contracts is casual to say the least, while the mechanisms for complaint and grievance-reporting by detainees are unsatisfactory – effectively involving the Home Office investigating complaints against itself.

Green concludes her study by suggesting that her findings are 'disturbing'. The 'total lack of public accountability ultimately protects the profits of Group 4 and ensures that the plight of the immigrants [sic] awaiting entry is subject first and foremost to the fortunes of commercial enterprise.' Based on my more limited observations, and the demonstrations in March 1994, I can but echo her concern.

The detainees

For illustrative purposes, I present below information on the experiences of five detainees. The cases are drawn from a newspaper report (Case 1), agency case notes (Cases 2 and 3) and from personal observation and interview (Cases 4 and 5). In the last two cases, some details have been changed to protect the anonymity of the individuals concerned.

Gulf War detainee – case 1: Ali al-Saleh

With the outbreak of the Gulf War, Kell's successor in MI5 generated a new list of suspected enemy aliens. Picked up in the net was Mr Ali al-Saleh, a computer salesman from Bedford who had lived in the UK for 20 years. He was visiting friends in London with his wife and two British-born children and only found out the police had called when he telephoned to remind the neighbour to feed the cat.

Curiously, Mr al-Saleh was released without interrogation after a few days, though he surmised (*Independent*, 13 Feb. 1992) that he was picked up on general grounds of suspicion both because of student activities in the 1970s and because he had once worked for the Saudi embassy. Another motive, which the Home Office amazingly confirmed to a persistent journalist formed part of the case against al-Saleh, was that his wife's sister had married a man whose uncle was Abu Nidal, the terrorist leader of the Fatah Revolutionary Council.

Overstayer – case 2: 'Cetin'

I have suggested already that the Home Office is unlikely to respond with any sympathy in the case of a detected overstayer. One of the cases dealt with by the JCWI (cited Gordon 1985: 64–5) concerned a Turkish seaman, Cetin, who had come to Britain on the advice of his doctor to recuperate from an illness. His passport stamp expired the day before New Year's Eve and he planned to travel to Italy on New Year's Day to start a new job which he had been promised. He did not bother to renew his leave to remain for the extra two days as, reasonably enough, he thought the Home Office might be shut over the holiday period. (Although he did not proffer this as an excuse, the mind-numbing wait at Lunar House for the renewal of documentation can exceed, on a bad day, the worst bureaucratic nightmare envisaged by Kafka.)

After a disturbance at a New Year party in the house where Cetin was staying, the police were called and discovered that Cetin's leave to remain had expired. He was able to show that his luggage was packed ready and waiting and that he held a valid air ticket to Italy. Despite this convincing evidence of his imminent departure, Cetin was arrested, held in custody for nine days before being taken to court, convicted of 'overstaying', recommended for deportation and held in Ashford remand centre *for three months* before being deported. Deportation following a court conviction means that Cretin will not be allowed to re-enter the UK without special permission.

Illegal entrant – case 3: Ahmed Bouzagou

Ashford remand centre was also the far from salubrious environment in which Ahmed Bouzagou found himself for five months during 1983. His crime? He came to Britain to renew his passport. Mr Bouzagou had legitimately been living with his Irish wife and two children in Eire since 1978. Required by the Irish authorities to revalidate his Moroccan passport, he travelled to London to the nearest embassy available to him.

Mr Bouzagou travelled from Dublin to Liverpool by ferry along with hundreds of other residents of Eire. Since 1925 (see Chapter 1), there have been no passport checks or immigration controls on the ferry routes from and to Liverpool. He proceeded to London only to be picked up and detained as an illegal entrant seven days later. Mr Bouzagou had indeed needed to request permission to re-enter the country as he had briefly overstayed his permit in the UK some years previously.

The Home Office attached no importance whatever to the fact that there was no IO to report to in Liverpool or that Mr Bouzagou had no way of knowing that he had needed to pass through immigration control. Though the arrest and detention were clearly legal within the terms of the 1971 Immigration Act, what followed seemed motivated by pure vindictiveness. Mr Bouzagou was detained *for five months*, then deported to Morocco, despite his repeated request to be allowed to return to his wife and children in Dublin.

Asylum-seeker – case 4: 'Fernando'

'Fernando' arrived from Chile via a third country and had been in detention for over six months when I read his case notes. He came from a poor family and left school at 14. As a young man he joined the Young Socialists and became active as a trade unionist in the mining sector. He was a party member and ardent supporter of Allende's Popular Unity government. When that government was overthrown, he fell victim to military and police harassment, torture and brutality.

He left Chile to join a sister in Argentina. There he was granted refugee status, but became subject to bouts of depression and homesickness and was committed to a mental institution for a time. Believing that the political situation in Chile had changed for the better, he returned home only to be picked up by the civil police, threatened with death and again tortured. His wife was raped by the policemen searching his home and he fell into a disconsolate depression, losing his job as a result.

Hearing of his condition, his sister in England, who herself had been granted refugee status, encouraged him to come to the UK and sent him a return ticket to do so. It seems she also had indicated that he would find work here with her husband, an independent tradesman. On arrival, and probably at her suggestion, Fernando told the IO that he was coming to the UK for a short-term visit. His baggage was searched and a letter from his sister was found, indicating that she expected him to stay for a longer period. Later he claimed asylum.

Fernando was immediately sent to the Harmondsworth detention centre, which, a psychiatrist reported, 'reminded him of the places where he had previously been tortured'. One agency concerned with immigration arranged for him to be examined by two psychiatrists, one of whom spoke Spanish. A voluntary charity concerned with the effects of torture arranged another examination. Both reports confirmed that Fernando had been tortured. One referred to the prospect of permanent mental disorder in the event of continued detention; the other mentioned the possibility of suicide.

Fernando's sister elicited the help of a sympathetic MP, who wrote to the Home Office minister on at least six occasions (I have seen copies of these letters) pleading Fernando's case for release, recognition as a political refugee and the withdrawal of his removal order. Only the last was achieved. The Home Office insisted that Fernando's attempt to mislead the authorities at the original airport interview constituted sufficient grounds for his removal and continued detention.

This ostensibly minor detail of the case illustrates how thoroughgoing are the Home Office's attempts to discover inconsistencies in the entrant's answers and the extraordinary lengths to which the agencies have to go to refute such 'inconsistencies'.

According to the Home Office, Fernando's 1976 claim to refugee status was invalid. The department baldly asserted that although Fernando had applied for asylum in Argentina 'this had been refused'. It is interesting to speculate how the department claimed such intimate knowledge of the decisions of the Argentine government seeing that, following the Falklands war, Britain had no diplomatic relationship with Argentina. The concerned agency had to use the good offices of the UNHCR to establish that Fernando *was* indeed a recognised refugee in Argentina and also managed to find a Uruguayan to make a sworn statement that he knew Fernando in the San Juan refuge in Argentina.

After this evidence was presented, the Home Office still did not consider that its erroneous statement on this issue might put into question its information on other related issues. The department remained unmoved by medical evidence and was unwilling to consider the simple interim solution of releasing Fernando to the care of his sister pending a decision. I was not able to establish Fernando's ultimate fate.

Asylum-seeker – case 5: 'Reza'

Reza arrived in the UK from France on a fake Dutch passport around Christmas 1986. His journey from his home country, Iran, had been a convoluted one. He had left Iran illegally on foot in 1985 and spent some nine months in Turkey. In Istanbul he had managed to buy an Iranian passport with which he had travelled to Yugoslavia (where he stayed for over two months) and thence to Greece (where he had stayed for three months). There he had obtained false Dutch papers which he had used to travel to Britain via Italy, Switzerland and France.

As the 1951 Convention permits the receiving country to download cases back to the country of first asylum, the question of his recognition in Britain was much complicated by this prior history. Negotiations with the Turkish, Yugoslavian and Greek governments ensued, but none of them would accept any responsibility for Reza's fate. Although Reza was only in France for one night en route to the UK, the Home Office decided to 'try' removal to France. This strategy backfired as the French authorities detained Reza, accused him of being a terrorist (apparently a sure-fire way of not having to recognise an asylum-seeker), broke his spectacles and returned him to Britain.

Apart from his European and Asian journeys, Reza had once been a student in the USA, where he had married, fathered a child and also established a close relationship with another woman. Unfortunately for Reza, neither of these women were prepared to vouch for him. As far as they were concerned, their relationships with him were over and they did not wish to persuade the US authorities to intervene on Reza's behalf. Why then did he leave the USA? According to Reza, he felt compelled to return to Iran to search for a missing and loved brother.

The Home Office official reviewing Reza's case did not take this story seriously. 'Paragraphs 41 and 205 of the UN Handbook put great store on an assessment of credibility, but this is a feature notably lacking in this case,' he rather pompously declared. Far from being involved in a quest for a missing brother, it seemed evident to the official that Reza had 'abandoned his wife in the USA to avoid domestic responsibilities'.

As with Fernando, the refugee agency concerned had to go to great lengths to establish, in this case from a former college roommate of Reza's in the USA, that there was indeed a missing brother. A sworn testimonial from the roommate, now a respectable computer systems engineer working for a leading US aeroplane manufacturer, established beyond doubt that many urgent family telephone calls were received and made regarding Reza's brother and that he was indeed agitated and preoccupied with his fate when leaving the USA for Iran. Officials at the Home Office also disbelieved other statements about Reza's political activities in Iran, but, as in the previous case, they apparently did not regard the refutation of one of their most damaging accusations (the missing brother issue) as questioning their Olympian certainty about the supposed lack of credibility of Reza's other statements. Reza was ultimately deported.

Although I have included details of only five cases, other client histories and the comments of case workers for the responsible agencies suggest that there are a number of disturbing features about Home Office evaluations.

- First, great credence is placed on the judgement of the IO at the initial interview or on outdated or superficial MI5 files. Little or no account is taken of the difficult situation genuine applicants may face in justifying themselves (in a second or third language) to an overworked or unsympathetic official after a long journey and possibly also after a recent loss of family lives, careers or property.
- Second, any inconsistencies in the entrants' statements are minutely recorded and used against them. Any positive evidence produced in favour of the applicant is rarely acknowledged in correspondence and does not lead to a reassessment of other negative judgements, often made after the event by desk officers who have

not seen the applicant.
- Third, very little advice is given on the limited rights an asylum-seeking detainee does possess.
- Fourth, official communications are distant and superior in tone, their writers held not to be impugnable by mere IADs or the refugee agencies. Although a certain indifference was perhaps to be expected in the case of foreign suppliants in view of the precognitions of many members of the immigration and intelligence services, I was surprised to find representations by lawyers, MPs and medical practitioners dismissed with similar rudeness and insouciance.
- Fifth, even where there is a clear conviction following a clearly illegal action, the punishment simply does not fit the level of the infraction.
- Sixth, there is evidence of gross inefficiency and overreaction by the police and immigration service. There is rarely any reason other than incompetence to explain why offenders have to stay for so long in detention while their deportations are being arranged. (Obviously legal complications sometimes do arise.) Equally, the case of the Turkish seaman seems to be one much better dealt with by a supervised departure, rather than by initiating an expensive and vindictive detention and deportation procedure.

Immigration control and social control

By the late 1980s there were some worrying signs that demands for greater efficiency in processing immigration cases were being used by the frontier guards to avoid allowing asylum-seekers (in particular) any meaningful access to representation in the pressing of their claims. On 3 March 1987, the home secretary stated that the normal expectation that an IO would refer an asylum-seeker's case to UKIAS was no longer to be honoured. Second, Douglas Hurd stated that the 'stop' powers of MPs to defer deportations pending consideration of the strength of the claim would no longer be respected 'where early removal is necessary'. Finally, Mr Hurd added: 'It follows that those who wish to seek to challenge in the courts decisions to refuse asylum cannot expect that they will automatically be allowed to stay here until proceedings are completed' (*Guardian*, 4 March 1987).

These three denials of hitherto accepted procedures signalled a new phase in immigration control. What this amounted to was a ministerial initiative to restrict the rights of representation and appeal by an asylum-seeker, an attempt to strengthen the hands of the Home Office or the IO and a push to turn the case around as quickly as possible so as to avoid any judicial reversal or adverse publicity. These practices, which had been initiated administratively, were given formal legislative effect in the Asylum and Immigration Appeals Act in 1993.

The increased capacity of the state to arrest, detain and deport aliens and asylum-seekers led to a subtle but definite relationship between immigration control and other forms of social control. The relationship between these two forms of control arises both through the overlap of enforcement personnel and the erosion of departmental boundaries in the zeal to detect illegal entrants. Overlap already existed in the Security Branch of the police which was created in the late nineteenth century to deal with the Fenian bombing campaign. The Branch was entrusted with the enforcement of early immigration controls (Gordon 1985: 10). When the Fenian campaign ended, the Special Irish Branch, as it came to be known, was not disbanded but continued to monitor the activities of Irish political refugees in Britain. In the 1905 Aliens Act, the Branch became responsible to the home secretary and provided intelligence reports on aliens.

In the modern period, the police also became involved in the supervision of aliens through the issue of an aliens' book which had to be stamped at the local police station. Aliens have to get the book restamped every time they change their address. I was also surprised to notice on my own university campus lines of desks staffed by the local police set up in the Student Union to facilitate the registration of foreign students. At one level this was a mere convenience, but again I could not help recall my own student days in Johannesburg and my days as a young lecturer in Ibadan (Nigeria) when we fought pitched battles against police trying to enter the campus. We thought our stance was legitimated by the historic British notion of 'university autonomy', which insisted that no forms of civic, military or political authority other than the university's own regulations should apply within the confines of the university. I was sad to see this tradition had died so silently and completely.

While these forms of overlap between the external and internal policing of the frontier are important, Paul Gordon (1985) is right to argue that up to the 1970s immigration control was still basically a matter of control on entry – of keeping people out of the country. He thought the switch in emphasis came with the 1971 Immigration Act which included the means to develop a fully-fledged system of post-entry controls. Even before the Immigration Act of 1971 came into force, however, the Illegal Immigration Intelligence Unit (IIIU), based at New Scotland Yard, was set up with a skeleton staff in September 1972 and became fully operational in March 1973. Its object was to 'receive, collate, evaluate and disseminate information on known or suspected offenders'. By 1980 this unit comprised 24 police officers and 2 civilians. Gordon (1985: 22–3) showed how this unit made the connection between 'illegal immigration' and 'drugs'. It needed but a short prejudiced jump to add the notion 'black' and thereby position the whole architecture of stigmatisation in the minds of the police.

The IIIU liaises closely with the Immigration Services' own intelligence unit which, by some unamazing coincidence, is based at Harmondsworth near the main immigration detention centre (31 officers and 8 civilians initially staffed this unit). By 1980 the IIIU had commenced the notorious 'passport raids' which sent a chill of fear around the minority communities in Britain. These comprised checks in supermarkets, places of work and places of leisure to confirm the immigration status of those selected. Temporary detention followed, pending confirmation of a legitimate right to be in Britain, followed by deportation for those held to be illegally in the country.

The enforcement of the immigration laws has also led to a violation of the traditional defence against the overweening big-brother state: the informal rule that one department of state should not share confidential information with another. In 1973, the year that the 1971 Immigration Act came into force, DHSS applicants were asked to produce passports, identity cards or birth certificates 'to confirm the accuracy of personal particulars required for National Insurance purposes'. The Home Office would be informed if there were any suspicions of illegal entry. Again Gordon (1985) records that the police used the Department of Employment's records on National Insurance to gather an address of a suspected illegal immigrant.

Passport raids and the sharing of information between departments of state are wholly alien to the British traditions of civil liberty which decry the use of internal identity checks. (Unlike in many countries, there is no agreed single identity card, while even so important a document as a driving license does not bear a photograph of the owner.) By contrast, it is common to observe French police 'fishing' for suspects at turnpikes like the huge Parisian metro station at Châtelet Les Halles by demanding proof of identity.[10]

The difference between the two countries arises from historical and geographic accident (British regionalism vs. Napoleonic centralism) and differing locations (an island vs. a part of a continent with lengthy permeable borders). This difference was characterised by strong on-entry controls and weak post-entry controls in Britain with the opposite situation obtaining in France. Unfortunately, what the prospect of European integration suggests is not that Britain will discard its own brand for a continental model, but that it will import an additional and parallel mode of social control.

---

10 Anyone who believes that the French police are less xenophobic than the British police is invited to spend a morning in the underground cafés at Châtelet. People of white phenotypes are rarely stopped, nor are those with black skins who are dressed respectably in a mainstream Parisian style. Those of Arab, Asian and African appearance are targeted, especially if they look poor. I was first alerted to the extent of this practice by a number of articles in *Le Monde* (see especially 27 May 1992 and 3 June 1992) examining 'racism' in the French police. According to these reports every year 200,000 residents are called upon to prove their national status.

Conclusion

In this chapter I have covered detentions in wartime and 'peacetime', if the Northern Ireland situation can allow the last description, together with detentions arising from security and immigration legislation.

If we take periods when war has formally been declared, it is perhaps unsurprising that the UK authorities should detain (or deport) aliens who are likely to give aid, comfort or support to the declared-enemy countries. However, the evidence adduced from the First World War, the Second World War and the Gulf War proves the old adage that reason is the first casualty of war. Nationalist sentiments needed to stir the populace to heroic efforts are easily turned to violent anti-alien expressions.

Instead of resisting such public hysteria, the frontier guards frequently condone or even galvanise it. I have shown how innocent German grocers, Italian restaurateurs, or Palestinian writers have been pulled into the maw of a Foucaultian nightmare. They are classified, declassified and reclassified as the fortunes of war intersect with the changing definitions of the familial and the strange, the friend and the enemy.

As to the period of formal peace, since 1975 security legislation relating mainly to Northern Ireland (but also to other terrorist threats), has generated a huge rise in the level of detentions effected by the authorities. Supposing, for the sake of argument, we added up the numbers involved in all forms of security and immigration detention in a sample year, 1986. The list would look like this:

- 60,000 detained for less than an hour under the PTA
- 1,556 detained under the PTA for at least 48 hours
- 26,000 detained in Secondary Examination Areas (estimate)
- 1,045 detained as illegal entrants
- 300 other immigration prisoners (estimate).

The result? Nearly 89,000 detainees not charged with any crime and not given access to traditional civil liberties.

The numbers involved are not the only disturbing feature of immigration and security detentions. An examination of international law on this issue suggests that British practice has fallen a long way behind best practice in other countries and, in certain respects, is legally suspect. The very large number of convictions on human rights grounds secured against the British government (see Chapter 7) is indicative of this broad departure from international standards.

Even in terms of the UK's domestic law, the steady erosion of *habeas corpus* in immigration and security cases provides a gauge of the increasing strength of bureaucratic and political power at the expense of judicial safeguards and individual liberties. It is a disturbing feature of the contemporary British political debate that so much emphasis has been laid on the liberties of the individual in the marketplace that the political and social aspects of liberty appear to have been overlooked.

The general lack of an effective opposition to the frontier guards is evidenced in the conditions found in the prisons and detention centres. Equally the impotence of critics is shown by the fate of individual detainees whose very human and poignant life-histories are brushed aside by administrative diktats sent down by Home Office officials who, characteristically, have never met the people whose fate they determine. The very limited judicial and appeal rights for immigration detainees mean that they are shuffled around by the force of bits of paper.

The general sense of a lack of fairness is particularly evident in the cases of asylum-seekers. There seems to be no good reason why, for example, applications for bail under the Bail Act of 1976 should not be permitted or why the asylum-seekers should not be able to apply for release on the grounds (i) that the state has abused its power; (ii) that the state is detaining the individual with no reasonable prospect of returning the asylum-seeker other than to a country where torture or danger are present; and (iii) that the period of detention has been unduly prolonged in view of the medical condition of the detainee.

The conditions under which wartime internees, IADs, security cases and asylum-seekers are held also give grounds for concern. All of these detainees are essentially accused of civil, not criminal offences. One may wish legitimately to question the extent to which criminality is also politically defined – as to some extent it is. But there seems a clear enough distinction between someone accused of being a murderer, thief or rapist on the one hand and someone who may be an enemy agent, a disguised economic migrant or an illegal entrant on the other. In particular, there has been too great a conflation between the conventional prison population and IADs.

Finally, the extent and nature of the policing of immigration and security legislation appears to have led to a steady seepage from external to internal control, from on-entry to post-entry supervision, from restrictions directed at aliens and asylum-seekers, to ones that are gradually affecting the minority and stigmatised parts of the home population.

CHAPTER 5

Sanctuary and the anti-
deportation movement

> The Lord spoke to Moses and said ... 'You shall designate
> certain cities to be places of refuge ... so that any man
> whether he be Israelite, resident alien, or temporary settler may
> take sanctuary in one of them.'
> — *New English Bible*, Numbers 35: 9–15

Much of the evidence in earlier chapters has been drawn from those
agents and agencies in the UK who seek to manage and control the
frontiers of British identity – notably the Home Office, the immigration service, certain politicians and the popular press. But aliens,
refugees and asylum-seekers also resist the exclusionary social
controls placed upon them and seek to effect links and alliances with
sympathetic groups in British society.

In this chapter, I look at two associated responses to exclusion and
marginalisation – the use of sanctuary in defence of a bid to stay in the
country and the construction of an anti-deportation movement linking
local communities and support groups to those threatened with deportation.

On sanctuary

As suggested in the opening quote, sanctuary is associated with biblical times, the Lord having enjoined Moses to establish six cities in
Canaan, to be designated as places of refuge. Therein, somebody
accused of manslaughter could be protected from the dead person's
next-of-kin – whatever the civic status of the accused person. Other
ancient cultures and civilisations,[1] including those of Egypt and

---

1 The Egyptian practice, in fact, antedated that of the ancient Judeans, as: 'Every
shrine ... royal altars, pictures and statues of the ruler, or site used for the taking of
oaths, was a protected region sought out by all the persecuted, by mistreated slaves,
oppressed debtors and political offenders.' Sanctuaries were also common in Greek
societies where they were 'converted into the resorts of murderous slaves, insolvent
debtors and notorious criminals' (Siebold 1934: 534). Romans fled to statues and
busts of the Caesars, and even to vestal virgins, in the hope of gaining temporary
immunity from prosecution. The Islamic tradition of sanctuary was similarly limited
and temporary. While Mohammed had expressly forbidden putting a thief or a murderer to death inside a mosque, the offender could be taken out by force and killed
outside the building (Stastny 1985: 26).

Greece, also established refuges, some created with the socially benign intention of preventing the decimation of innocents arising from the blood feuds between warring kinsmen.

In England, sanctuary was authorised by the Normans in two arenas. First, the major churches were regarded as inviolate and second, a number of cities were granted sanctuary status by Royal Charter. Henry VII reduced the number of sanctuary cities to seven and, in 1623, the general right of sanctuary was abolished by statute.

At a national level, the political asylum granted by one state in the case of a national from another state can be seen as the functional equivalent to sanctuary at the level of a municipality or church. Indeed, the German ethnologist Emil Mühlmann argued that the moral and legal origins of modern nations (a process he called 'ethnogenesis') were rooted in the protection granted by fledgling nation-states to escapees from neighbouring territories (the *droit d'asile*).

Thomas Paine's flight from England to France and thence to the USA after he published his radical works on human rights, provides one well known example that lends support to Mühlmann's idea. Paine himself made a passionate appeal to the American authorities to recognise their historical obligations to dissenters, like himself, seeking freedom. His words (cited Schneider 1989: 164) provide an important part of the founding mythology of the American nation and are commonly quoted in civics textbooks in the USA:

O! ye that love mankind! Ye that dare oppose not only the tyranny but the tyrant, stand forth! Every spot of the old world is overrun by oppression. Freedom has been hunted round the globe. . . . O! receive the fugitive and prepare in time an asylum for mankind.[2]

Subsequent to its apogee in the tussles between church and state in the Middle Ages and in the 'ethnogenesis' of the European and American nation-states, the practice of sanctuary survived in a number of indirect ways:

- The underground railroad of the pre-Civil War period in the USA provided aid to slaves evading the Fugitive Slave Laws and seeking to find freedom in Canada.
- Jews escaping the holocaust found help in the French village of Le Chambon-sur-Lignon where the inhabitants had collectively decided to turn their village into a place of refuge.
- In fragile Latin American democracies, the military and police forces have been reluctant to enter parliamentary buildings in

---

2 To update and complete the paradox, in the period of the Vietnam war, war resisters (known by the political right as 'draft dodgers') fled *from* the USA, Paine's country of refuge, to neighbouring Canada. The refusal of the Canadian authorities to send any deserters or resisters back across their southern border meant that the whole of Canada had, in effect, become a sanctuary for US war dissenters (Kasinsky 1976).

pursuit of those defending democracy.

• The protection granted to embassies and consulates and their staff ('diplomatic sanctuary') can also be seen as another survival of earlier sanctuary practices.

The modern revival of sanctuary can usefully be marked by an address from the pulpit by Yale University's chaplain in 1970. In referring to those resisting their call-up at the time of the Vietnam war, he (cited Stastny 1985: 25) asked: 'Now if the Middle Ages churches could offer sanctuary to the most common criminals, could they not do the same for the most conscientious among us?'

By the end of 1985, the US movement claimed the adherence of 300 congregations and 70,000 supporters (Stastny 1985: 24). The nature of the US movement can be glimpsed in a typical resolution (cited Saperstein 1987: 671) adopted on 5 June 1985 by the Temple Shir Shalom congregation of Mar Vista, California:

Today, Temple Shir Shalom declares itself a member of the Sanctuary Movement. We join over 200 synagogues, churches and communities of faith providing protection and advocacy to refugees from El Salvador and Guatemala fleeing armed conflict and seeking safe haven in the United States out of fear of persecution. . . . We Jews are taught not to oppress or harm the stranger residing in our midst, since we know what it is like to be a stranger (Exodus 23:9). We are a people who have lived in many lands and who have been forced to flee many lands: repelled often in times of our needs. . . . Certainly we remember the Holocaust when millions of our people were murdered by the Nazis because the nations of the world – including the United States – did not offer sanctuary to those fleeing to safety. There were, of course, those few people who did help many of us. We want to remember those acts and acknowledge that their courage is also part of our heritage which impels us to make this declaration.

The Jewish and Christian congregations joining the sanctuary movement were later strengthened by over two dozen cities declaring themselves to be 'sanctuary cities'. But despite its extent, most supporters of the US movement have been careful not to stray too far outside the law and have sought not to provoke the immigration authorities. A partial exception to this rule occurred in the case of some Quakers, who have been particularly prominent in opposing the moral basis of the US immigration law. One Quaker, Jim Corbett, has become something of a folk hero to his acolytes in smuggling refugees from other Latin and Central American countries over the Mexican border to the USA. So threatening had this throwing down of the gauntlet become to the US authorities, that a number of the supporters of the sanctuary movement, including several nuns, were prosecuted by the US Immigration and Naturalisation Service. One is regarded as a prisoner of conscience by Amnesty International – the first offender in the USA to be so recognised since the anti-Vietnam war movement of the 1960s and 1970s.

A 'right' to sanctuary was increasingly also asserted in a number of European countries during the 1980s – notably in Germany, Switzerland, Belgium, the Netherlands and the UK. Within the USA, it is probably no exaggeration to assert that a 'sanctuary movement' began, normally involving Christian churches or Jewish synagogues, which allowed their places of worship to become sanctuaries, or encouraged their congregations to shelter those who fell foul of the immigration authorities.

In both the contemporary European and North American cases, the customary use of sanctuary is for those who have violated immigration law by 'illegal entry' or 'overstaying'. Characteristically, those supporting sanctuary use the expressions 'unauthorised' or 'undocumented' migrants to describe their charges – thus indicating their disagreement with the legitimacy of the state's determination to label such migrants as 'illegal'.

The growth of sanctuaries in Britain during the 1980s paralleled the comparative cases mentioned, but any notion of a 'movement' is as yet premature. Additionally, the British case has certain distinctive features. For example, sanctuary in Britain has been politically linked to the anti-deportation campaigns and (with more difficulty) to anti-racist work more generally. Another particular characteristic is in the participation by religious groups other than the Christian and Jewish – Sikh gurdwaras, Muslim mosques and Hindu temples have all given refuge to various individuals threatened with deportation (Weller 1989).

Despite the venerable precedents of sanctuary and its increasing familiarity in the 1980s, when government ministers and Home Office officials argue that the right of sanctuary does not legally exist in modern Britain, they are correct in terms of a narrow interpretation of the historical statute of 1623. However, as most sophisticated lawyers would agree, if social conduct of a particular sort becomes customary, the law slowly but eventually adjusts to the reality of normal social behaviour. A Home Office official thus made a probably unwitting concession to the principle of sanctuary when he declared of Rajwinder Singh who had taken refuge in a Sikh temple, that, '*We would not enter a place of worship*, but he will be deported' (cited Weller 1987: 16). David Waddington, the under-secretary of state at the Home Office, matched this statement by saying, 'We have no intention of offending people's susceptibilities by going storming into a church' (cited VMDC 1988a: 18).

As is shown later, within some religious circles contemporary sanctuary has already fully regained its moral legitimacy. Whether sanctuary is able to regain some legal basis, however, will turn on the extent to which the authorities are prepared to enforce and assert the statute of 1623. Despite the Home Office statements quoted above, as

we shall see, in the crucial case of Viraj Mendis that was precisely
what they decided to do.

The revival of sanctuary in Britain

Weller (1987: 10–12) has suggested that the origins of modern sanctuary in Britain lie in the late Bishop Colin Winter's use of his home,
called the Namibia International Peace Centre, in Cephas Avenue,
London, as a place of safety and security for refugees from apartheid.
However, the Centre was soon involved in extending its refuge to
Chilean exiles, then Filipina migrant workers, and finally to Bengalis
who were under threat of deportation for violations of their entry
conditions.

In 1979, two Moroccans were given sanctuary in the Regent's Park
Mosque in London, and Weller was aware of other groups in Dews-
bury, Leeds and Luton who had sought to emulate the Winter Centre in
London. Shelter was often provided in the homes of anonymous
citizens. Far from courting publicity, the hosts often cultivated a
somewhat exaggerated cult of secrecy, on the lines of Anne Frank's
protectors in Nazi-occupied Holland.

Those who sought and gave sanctuary in this period hoped that the
police would eventually give up the pursuit of migrants who had fallen
foul of immigration law. On the ground, there was some sense to this
tactic. Notwithstanding the gradual internalisation of immigration
control and the formation of groups like the IIIU at Scotland Yard (see
Chapter 4), there was a degree of consensus in many local police
stations that the enforcement of post-entry controls was a distasteful
and inappropriate task – the proper business of the immigration
authorities, not the police. Moreover, where the anti-racist movement
had gained some local authority support, chief constables were
concerned that raids for immigration violators were likely to cause
damage to their various programmes for better community relations.

Despite this initial reluctance to become involved, the police have
gradually been sucked into the pursuit of 'overstayers', either through
legislative enactment (for example, in one of the important Clauses of
the 1988 Immigration Act) or in the form of a reciprocal amplification
of response and counter-response as defence campaigns took on a
more public stance and right-wing politicians and newspapers in turn
demanded an enforcement of the law.

The case of Vinod Chauhan, in October 1983, was the first to
follow this newer pattern. Chauhan's marriage to a British citizen had
broke down and he had fallen foul of the 'primary purpose' rule (this
rule states that marriage cannot be made for the purpose of evading
immigration controls). Chauhan undertook a fast while in sanctuary in
Ashton-under-Lyme's Baptist church, following the failure of legal

appeals against deportation and the receipt of a letter saying that the police would be making arrangements to arrest him for deportation. He sought publicity and the involvement of Christian church leaders unconnected with his own beliefs. The campaign lasted six months and failed to prevent Chauhan's deportation, but some short-term successes were recorded. The threat of arrest was lifted, while the local MP and town Mayor plus Chauhan himself, secured an interview with the responsible Home Office minister to plead their case.

On 25 February 1985, a second public sanctuary was commenced by two Cypriots, Katerina and Vassilis Nicola, who established themselves on camp beds in the south aisle of the Anglican church of St Mary the Virgin, Eversholt Street, London. They had been living in the UK for over a decade after their village in Cyprus had been occupied by the Turks. The couple were part of a group of about 10,000 refugees who gradually found their claims for refugee status undermined as the British Foreign Office changed its policies in favour of recognising the permanent division of the island into Greek and Turkish zones (see Chapter 3). Some 8,000 refugees, including the Nicolas, were told that conditions on the island were now sufficiently settled for them to 're-establish themselves' (CCWAG 1982: 9–10).

Although the Nicolas succeeded in winning a considerable amount of publicity and the (somewhat grudging) support of a number of church leaders, living conditions in the church made a long-term stay difficult and their endurance cracked after four months. Mr Nicola made an emotional appeal for justice before being deported. He told *The Times* (13 July 1985):

I feel very angry when a man has a just case and cannot find justice. Next week it will be the eleventh anniversary of our leaving Cyprus and now we are being thrown out of our home in England. I do not know where we are going to stay. My relatives have many problems and they have nowhere to live. My wife is finding it very difficult to cope with the strain we are going through.

On 15 March 1985, not quite three weeks after the Nicolas had started their protest a Filapina, Pina Manuel, and her son Arman took refuge in the Roman Catholic church, St Aloysius, only a few hundred yards from the Nicolas. Señora Manuel had been working in England on a domestic worker's permit which ran out when her employer failed to make a proper application for its renewal. The conditions in the church were easier and the supporters of Señora Manuel waged a quieter campaign, without much press publicity – one that was successful six months later.

Finally, amongst the first cases of modern sanctuary in Britain, I should also mention the case of 60 Tamils being given refuge in the Ghandapathy Hindu Temple in Wimbledon when they found themselves in the UK without visas immediately after the UK government imposed visa restrictions. The sanctuary was quietly ended by the local authority on health and safety grounds.

'People like me don't win': the case of Viraj Mendis

While it is only proper to remind ourselves of the path-breaking precursors to the use of sanctuary as a form of resistance to the immigration laws, by far the most publicised case was that of Viraj Mendis, who started his sanctuary in the Church of the Ascension in Hulme, Manchester, on 20 December 1986. Mendis was not only the longest example of someone in sanctuary in modern Britain – he stayed in the church for nearly two years – he was also compelled to leave by force. He and his supporters fought a highly public, extremely active and increasingly bitter campaign, seeking to link Mendis's plight to a more general anti-deportation movement.

In the welter of pro-Mendis publicity and anti-Mendis denunciation, some of the essential facts have been lost. So here is a quick résumé. Mendis, a son of a middle-class Sri Lankan plantation manager, came to Britain in October 1973 at the age of 17 to study at the University of Manchester Institute of Science and Technology (UMIST). He was granted leave to stay in Britain, as a student, until 1975. After failing his exams, he earned enough to continue studying for a further period. Then he started drawing social security.

On 23 May 1984, the Manchester police visited him, asserting he had been an overstayer since October 1975. He surrendered his passport to the police two days later and also announced that though he was Sinhalese he was a political opponent of the Sri Lankan regime and a supporter of the Tamil movement for self-determination.

According to his own account, he became 'politically active and saw the irrelevance of education to the struggle' (B. James 1988: 9). 'The struggle' was allied first to the Socialist Workers' Party and then to the Revolutionary Communist Group (RCG), a group he joined in 1980 as a result of buying their pamphlet, *Fight Racism, Fight Imperialism* (Batsleer 1988: 77; VMDC 1988a: 3).

The Viraj Mendis Defence Campaign (VMDC) was formed in June 1984. On 25 July 1984 Mendis applied to be allowed to stay in Britain on the grounds that he had married a British citizen, Linda X. In August 1984 the Department of Health and Social Security (DHSS) withdrew the couple's benefit. According to Mendis's account: 'Swift action by the VMDC forced the DHSS to abandon this attempt to starve [me] out. The pressures of the campaign, however, led to the marriage breaking down.'

On 29 October 1984 Mendis was interviewed by the Home Office at the odd location of Manchester Airport, where he again asserted his opposition to the Sri Lankan government and his support for Tamil self-determination. In August of the following year he was arrested in the street. He claimed he was 'racially abused, physically assaulted, strip-searched and charged with "conduct likely to cause a breach of the peace"'. In response to this intimidation the VMDC, with the support of the chair of the Manchester City Council, led an emergency march through the city centre. The charges were dropped two days later. This victory for the VMDC undoubtedly gave the campaigners a sense that their tactics of publicity and confrontation could pay off.

Subsequently, Mendis went through various judicial procedures and appeals heard by the chief adjudicator, the immigration appeal tribunal, a judge of the Divisional Court and then the Court of Appeal. Perhaps the most controversial of the legal decisions arose from the chief adjudicator's comment that, far from being an unsafe place to return someone (the crucial inhibition that the Geneva Convention places on the country of deportation), 'Sri Lanka is inherently a democracy where the rule of law obtains.'

When the High Court rejected an appeal by Mendis against the dismissal of his 1987 judicial review on 17 June 1988, Home Secretary Douglas Hurd reacted by saying that he would abide by anything the court said. He hoped Mendis would too. He had put his case in the British courts; had been given fair hearing. Now he should go. This statement was precipitous in that another appeal was still possible – to the House of Lords. When that too failed, Mendis entered sanctuary in the Church of the Ascension. The long siege started on 20 December 1986.

The campaign

The RCG was at the heart of Mendis's support group, ran the 24-hour vigil at the church and was the major force behind the 'defence campaign'. Batsleer (1988) argued that the RCG did not act in an overly sectarian way and that what could have been 'a fatal flaw' given 'the experience of many campaigns led by aspirant vanguards' was offset by the RCG's commitment to 'open and democratic organisation' within the campaign. 'This means', she continued, 'that although members of the RCG retain a commitment to the RCG's collective line, this is expressed and argued openly alongside the perspectives of other groups.'

It is difficult to come to a final judgement on this question. Undoubtedly, the tightknit, dedicated nature of the group led to a great deal of organisational effectiveness. By 1988, the VMDC was able to announce support from 42 other anti-deportation campaigns, 160 organisations ranging from the All London Teachers Against Racism and Fascism to the Workers' Press of the Workers' Revolutionary Party, 8 local councils (including Manchester), dozens of councillors, MPs, former MPs and MEPs, 15 bishops, 9 moderators of the United

Reform Church together with over 100 other clergy and religious bodies, numerous constituency and ward branches of the Labour Party, many trade unions, trades councils and trade union leaders, 14 student unions and finally, a number of prominent individuals. Amongst the individuals was one surprising name, Lord Jenkins, formerly a Labour home secretary, one of the 'gang of four' that formed the breakaway Social Democratic Party. Jenkins is normally regarded as a cautious politician, not easily given to rash enthusiasms.

It was a formidable list and showed the enormous energy and dedication of the members of the RCG involved in the campaign. The VMDC organised rallies and marches, poster displays and council resolutions. A petition containing 40,000 signatures demanding that Mendis be allowed to stay was collected. The VMDC convened a number of conferences, the most notable of which, on 11–12 April 1987, brought together delegates from other anti-deportation campaigns and sanctuaries, political activists, journalists, and religious leaders, Labour Party and union supporters of the campaign. (I also attended this conference in furtherance of my research.)

The conduct of the campaign provided an interesting example of the way in which images and slogans were used to vindicate a political cause. At the centre of the campaign, naturally, was Viraj Mendis himself – with the compulsory beard and long hair of the revolutionary, but also looking vulnerable, with owlish Billy Bunter spectacles, a pinched face and an seemingly endless interruptive stammer. Could this shy, uncertain, youthful-looking man (more like a boy) truly represent a threat to the state? And just next to the central character was a short, genial, befrocked, beautifully spoken priest, with a deceptively mild manner: Father John Methuen, ex-chaplain to Eton College. Was he really such a meddlesome priest, let alone the stuff of revolutionary anarchism as some right-wing commentators alleged?

The campaign was cleverly targeted virtually exclusively on these two sympathetic individuals and the mass marches and demonstrations in their support. The members of the VMDC, particularly the RCG, kept well out of the spotlight. In true conspiratorial fashion many of the RCG's 200 members adopted a pseudonym for their political activities. The campaigners also had the good sense to follow the spin doctor's rule never to publicise their opponents' case. In the VMDC campaign literature, Douglas Hurd, Timothy Renton and David Waddington, the ministers responsible at the Home Office, remained faceless, grey, stony and remote.

Campaign slogans are also a useful indication of the intentions of the organisers. Here is a sample of the posters and placards used, drawn entirely from the Viraj Mendis Defence Campaign's *Bulletin*:

'Viraj Mendis Will Stay! Deportations No Way!'
'Viraj Mendis Will Stay! Stop all Deportations Now!'
'Viraj Mendis Will Stay! No to Death in Sri Lanka!'

'Viraj Mendis Life or Death? Which Side Are You On?'
'Viraj Mendis Defence Campaign. Stop All Deportations.
   No to Britain's Pass Laws!'
'Fight Deportation! Unite Families! Fight Racism!
'Timothy Renton. "Herr" [*sic*] Us Say, Deportation No Way!'
'Stuff Their States, Passports and Borders.
   We've Had Enough!'

The first five of these slogans were 'officially' issued by the VMDC
in pre-printed form and they again show a reasonably sophisticated
sense of the rules of Madison Avenue – always make sure your own
brand name is at the top, then provide the subsidiary message. The last
slogan, scrawled in a less authorised style, is perhaps the most revealing of the underlying sentiments of the campaign – in effect, it
demanded the free movement of peoples across all boundaries.[3]

Despite the large number of supporters generated by the campaign
and the acres of publicity in the printed and electronic media, I would
argue that the campaigners antagonised leading decision-makers,
opinion-formers and potential supporters – whose alienation in the end
proved decisive. For example, the top church leaders saw the campaign
as leading to a generalised demand for the reassertion of the right to
sanctuary – a prospect that they were simply not prepared to contemplate (see below for a discussion on the Church's role).

Next, a key figure in the Labour Party, its former home secretary
and deputy leader, Roy Hattersley, was far from convinced that
Mendis had a particularly meritorious case. Despite the many Labour
Party constituency resolutions in Mendis's favour, Hattersley (who has
always liked the sound of his own pen) was positively surly in his
retrospective assessment of the case (*Guardian*, 21 Jan. 1989) just
three days after Mendis was dragged from his sanctuary:

On the evidence available to me, I have little doubt that dozens of more
deserving cases pass through my bureau each year – straight into the Immigration Detention Centre at Harmondsworth. ... Mr Mendis also had problems
with his friends. Many of them were hardly the sort of people one would
expect to find at a bishop's tea party. Some were, in fact, bishops. But it was
his least Episcopal supporters who made the headlines. They had strange hair-
cuts, chanted offensive slogans about racism in Britain and exploited their
hero's predicament by using it to promote bizarre political views. ... Viraj

---

3 The demand for no borders, in other words for a free market in the migration of
   labour, is one that curiously unites the far left with the far right. It is not that well
   known that important elements of the Bow Group (the right-wing ginger group of
   the Tories) support the removal of all immigration restrictions. Their position has the
   virtue of consistency, as their sacred cow, the free market, would reign supreme
   throughout the economic and social structure. By contrast, the 'Thatcherites' and
   'Majorites' support a free market for capital, while vigorously denying the same
   freedom to labour. In Lord Tebbit's version, workers should get on their bikes, but
   they should not board planes, ships or ferries.

Mendis buzzed about in the most inconvenient and infuriating way and there were many occasions when I would gladly have swatted him with a rolled-up newspaper.

Hattersley concludes this negative, patrician vision of Mendis and his campaign with a surprising declaration of his support: not, however, because of any strength in Mendis's case but, apparently, because Hattersley could not stand the sight of 'a smirking Douglas Hurd (Eton and Trinity College, Cambridge)' describe Mendis as 'certainly not fortunate in his student career'. While some might sympathise with Mr Hattersley's reaction, his views on Mr Hurd's manner were hardly the basis for an informed judgement of the strengths of Mendis's claims.

In addition to losing the sympathy of leading members of the Church and Labour Party, the usual clutch of right-wing populist newspapers, notably the *Sunday Express* and the *Daily Star,* ran a good number of hostile stories. Using every cliché in the book, one story referred to Mendis as both 'a bearded Bolshie' and a 'Trotskyist rabble-rouser'. In an unusually tasteless touch, police were invited to 'march right in, grab him by the tamils and put him on the next plane to Sri Lanka' (*Daily Star*, 24 March 1987).

More serious than the kneejerk right was a good deal of caution and scepticism from newspapers like the *Guardian, The Times* and the *Independent*, all of which (with the possible exception of *The Times* in its post-Murdoch phase) might have been expected to give Mendis a fair hearing. One commentator, the former Labour MP Robert Kilroy-Silk, expressed strongly hostile views to Mendis in *The Times*, the *Police Review* and during the course of hosting his television chat show. The shadowy support of the RCG for the campaign was also either an explicit (as in the case of Hattersley) or implicit ground for the suspicion attached to Mendis's case.

Given this range of antagonistic or distrustful views, we would have at least to question Batsleer's conclusion that the secret vanguardism at the heart of the campaign was not a disadvantage to its successful conclusion.

A dialogue with Viraj Mendis

The amount of documentation about Viraj Mendis in the form of newspaper interviews, campaign leaflets and bulletins is voluminous: but much of it is suspect, either because his statements have been edited for publication in his own campaign literature, or edited out by journalists to serve the purposes of their paper's politics. I have there-fore reproduced below extracts from my own dialogue with him on 12 April 1987. I prefer the word 'dialogue' to 'interview', as I was trying to press the limits of his beliefs, share my own views and learn about his opinions in a more direct way than was possible to discern from the material I had read.

After talking generally about the nature of previous sanctuaries and other anti-deportation campaigns, we turned to his own situation:

VM: In my case I'm a political person, anyway. . .

RC: So, there's no point in concealing it?

VM: I *don't* conceal it. It's part of my case. If I go back to Sri Lanka, I'll be persecuted. And, on the other hand, because I'm political, the Home Office want to deport me. Of necessity, the campaign becomes political. . . . In other cases [examples given], a different campaign is necessary. In each case – that is my starting point anyhow – I start with the person's right to stay. . . . In building a campaign, a certain movement grows up against deportation. But you do it because it's the person's right to stay, not because [hesitation] of the anti-deportation . . .

RC: That's a spin-off?

VM: Yes, that's right. In *doing* it, you automatically politicise a lot of people. The different layers get involved. For example, in [X's] campaign, the [Y] women's centre got involved. Now they're in my campaign. You know what I mean? It might not have happened if they had not been involved in [X's] campaign and not understood what the immigration laws were. Once you get involved in a campaign about one person, you learn it's not one person, but hundreds or thousands who are affected by the immigration laws. So you automatically learn.

RC: I'm wondering – I don't say this in any mean spirit – whether all of your friends necessarily help your case? I mean, you are dealing with a Conservative administration (with a big and little 'c'). They are bound to be a little pious and moralistic and prefer to deal with 'respectable' people. Does it help, for example, that you are being supported by the Wages Due Lesbians Campaign or the English Collective of Prostitutes?

VM: [sharply] That's up to them. If they want to support me I cannot say 'no'. That's not up to me. I mean it's *their* decision . . .

RC: Is there a natural cycle to these cases. I mean, do you find yourself first going down the route of representation and legal advice. Then, when it's not working, find you have to widen the individual's case into a campaign?

VM: It just depends on the case. Sometimes you only have two days to do something. Then it's a matter of the lawyer. Or often getting the MP to put a 'stop' on the deportation, so that the legal thing can be sorted out later. But legal matters *are* important. That is where, if you like, the negotiations take place. But you build up a case when the people involved build a strong campaign, when the support from the people is strong enough, that's when the Home Office back down and find a legal reason – and there's always a legal reason why they *can* back down.

RC: So the purpose of the campaign is to build up sufficient public support . . .

VM: That's right.

RC: So the end is always a political contest, then after that's resolved some legal pretext is found.

VM: That's right.

RC: This then raises another point about legality. If you were reforming the immigration laws, you would perhaps run into another danger. Reform means rationalisation and rationalisation means limiting discretion. At the moment the Home Office is always able to back down by using the discretionary powers of the home secretary. If you tried to reform the immigration laws wouldn't you also make it more difficult for him to exercise discretion in your favour?

VM: The thing about discretion is that the Home Office has the widest powers. It's a very wide margin. They have control over everyone. The thing is, that it is racist. It doesn't actually ever operate the other way. That's the point of it, the context of it. It only acts *against* people from the third world countries. The legal framework is built up to make it not appear racist. But it is a smoke screen. I mean, there's no real difference with the laws of apartheid, influx control, pass laws. Apartheid is the law of the land. It *is* the law of the land. In the same way, although it's not so obvious, our immigration laws are almost exactly like the influx control and the pass laws in South Africa. The immigration laws are just a method of moving people up and down. When they're needed they are let in, when they are not they are told to go. So the immigration laws are being strengthened all the time. I mean they don't need immigrants: there are 4 million unemployed. You don't even have a birthright here [in the 1988 legislation]. This is more explicit in Germany [discussion of the *gastarbeiter* system]. If you were to remove the racism from the immigration law, there would be no immigration law.

RC: Suppose we switch the scenario a moment and imagine a world where non-racist immigration laws obtain. Take for example, Canada or Australia. Historically, they were, of course, highly racist in their admission policies. Now they claim to operate other criteria like skill, education, qualifications and vacancies in the labour market. In other words, they have turned their immigration policies into an extension of their economic policies. What do you think of such a policy? Is it relevant to Britain? Can you imagine, in short, a policy that doesn't allow free entry to all on the one hand and isn't racist on the other?

VM: The problem is, whether we can construct such a thing in the abstract, it is not going to happen. Looking at the last fifteen years, there is no reason to believe that the immigration laws are going to get better in this country. It's been one way all the time. I'd prefer to deal with concrete things.

RC: Are you saying there are *no* possibilities for reform?

VM: I'm just saying, how can it happen? There must be a lot of people saying things have to change. Until the people force the changes, nothing will happen.

RC: I think I disagree with you on where reform and change can come from. For example, British immigration law will have to respond in the next few years for demands for harmonisation in Europe.... This raises in my mind the sorts of demands associated with your campaign, for example, the slogan 'End All Immigration Control'. This is so unrealistic as to be absurd. It takes no account of the fact that every country in the world has immigration control.

VM: It's a demand not because it's achievable in the immediate future...

RC: It's not achievable at all!

VM: ... No! The reason we oppose all immigration laws is that we have to support everybody. I can't say so-and-so's case is no good and mine is OK. I mean, if you start discriminating, there'll be one person who fits into every category. What we are saying is that we defend *all* those who are attacked by the immigration laws. That's why we have to have the slogan.

RC: I suspect your argument. But let me put mine more clearly. Suppose we say that all asylum-seekers should have clear rights of appeal and that, in a public hearing, expert testimony concerning the country from which they have fled can be presented. These are features of the immigration and deportation laws in other countries. Why can't one construct a more modest set of demands around such obviously unjust aspects of our laws?

VM: Well, in my case we *had* expert witnesses. Sinhalese who told the court what it was like in Sri Lanka. Members of the bar from this country. Extremely impressive testimony was given in

my defence. This didn't make any difference to the Home
Office.

RC: But, surely, the Home Office should at least be formally
required to consider evidence about conditions in the countries
of the refugees? I mean they may genuinely be ignorant or
relying on imperfect press stories, etc.

VM: I disagree totally. It's not a matter that the Home Office does
not know. In the case of Sri Lanka, all the economy is run by
London. Forty per cent of the exports [... unintelligible]. I
mean, I know that Douglas Hurd knows all about it. And David
Waddington, one of his best friends is the prime minister [of Sri
Lanka]. Even the chief adjudicator of the Home Office who
dealt with my case goes for his holidays in Sri Lanka. It's not a
matter of what you know; it's a matter of interests. The answer
is not having more democracy or better courts – that will only
happen as a result of other things happening.

RC: So, in your case you felt you were dealt with fairly, within the
framework of unfair laws?

VM: Oh, no! If you look at the chief immigration officer's report he
says there, I mean, that here, standing before him, was somebody who campaigned against the immigration laws. And if I'd
done it quietly, I might have my right to stay. . . ?

RC: Is there something in that? Of course, it's *morally* indefensible,
but *practically speaking* does one stand a better chance through
private representations rather than public confrontation?

VM: He *did* say it; but the immigration tribunal were more subtle.

RC: How far would you carry your defence of someone who had
come here as a student, say, or a visitor and who simply had
overstayed because they liked it better here? Would you defend
such people even though they were not refugees?

VM: Yeah, I would defend all people from oppressed nations and
black people.

RC: So I take it you would not defend, say, an American who had
overstayed.

VM: There are no immigration restrictions on people from rich coun-
tries. Immigration laws are meant for third world people.
Americans, Australians have the right to stay if they want to.
No legal restriction at all.

RC: I can assure you, you are utterly wrong. The CRE has just
published a report that shows that US citizens have the highest

rates of overstaying and illegal entry.[4] However, the rate of enforcement against US citizens is low. Would you support a greater enforcement of the law in the case of US overstayers? Would you perhaps want to make a distinction between black and white Americans?

VM: [hesitates] I wouldn't want to kick out anybody.

RC: So, let's get this clear, you are not so much interested in the fair application of laws between black and white, you don't want any immigration laws.

VM: [hesitates] Yeah, that's right.

After, to my mind, this interesting revelation of Mendis's views, we chatted for a long while. I then concluded the dialogue with a question about the likely outcome of his campaign. His response, in a moment of pessimism, proved all too prescient.

RC: Tell me, Viraj, do you think, honestly, you are going to win?

VM: Waddington and Hurd are not going to let me win. The political issue is too important. They can't let a communist win and the Home Office lose. People like me don't win.

The Church

The most brutal and dramatic violation of sanctuary in England occurred with the murder of Thomas à Becket, the Archbishop of Canterbury, in 1170. (T. S. Eliot's *Murder in the Cathedral*, published in 1935, dramatised this event.) After an intemperate outburst by Henry II, four knights, who thought they were acting with the king's consent, brutally murdered his old friend and adversary. Certainly the contest between Henry II and Thomas, between state and Church, had reached boiling point. Paradoxically, so shocking was the assassination that the immediate result was to *ensure* the preservation of ecclesiastical prerogatives against monarchical power for some decades.

Gradually, however, the doctrine of the absolute sovereignty of the state (first for the monarch, then for parliament and 'the people') was asserted over Church authority. However, something of that original

4 I was referring here to the CRE's (1985) formal investigation of *Immigration Control Procedures*. Table 10 (p. 170) shows that the percentage of 1981 arrivals from the USA who violated their entry conditions by overstaying or were illegal entrants was 29.5 per cent. The nearest rivals to the USA were Canada (with 4.75 per cent illegals) and Australia (with 4.11). Only 0.43 per cent of Sri Lankans arriving in 1981 were classified as illegal entrants or overstayers. Country-by-country the apprehension figures rarely positively correlate with the rates of violation (many are inverse). Mendis was thus right in implying that immigration laws are highly differentially enforced by race and nationality, but wrong in stating that no non-racial laws existed.

discord between Church and state still persists, the Church ultimately claiming a moral authority (derived from God's law) that is superior to the power of the state (which merely expresses temporal law).

With respect to sanctuary in the UK, a sign of a new assertion of religious authority was seen in November 1987 when a resolution at a conference sponsored by the Community and Race Relations Unit of the British Council of Churches (BCC) and the Programme to Combat Racism of the World Council of Churches called on the British churches (cited Weller n.d.: 10) to 'provide accommodation and bail for refugees and asylum-seekers, to oppose deportations wherever appropriate and to support those seeking sanctuary in churches and other places of worship'. Fourteen months later, the Community Relations Committee of the Catholic Bishops' Conference concluded:

Because the right of free movement and other rights are not sufficiently recognised in the immigration policies of states, illegal immigrants may often be victims of unjust law. They may be morally justified in evading the repercussion of their illegality and others may be morally justified, or even obliged, to assist them. In such a context, the increasing phenomenon of sanctuary can be understood as an authentic expression of morality and Christian principle.

In the same year the BCC explicitly unfurled its moral banner by proclaiming that, 'if unjust law is no law, and if indeed immigration law and practice have become unjust, and if human rights are being diminished, it may be a *requirement* of contemporary Christian discipleship to grant sanctuary if it is granted'.[5]

Even before sanctuary was sought, church leaders, especially the Bishop of Manchester, the Rt Revd Stanley Booth-Clibborn, had become concerned about his case. He sent a message of support in March 1986. Equally, the BCC voted £500 to the Viraj Mendis Defence Campaign in July 1986 and, two years later, the Executive Committee wrote to the home secretary documenting the unrest in Sri Lanka and asking that some way be found to keep Mendis in the UK. Further correspondence followed and in December 1988, subsequent to the House of Lords' rejection of Mendis's final appeal, the general

---

5 In this sub-section, I am concentrating on the recent debate in the Christian churches, as it was ultimately an Anglican church that gave sanctuary to Viraj Mendis. But it is worth noting that the National Council of Hindu Temples 'felt strongly that religious places should be recognised, as in the past, for sanctuary. ... After having tried all possible channels, one should be able, as a last resort, to turn to God for shelter.' Leading Muslims, including the Imam of Regent's Park Mosque, more cautiously agreed that 'as a last and final step sanctuary may be sought ... in such cases of clear innocence it would be justified to offer temporary refuge in a place of worship so that efforts to secure justice might be continued.' Likewise, prominent Sikhs have affirmed that, 'Sikhs are duty bound to assist in all possible ways ... those fleeing persecution. It is the clear duty of every Sikh home and every Sikh institution to provide such people with food, shelter and sanctuary' (Weller n.d.: 11–12).

secretary of the BCC pressed for Mendis to be allowed to stay 'in the spirit of Christmas'.

At the core of the Church's support was the quiet but determined figure of Father John Methuen. The decrepit and miserable housing estates that surround the gimmicky Church of the Ascension give a lie to his more establishment background – he was formerly the chaplain at Eton College and is High Church. The relationship between Methuen and Mendis is redolent of the relationship between priest and communist in Graham Greene's novel *Monsignor Quixote*. Perhaps, as Northam (1987: 7) suggests, 'a true communist is a sort of priest. ... They are both protests against injustice.' Father John himself talked about the 'congruence of the incongruent', as he witnessed members of the VMDC joining the Church and vice versa. He also welcomed the language of 'solidarity' entering the Church's language and grew increasingly certain that Christianity should not be identified with either capitalism or communism.

In March 1987, the Church of the Ascension was attacked by six men wearing balaclava caps and armed with screwdrivers and carving knives. One of the members of the VMDC was stabbed in the back of his head as he shouted a warning. A few days later a woman member of the VMDC was set upon outside the Church and a swastika was carved into the back of her hand. Methuen's reaction to these events was quietly determined: 'If you take a stand because a man's life is in danger, and then the danger appears not just in Sri Lanka but also in Great Britain, then you have to harden your resolve.'

His own statements on the right to sanctuary have always been consistent, were carefully qualified and have followed extensive discussions with his congregation. The five criteria specified by Methuen for the approval of sanctuary were:

- that the person concerned had to be a member of the local [Hulme] community or very closely associated with it;
- that the person concerned was not involved in violence;
- that he or she was not wanted for a criminal offence;[6]
- that all the legal proceedings and appeals had been gone through and this was the last resort; and
- that there was the danger of a monstrous injustice being committed. In this respect Methuen quoted with approbation the Bishop of Milwaukee's comment that: 'Sanctuary is not a way of avoiding justice, but a holy respite so that justice can be done.'

Behind Father John Methuen and his fellow priest Father Henry West, were a group of religious supporters from churches in the Manchester area. Most formed themselves into a Viraj Mendis Defence Campaign–

---

6 Subsequent statements by Father John qualified this criterion to 'not wanted for any *serious* criminal offence' (*Sunday Telegraph*, 15 May 1988).

Religious Support Group (VMDC–RSG) which remained organisa-
tionally distinct from the RCG-dominated VMDC. The RSG organised
the first national conference on sanctuary which was held in the
Church of the Ascension on 12 December 1987. Some 180 people
from many faiths were brought together for this occasion. The
proceedings of this conference (VMDC–RSG 1988) included a notable
speech by Revd Kenneth Leech, then director of the Runnymede Trust,
who said: 'All our claims to worship God have to be tested against the
criterion of how we respond to the alien, the orphan and the widow.
. . . By giving sanctuary to Viraj Mendis, the Church of the Ascension
is doing no more than standing for the traditions of biblical and
orthodox Christianity.'

The RSG also conducted a Good Friday procession in which one of
the marchers who carried a rough wooden cross with the slogan 'Viraj
Mendis – Life or Death' attracted much comment by passers-by who
thought this act blasphemous. To the comment that 'Viraj Mendis is a
communist, not a Christian' the campaigners replied: 'God calls us to
be vehicles of his love and not to be the judge of people. He alone is
judge. The good Samaritan parable was used by Jesus to help us look
beyond the label a person is marked with, to her or his inner self, to
how he or she lives their life.' The RSG also contacted 38 'faith
communities', who wrote in support of the sanctuary and held a prayer
vigil outside the Home Office in St Anne's Gate in London.

Despite the protestations of their faith and the dignified affirmations
of Mendis's right to sanctuary by the BCC, the local priests, several
bishops and the RSG, the appearance of religious unanimity was
deceptive. At the top of the church hierarchy serious doubts prevailed.
For example, the Archbishop of York, Dr John Habgood, who was
known to be on the conservative wing of the Church, cautioned against
clergy allowing refugees into sanctuary: 'I am very dubious about the
whole thing. The Church must obey the law. To do otherwise is not a
proper Christian attitude in a law-abiding country.' Similarly, the then
Archbishop of Canterbury, Dr Robert Runcie, while allowing that
there was 'unease in many church circles about the government's
immigration policy and practice', bluntly warned that 'churches are
not above the law. However objectionable a particular law may be
thought to be, everyone in a democracy must obey it or accept the
consequences of disobeying it' (*Observer*, 22 Jan. 1989). One wonders
whether Thomas à Becket would concur with these words of his
successor? Was his murder in Canterbury cathedral the effective start
of the sapping of the Church's moral will?

Press reactions

The forcible eviction of Mendis and his deportation to Sri Lanka on 18
January 1989 provided the editorial writers of many of the country's

newspapers with the opportunity for much reflection and posturing on the justice or injustice of this action and, more generally, on the morality of Britain's immigration policy. I provide below extracts from seven editorials that appeared on the day after Mendis's arrest.

Under the heading 'Justified Eviction' the *Daily Telegraph* described Mendis as a:

self-styled Sri Lankan revolutionary. . . . Since he was discovered to have overstayed his entry permit as a student after repeatedly failing his exams, he has found one pretext after another for remaining here. . . . We hope Britons of every ethnic background will see the removal of Mr Mendis as a victory for common sense and fair play.

Prefacing its editorial, 'A Case and a Symbol' the *Guardian* suggested that:

no recent case has helped focus so much attention on British deportation procedures . . . Mr Mendis has attracted widespread support. . . . This support is wholly understandable, because British deportation procedures are a disgrace; but it should also be acknowledged that Mr Mendis's case is no ideal focal point for such wider outrage.

The Times allowed that:

Hypothetical and extreme circumstances can, of course, be imagined in which a well-informed Christian conscience could command disobedience by a Church of the laws of a state. But this was certainly no such case. . . . In fact the Home Office has been scrupulously fair: it is impossible to imagine what else it could have done. Mr Mendis's continued presence in Britain under the spurious protection of supposed sanctuary merely brought the law into contempt, inciting imitation.

As to the *Daily Mail*,

on the central issue, [it] had no doubt. . . . This newspaper finds Viraj Mendis an utterly unconvincing martyr to the cause of human rights. The Home Office is fully justified in returning him to his native land.

The *Glasgow Herald* concentrated on the:

nature and the timing of the police action. . . . As far as public policy is concerned the point is not whether the clergymen concerned were setting themselves above the law; it is that the police action was unnecessarily heavy-handed and the timing was dubious in view of the negotiations evidently going on with the Home Office to arrange a destination other than Sri Lanka for Mr Mendis.

Also alluding to the nature of the arrest, the *Northern Echo*, published in Darlington, thought that:

Fifty police officers breaking down church doors and bursting in on a lone and unarmed Sri Lankan at dawn simply does not fit in with most people's perception of British life. It is all too easy for the Opposition to shout 'Sieg Heil' from across the benches but on this occasion such an image must have flickered through the memories of many others; particularly when this wholly unnecessary breakfast-time drama was followed by a stern warning to the Church to get in line.

Another out-of-London newspaper, Bristol's *Western Daily Press*, disagreed:

This selective sanctuary smacks more of mischief-making than of humanitarianism. At the very least it was dangerous naiveté. Those who have campaigned on Mr Mendis's behalf cannot say the law has been unfair. Every proper procedure has been used, every avenue examined. And Britain's proud reputation for giving comfort and shelter to genuine refugees is intact.

These comments are interesting both in their diversity and in their iteration of the notion of fairness, justice and the *British* way of life. Those editorial writers who were concerned to justify the Home Office's policy, the home secretary's decision and the police's action were equally concerned to assert that Mendis had a 'fair' chance. He had been allowed to 'have his say'. It was not 'our fault' that his case had been found wanting, *British* common sense and *Britain's* reputation were 'intact'. Those, on the other hand, who were not convinced by the authorities' actions did not go so far as overtly to support Mendis, but concentrated their fire on the disgraceful nature of *Britain's* refugee policy and the *unBritish* way in which the police exercised their tasks.

Not for the first time, the interface between the stranger and the host, the alien and the citizen, between the British and the other, had triggered a contested debate about the nature, values and qualities of British identity itself.

Other sanctuaries and the anti-deportation movement

The case of Salema Begum

Salema Begum, a 13-year-old Bangladeshi girl, started her sanctuary experience in 1988. After getting nowhere with the Home Office, the solicitor involved in her case pleaded for her at a church meeting at the Chorlton Central Baptist Church in Manchester. Her father had lived in Oldham since 1963 and had visited Bangladesh regularly. In 1981, after visa checks lasting several years, his wife and family joined him, leaving behind Salema – who remained with her grandmother. In 1986, however, when it became clear that the grandmother was dying, Salema's parents arranged that some friends should bring her to the UK to be reunited with her family in Oldham. Some months after Salema's arrival in the UK her grandmother died. The pleas by her father's local MP and the Bishop of Manchester that she should be allowed to stay with her parents were met with an obdurate response at the Home Office. The officials' position was that Salema should go back to Bangladesh, prove her kinship and take her place in the queue for an entry certificate just as her mother, brothers and sisters had done before her.

The church meeting of the Chorlton Central Baptist Church agreed almost unanimously to offer her sanctuary, even though her life was not in danger and she could not claim to be a political refugee. The central argument made by the congregation was that it would be cruel to return the child to one of the poorest countries of the world where there was no one ready to look after her. The church members organised duty rosters, provided for her education and welfare, and issued press releases. Within 24 hours, the immigration authorities wanted to talk. After eleven days of sanctuary an agreement was reached. Her father would be reinterviewed. Salema would be given temporary admission and would not be detained while a sympathetic reconsideration of her case took place. The Home Office continued to disbelieve the father's and mother's claims that Salema was their child.

In the end, the case turned on this issue of identification. The family was forced at its own expense (the test cost £500) to expose Salema to a DNA test (a form of genetic fingerprinting) which had become commercially available in June 1988. The results were a dramatic vindication for the family and the church's belief in them. Thirty-eight bands of Salema's blood were isolated and compared with those of her stated parents. They matched. The odds of a total match were more than 390,000 million to one.

The use of a DNA test to establish consanguinity has some unfortunate resemblance to the 'racial science' of the 1930s, though this reason has never been advanced by the Home Office itself for its refusal to adopt genetic fingerprinting where there is a dispute about a parental relationship. Instead, it has been poor Bangladeshi and Indian families who have been forced to pay for modern science to prove their paternity and maternity. Amazingly enough, after the results of the test were announced, the Home Office did not immediately bury its head in shame, but turned on another of the couple's children who had been adopted since Salema's aunt had died at his birth. Only a picket at the House of Commons finally ended this family's struggle to reconstitute itself in England. Salema and her brother were allowed to stay.

Rajwinder Singh

In February 1987 the family of Rajwinder Singh sought sanctuary for their son in the Guru Nanak Sikh Temple in Bradford. At that time Rajwinder was a 29-year-old epileptic who had been mentally handicapped from birth. His father, Gurdev Singh, migrated to the UK from India in 1967. Mr Singh conformed to the pattern of many heads of household migrants in working and saving for a family home. At long last he achieved his object. In 1976, Mr Singh applied for his wife and two sons, Kulwant and Rajwinder. His application was turned down in the case of Rajwinder, but the family continued to visit him in India at great expense (they made return trips on no less than six occasions) and were distressed to see his condition worsen.

The family involved their local MP, a firm of solicitors, a leading Asian supporter of the Tory Party and the Indian High Commissioner in pleading their case for the exercise of 'compassionate grounds'. All these representations were turned down. Finally, Gurdev Singh's patience snapped and he (apparently) intentionally violated the immigration rules by obtaining a passport for his epileptic son under a false name.[7] The Home Office soon tumbled that they were dealing with one and the same person and, somewhat surprisingly in view of the deceit, allowed Rajwinder temporary admission after Mr Singh's MP had intervened on his behalf.

A consultant psychiatrist at Lynfield Mount Hospital in Bradford, Mr J.T. Bavington, reported that Rajwinder's:

mental handicap had left him with a limited capacity in many areas of his life. His speech and appearance suggest a person younger than 29. . . . he is timid, diffident and [has] a dependent personality. . . . It is probable that the cause of his mental handicap is some form of brain damage occurring in the early infancy, possibly resulting from birth trauma.

Despite this sympathetic account of Rajwinder's handicap, IOs from the Leeds–Bradford airport called at the family home to arrange a removal for 25 February 1987. According to the family's recollections: 'A public meeting was called for, when the local community heard about our family's plight and our son Rajwinder Singh. From this meeting of over a hundred people, Rajwinder's defence campaign was launched. [Six days later] 400 people marched in the streets of Bradford chanting slogans that Rajwinder was here to stay.'

The obvious sincerity and popularity of the Singhs (which was partly derived from Gurdev Singh having been an Olympic Gold

---

7 Just to complicate matters his original name was Rajwant and his newly adopted name was Rajwinder. As the case was fought and has been reported using the second name, I have followed the use of 'Rajwinder'. When I interviewed him Mr Singh was evidently ashamed at having deployed this clumsy subterfuge, but insisted he did so at the urging of some local Tory advisers.

Medallist) led to a great deal of community support for the family and the intervention also of some of the more 'professionalised' anti-deportation campaigners – who organised a 'write-in' to over 120 MPs and made a video titled 'Rajwinder's Story'. Perhaps fortunately for the Singhs, the essential appeal of a family in distress was never subordinated to a wider political campaign.

It took over a year after the sanctuary was entered for the Home Office to agree first to re-examine Rajwinder's medical history then, finally, to grant him the permanent right to stay.

Afia Begum

Afia Begum's case conforms to a policy announced at the end of 1982 when William Whitelaw, the home secretary, published a White Paper 'tightening up' the rules to prevent abuse of immigration procedures through 'marriages of convenience'. The White Paper significantly changed the burden of proof – with the couple concerned having to demonstrate the validity of the marriage rather than the Home Office having to demonstrate its invalidity. Couples would have to live together for two years (this was changed later to one year, after parliamentary discussion).

If the marriage ended before one year, or there was a separation, automatic deportation would follow 'irrespective of the reasons that led to the termination of the marriage . . . and irrespective of the length of period of residence'. As an editorial in the *Guardian* at the time (7 Dec. 1982) noted: 'The genuineness of the relationship no longer matters; marriage breakdown is henceforth a deportable offence.'

Afia Begum had been granted an entry clearance in 1982 to join her prospective husband who was legitimately settled in the UK. Unfortunately in her case the quality of the marriage was not in dispute as her betrothed died before the marriage could take place. Afia Begum was then told that as her status was dependent on the deceased man, she could no longer stay in Britain permanently. The fact that she had lost her fiancé and that most of her relatives were in the UK cut no ice. Early in April 1984 she was deported.

This sad story attracted a great deal of press publicity and considerable support, on humanitarian grounds, for Afia Begum. The case gained its particular political salience, however, by a coincidence of timing. Shortly before Afia Begum was arrested and deported for over-staying, Home Secretary Leon Brittan had recognised the claims of Zola Budd, a 17-year-old South African runner, to British nationality. This would enable her to compete as a British athlete in the 1984 Olympic Games. The ethnic press (for example, *Asian Times* 11 April 1985) wondered bitterly why there had been room in Britain for Ms

Budd but none for Afia Begum.[8]

That accusations of racism were rife was to be expected. Moreover, as the *Guardian* (9 April 1984) editorialised:

Discretion is being applied ruthlessly, without a shred of pity or humanity, in hundreds of cases which do not attract the publicity that has attended Afia Begum. People are being thrown out of the country who have lived here for many years, sometimes quite unaware that they have broken any rule at all. They may have come here as children, or been made redundant, or seen their marriages break up, or found that the rules have been changed without their knowledge. ... As a result immigrant communities are riven with fear and distrust. ... It is hard to imagine how the Home Office can equate such tensions with its alleged goal of good community relations.

Towards Britain's underground railroad?

In the wake of the Mendis affair and other instances of harsh Home Office actions, the anti-deportation movement moved away from public campaigns and confrontations with the authorities. Observers of sanctuary in the UK have suggested that by 1988 as many as 36 quiet sanctuaries none the less continued. Unlike in the Mendis campaign, these were not intended as a general critique of immigration policy or the xenophobia current in Thatcher's Britain, but rather were small-scale, unco-ordinated acts directed to helping particular individuals.

Early in 1989 the *Observer* (8 January 1989) carried a more startling claim – that an 'underground railroad' had been started by the Refugee Forum, a lobby group which has always prided itself on its close grassroots contacts and sought to distance itself from the more established agencies like the Refugee Council. The expression 'underground railway' was obviously meant to resonate with the similarly-named movement in the USA which helped in the escape of fugitive slaves.

---

8 Under the patrial Clauses of the British Nationality Act, Zola Budd was able to use her grandfather's putative British descent as a bargaining counter. But there was undoubtedly some ambiguity in her claim, which could have permitted the exercise of discretion in either direction. In terms of the justice, rather than the legality of the claim, Ms Budd had little going for her. Her family had become strongly identified with the Afrikaners of the Orange Free State and had little time for the British; she hated living in the UK and blandly indicated, when her minders did not stop her, how instrumental was her claim. Sections of the South African press rooted for her in a rather undiplomatic way, gloating that this was one way of securing South African participation in the Olympiad, despite the sports boycott of their country. Two other ironies should be noted. First, the greatest advocate of Ms Budd's cause was the immigrant-bashing *Daily Mail*, which ran an incessant campaign on her behalf. Second, the new home secretary, the frontier guard who made the vital decision, was a descendant of two of the Lithuanian Jews whom Sir John Pedder had suggested 'do not want to be assimilated and do not readily identify themselves with this country' (see Chapter 2).

According to its spokesperson, Ronnie Moodly, there were 100 contacts or 'stations', where people were prepared to protect from deportation those considered to be refugees. He claimed that 52 people were currently living at the underground stations and that the 'railroad' had helped 125 people *in toto*. In addition to those sheltering a refugee, the organisation relied on money 'given by some rich people who do not think they could manage a refugee, but want to help.' 'Some people', he continued, 'give food and others are teachers and come for a few hours to teach English, or teach children.'

I do not dispute Mr Moodly's claims, but I cannot support such claims from research evidence and it may be wise to be a little cautious in fully accepting all the refugee organisations' own accounts. One reason for scepticism is that several agencies often helped the same client and there was likely to be some double counting. There is also a certain amount of competition between the different groups in giving aid to asylum-seekers and this sometime leads to exaggerated claims.

Conclusion and critique

Sanctuaries and the anti-deportation movement in the 1980s in Britain acquired a number of distinctive features, the most important of which (in contrast to the USA and continental Europe) was their multi-faith character. It is perhaps remarkable that religious leaders from Christian, Jewish, Sikh, Muslim and Hindu backgrounds were all capable of finding a justification and defence of sanctuary in their different religious tracts. But I have been careful not to argue that a 'sanctuary movement' had begun in Britain on the scale that developed, say, in the USA and perhaps the Netherlands.

There were two major inhibitions to the growth of such a movement. The first was the cautious, some might judge it pusillanimous, attitude of the top of the church hierarchy who, fundamentally, were disinterested in challenging the state's authority, even where they accepted it was morally deficient. The four hooded knights of Canterbury cathedral had won the day. The second is my own gloomy conclusion, after trying to weigh the evidence as fairly as I can, that the high ground in the crucial Mendis case was ultimately won by the frontier guards and not by the anti-deportation movement.

Mendis (cited Steve Cohen 1988: 7) himself correctly analysed the wider significance of his campaign:

The reason for the Home Office's determined efforts to destroy our sanctuary was because of the potential that sanctuary has as a means of fighting deportations in Britain. The new Immigration Act [of 1988] is a full-blown attack on anti-deportation campaigns. It destroys the right of appeal for people who are threatened with deportation. The withdrawal of appeal rights eliminates the time to develop support and threatens them with imminent expulsion. The only viable response will be sanctuary, because sanctuary will give a breathing space to start a campaign. It is in this context that the attack on me must be looked.

But if his training in revolutionary politics gave him the capacity to diagnose (and, in my view, also sometimes misdiagnose) the mystagogy of state power, the inherent flaws of his own case made it difficult for him finally to overcome that power. Let me provide some evidence for this conclusion.

First, probably the strongest part of Mendis's legal claim was that he had been living in England for thirteen years at the time when his deportation order was signed (in December 1986). It has long been Home Office practice to regard residence over ten years as *de facto* evidence of settlement. At that point, so the informal official argument runs, it is easier to throw in the sponge and formalise the arrangement, if for no other reason than that it may be difficult to persuade another country to accept the person concerned. Douglas Hurd himself acknowledged this practice in a letter to Alf Morris MP on 21 April 1986:

Where any person has lived continuously in this country for ten years or more, it has to be recognised that they will have established a way of life in the United Kingdom and this is taken into account when considering any application for indefinite leave to remain. Continuous residence for 10 years is normally considered a *prima facie* reason for granting indefinite leave to remain, even though the person may not qualify for this under the general provisions of the Immigration Rules.

The difficulty that faced Mendis was that the power of the home secretary to accept this informal rule of thumb was entirely discretionary. It would not be too difficult to imagine that discretion is characteristically exercised more favourably in the cases of law-abiding, hardworking, white-skinned, clean-living people ('just like one of us'). By contrast, Mendis had three distinct disadvantages:

- First, he was a member of a visible racial minority, only had two years of legitimate residence (1973–75) and had lived on social assistance for nearly nine years: hardly the image of a solid citizen producing tax revenues for the state.
- Second, Mendis's marriage took place just two months after he was apprehended by the police. According to one hostile report (*The Times*, 2 Aug. 1988), which is not independently corroborated, his wife admitted that the marriage was not consummated. Certainly the timing of the marriage and its eight-week duration seem suspicious. It was also notable that, after the first few weeks, the VMDC never sought to press Mendis's marriage as a legal reason for him to stay in the country.

- Third, something of the same quality attached to Mendis's declared political position on Sri Lanka. This is admittedly a much more difficult contention to demonstrate. In his defence the VMDC (1988b) reproduced a letter from the secretary of the Eelam Solidarity Campaign (a pro-Tamil group) that Mendis participated in a march in August 1983, i.e *before* he was picked up by the police or served with a deportation order. On the other hand, this letter was *dated* no less than eight years after his legal stay had expired and ten years after his arrival.

The late association with the cause he espoused was clearly the Achilles's heel of Mendis's case. The Home Office's chief adjudicator, M. Patey, commented in his 1985 report: 'There is, regrettably, a more sinister aspect to this case in that I find it impossible to disassociate the appellant's actions in openly and publicly espousing the Tamil separatist cause from his campaign to avoid deportation.' Lord Justice Balcombe of the Court of Appeal (*The Times*, 2 Aug. 1988) was also concerned at this aspect of Mendis's appeal:

... a person is not at risk of being persecuted for his political opinions if no events which would attract such persecution have yet taken place. If this were not so, a person could become a refugee as a matter of his own choice: all he would have to do would be to establish the following two propositions: (1) if, when I return to my native country, I speak out, I will be prosecuted; (2) I will speak out. This is tantamount to saying that a person who says he proposes to invite persecution is entitled to claim refugee status. That I do not accept.

The very least one can conclude is that Mendis's advocacy of the Tamil cause was both not very public and not fully articulated until after he was threatened with deportation.

Only on one crucial matter did the Home Office lose the argument, i.e. the issue as to whether Sri Lanka was a safe place to which Mendis could be sent. It was important to the frontier guards to press the image of a peaceful and democratic Sri Lanka – as the Geneva Convention, signed by the British government, prohibited *refoulement* to a place of danger. As previously mentioned, the chief adjudicator of the Home Office rather implausibly advocated the view that 'Sri Lanka is inherently a democracy where the rule of law obtains.' This was on the equally odd grounds that the Communist Party was not banned. The idea that, in 1986, communism – rather than ethnic separatism, religious zealotry or self-interested banditry, to name but a few possibilities – provided the main danger to the state, was risibly out of date.

Amongst the many inconvenient realities of Sri Lankan life the VMDC were able to present were that 20,000 people had died in various manifestations of civic unrest and that there were 815,000 internal refugees. The campaign also publicised Amnesty International's reports based on numerous testimonies from released prisoners (some accompanied by medical records) that 'they have been hung by their thumbs or upside down by their toes, beaten with clubs or iron rods, had chilli powder rubbed into their wounds or had their nails torn out while under interrogation in army or Special Task Force camps or police stations.'

Both Mendis's detractors and supporters used the argument that the final proof of whether it was safe to return him to Sri Lanka could only be demonstrated by that very thing happening. This was, in fact, a weak argument – an 'experiment' that was rigged by the publicity attracted to the case. One can hardly imagine the British government sending Mendis to Sri Lanka without stern warnings of what might happen to that country's trade, aid and diplomatic ties in the event that he was in any way harmed.[9]

However, that Mendis was treated with kid gloves on his return could not in any way refute the decision of *all* other western European governments not to send Tamils, or supporters of the Tamil cause, back to Sri Lanka on the grounds that it was unsafe to do so. Nor should Mendis's good treatment obscure the bad treatment meted out to other, unknown, returnees from the UK. For example, the *Observer* (22 Jan. 1989) was able to establish that at least two of the Sri Lankans who were forcibly returned to their home country were detained on more than one occasion and mistreated. Moreover, the details of these cases were known to the Home Office before Mendis's departure.

What were the effects of the Home Office's victory in the Mendis case on the sanctuary and anti-deportation campaigners? Probably the most visible reaction was that sanctuary returned to its earlier form. To use Weller's (n.d.) distinction between sanctuary as 'concealment' and as 'exposure', the tendency to revert to secret sanctuaries was reasserted. After the Mendis case, public confrontations with the authorities were now no longer so obviously the route forward. Simply mobilising a sufficient body of the great and the good was not going to be enough either to melt hearts at the Home Office or significantly to undermine the electoral advantages of being seen to take a tough stand on 'illegals', overstayers or 'bogus' refugees.

Within the wider anti-racist movement the Mendis case also occasioned much debate. The main critique made of the anti-deportation movement was that each campaign was individualised and not tightly woven into the general fabric of anti-racist struggle. So long as the struggles of refugees, asylum-seekers and those awaiting deportation remained isolated or relatively independent of the more general anti-racist movement, so the argument ran, the government would be able to isolate its opposition and pick off deportees one by one.

---

9 After he was deported to Sri Lanka Mendis was not maltreated. With a loyal female supporter of the campaign as his partner, Mendis successfully applied for and was granted residential rights in Germany. Ironically, as soon as these are secured, under EU travel rules he will be free to return to the UK.

This line of argument was, I believe, seriously flawed, for these four reasons:

- First, as illustrated in the two cases of successful anti-deportation campaigns (those of Salema Begum and Rajwinder Singh), a change of heart often turned on the identification that neighbours, friends (and the more influential, like priests, MPs and solicitors) were able to make with the individuals concerned. In one case a young and vulnerable girl was to be sent back to a country where there was no one to care for her; in the other, the God-fearing and respectable parents of a mentally retarded man simply asked to be allowed to look after and love him. By seeking to dilute the specificities of these cases, the anti-racist movement risked alienating the 'non-political' support given to those facing deportation.
- Second, on the other hand, wanting to fuel a general political movement on the back of a particular case or set of cases fell into the old leftist trap: the misguided belief that a mass movement would be bound to defeat the narrow interests of the ruling class. It was indeed apparent that this notion underlay the misguided vision of Mendis and the RCG. The fallacy was this: however many organisations and individuals signed up for the cause, the frontier guards were bound to be able to identify such a campaign as 'political' not 'humanitarian'. Moreover, if they were successful in that objective, the frontier guards could rely on many more votes gained than lost, and many more than could possibly be shown as supporters of the campaign.
- Third, the political groups who sought to use anti-deportation campaigns for a larger goal had a very crude understanding of the basis of the Home Office's decisions, which were invariably and routinely described as 'racist'. The simpler versions of this notion did, of course, have a historical basis. Between the 1950s and 1970s popular xenophobia in Britain mainly took the form of identifying particular racially visible target groups, namely the labour migrants and their descendants from the Caribbean, India, Pakistan and Bangladesh.
- Fourth, those opposing these manifestations absorbed the taunts of their tormentors by forging a precarious alliance around the category 'black' and around the slogan of 'anti-racism' – thereby implicitly accepting the racial language of the press, the pub and the street. The limitation of so doing in the case of the anti-deportation movement is that the *official* mind had moved beyond racial categories to more general categories of undesirability and exclusion.

The failure to recognise these four differences between the anti-deportation campaign and the anti-racist struggles of earlier years meant that those cases which did not conform to the 'black' label were side-tracked and misunderstood. Many individuals threatened with deportation, or who were actually deported, did not have links with the Caribbean, Indian, Bengali and Pakistani minorities in the UK. Their ranks included Africans (from Uganda, the Sudan, Ghana, for example), Iranians, Cypriots, a range of South Americans, in addition to those from the Asian subcontinent, like the Tamils and the Hong Kong Chinese who were not part of the migrant waves of the 1950s and 1960s. The *refoulement* of 36 Bosnians to 'safe third countries' in August 1992 was also a strong indication that the frontier guards were bracing themselves for a contest with white asylum-seekers from the former communist East, as much as with black applicants from Britain's former colonies.

The insistence by a number of campaigners on using the rhetoric of race not only left out a large proportion, indeed increasingly the majority of potential deportees, it failed to recognise that the main axes of organisation, particularly in the case of sanctuary, turned on religious conviction and humanitarian concern not on interracial solidarity. A number of activists also overlooked certain distinctive strengths of the UK setting. While sanctuary in the UK was underdeveloped by comparison with the USA in terms of its level of support, it was more advanced in linking a number of communities of faith around a common pursuit. Sanctuary also provided a small-scale, but deeply moving, form of participation that was broadly non-racial in character and linked neighbours and friends in a common voluntary enterprise.

Both the sanctuary and the anti-deportation movements depended for their success on cross linking the campaigners by class, religion, culture, interest or simple common humanity. In the terms used earlier in this book, the self–other, familial–stranger, British–alien dichotomies had to be broken down. Only by showing that these bridges could be crossed could the power of the frontier guards be sapped and undermined.

CHAPTER 6

Inclusion and exclusion:
Britain in the European context

> And if a stranger sojourn with thee in your land, ye shall not
> vex him. But the stranger that dwelleth with you shall be unto
> you as one born among you, and thou shall love him as thyself;
> for ye were strangers in the land of Egypt.
>   – *The King James Bible*, Leviticus 19: 33–4

From the middle of 1992 the newspaper headlines told a grim tale of
'ethnic cleansing' in Bosnia and the creation of a massive displaced
population in the former Yugoslavia, desperate to find shelter in
neighbouring European countries. But if this was the most dramatic
instance of western Europe's reluctance to respond adequately to the
pleas of refugees for admission, it was but the climax to a decade of
hostility to the increasing numbers of people seeking asylum in individual European countries.

The general causes for the surge of applicants in the 1980s are not
difficult to identify – the continuing and accelerating poverty and
political instability of poor (so-called 'third world') countries on the
one hand, together with the collapse of state socialism in the Soviet
Union and eastern Europe on the other.[1]

The surge in the number of applicants occurred in the mid-1980s.
Over the period 1984–86, the UK considered 13,300 cases, France
screened 71,300 claimants, while the Federal Republic of (West)
Germany processed 208,000 applicants (Layton-Henry 1990: 18).
With the advent of large-scale East–West migration, the numbers of
asylum-seekers arriving in the three countries in 1991 totalled about
360,000 to Germany, 120,000 to France and 45,000 to the UK, representing 68.5 per cent, 23 per cent and 8.5 per cent of the total arriving
in EU countries. The inter-ethnic violence in 1991/2 in the former
Yugoslavia, especially in Bosnia and Croatia, led to the largest number
of displaced people in Europe since the Second World War.

---

1 To keep some sense of political balance here, one should add that the early free-
market experiments in the former communist countries have been abysmal failures,
resulting in massive unemployment, food shortages, unstable currencies and
inflation. These conditions, combining with increased contact with the West, also
provide a potent stimulant to international migration. There is still room for
argument as to whether the failure of the market alternative to state socialism lies in
the heritage of the old system, the need for more time for the prescription to work,
or, finally, is evidence of an intrinsic design fault in the ideology and practice of
neo-liberalism itself.

Germany's 1992 asylum-applicant figures soared to 400,000, while a further 160,000 arrived in Germany in the first four months of 1993 alone.

Whereas the newly unified Germany agreed to take 200,000 refugees from ex-Yugoslavia, both France and Britain have refused to take anything but a token number. The scale of the German gesture was exceptional. It was precipitated partly by the recognition that the long history of Yugoslavian migration to Germany would in any case create demands for admission and a sense that the desperate situation was partly brought on by Germany's premature insistence on the EC's diplomatic recognition of Croatia. Neither of these arguments diminishes Germany's generosity compared with France and Britain's miserly response to the emergency conference convened by the UNHCR in July 1992. Nor, however, does Germany's one-off gesture contradict the general disinclination of EU countries, including Germany, to recognise asylum-seekers as legitimate 'Convention refugees'.[2]

Again the general cause of this recalcitrance is not difficult to find. Amongst significant sections of the EU population, the degree of social toleration for aliens and foreigners – always a scarce commodity – has further eroded. Western European governments of whatever political hue (social democratic or conservative) have felt themselves compelled to respond to escalating internal and Europe-wide political demands to restrict the entry of asylum-seekers.

As I argued in Chapter 3, the right of asylum historically has always firmly belonged to the state granting such a status, rather than to the individual claimant. This places the state and its representatives in an inherently more powerful position in determining an asylum-seeker's status. However, this aspect of state sovereignty is exercised by the British government both individually and (increasingly) in harness with its EU partners. In this chapter, I compare the British with the French and German states' records on refugees and the exercise of their powers to confer asylum status. In order to do this I have to provide, particularly in the German case, some background information on immigration policies in general, before turning to the particular issues of refugee admissions and settlement patterns. The rather different practices and histories of the three countries, it will be shown, are now converging into a new European pattern of exclusion.

---

2 That is, those recognised under the international refugee conventions. The UN (Geneva) Convention of 1951, the 1967 Protocol and Declaration and the 1977 Draft Conventions are conveniently reproduced in Goodwin-Gill (1983: 247–77). The proportion of asylum-seekers recognised by West Germany under Article 1 of the Geneva Convention steadily dropped from 87.6 per cent of a total of 11,664 applicants in 1969 to 19.9 per cent of a total of 51,493 in 1979.

'More hands, more hands'

Because contemporary European frontier controls are marked by immigration restrictions, increasingly tight definitions of nationality and citizenship and a hostility to refugees, it is sometimes difficult to remember that attitudes to migrants in the immediate postwar period were far different in the three chosen European countries.

In France, for example, the leading demographer at the influential Institut National d'Études Démographiques, Sauvy, pronounced that France needed at the minimum to import 5,290,000 permanent immigrants to renew its labour force, stabilise the skewed demographic structure arising from wartime losses and reinforce its claims to Great Power status (Freeman 1979: 69).

In Germany, the postwar constitutional provision for reunification allowed millions of East Germans to cross the frontier. These expellees and refugees, together with those from the former eastern territories of the Reich and demobilised soldiers, all unprotected by the weakened labour movement, 'provided ideal conditions for capitalist expansion, and were the essential cause of the economic miracle' (Castles *et al.* 1984: 25). With expansion, West Germany's demand for labour increased dramatically. Though a more cautious attitude prevailed on the question of according citizenship to 'foreign' newcomers, a massive guest-worker programme from Turkey and elsewhere was initiated.

Across the Channel, the budding Labour Party politician, James Callaghan (later to become prime minister), ignored the potentially adverse reactions of his working-class supporters and proclaimed in the House of Commons:

We are living in an expansionist era. Surely, this is a Socialist government committed to a policy of full employment? In a few years' time we in this country will be faced with a shortage of labour, and not with a shortage of jobs. Our birth rate is not increasing in sufficient proportion to enable us to replace ourselves... We are turning away from the shores of this country eligible and desirable young men who could be added to our strength and resources, as similar immigrants have done in the past (cited R. Cohen 1987: 124).

The end of the migrant labour boom

As is well documented in the literature on European migration, the authorised importation of co-ethnic Germans and other migrant workers to the European industrial economies lasted roughly until the mid-1970s, when sharp restrictions were imposed.

It is now no longer necessary to mount an elaborate argument listing the advantages that were conferred by the deployment of migrant labourers by the host countries and employers in the postwar period, as there is now a remarkable unanimity of views between liberal (see Kindleberger 1967; Böhning 1972), Marxist (see Castles & Kosack 1985; Castells 1979) and official accounts. Perhaps one, remarkably frank, paper prepared by the West German government for a conference on 'The Future of Migration' organised by the OECD in May 1986 is sufficient to make the point. The paper (cited Cross 1988) accepts that the German economy had gained considerable benefits with negligible costs from migrant labour, and continues:

Until far into the 1960s, the employment of foreigners helped to satisfy the rising demand for labour ... at a time when the labour volume was getting scarcer and scarcer. ... Their considerable flexibility in the economic cycle helped to offset negative employment effects in times of recession and to avoid inflationary shortages in times of upswing. The need for infrastructural facilities, integration assistance and social benefits which followed from the employment of foreigners was almost insignificant because of the short periods of stay of the individual foreigners and the low numbers of family members who entered in the course of family reunion.

If the benefits of migrant labour were so apparent, why did the import of labour throttle off so dramatically in the mid-1970s? On this question there is no final agreement, but a number of mutually reinforcing explanations, or at the very least contingent factors, may be advanced:

- There is an obvious coincidence of dates in the early 1970s which may lead to a simple association between the dramatic increase in the price of oil and the end of the migrant labour boom. Certainly, the immediate wave of redundancies that followed in energy-intensive industries led to a political situation which would have made the importation of large numbers of 'alien' labourers untenable for most European governments. But, while the oil crisis can partly explain the timing of particular measures, any explanation of the end of labour migration must also be concerned with other deeper, underlying, factors.
- One of the key variables was the rise of a virulent indigenous xenophobia in a number of European countries often in the working classes. In Britain, old protective practices like closed shops and demarcation agreements were used to freeze out migrant labour (Duffield 1988), while in France a municipal branch of the Communist Party bulldozed the hostels erected for migrant workers in response to the demands of its supporters. In short, both industry and governments were increasingly constrained in employing migrant workers because of the countervailing racist sentiments such a policy provoked.
- Migrants were not so much hopeless chaff blown about by titanic

political controls and storm-force economic winds. Whatever the variation in activity across the different European countries, community associations, religious bodies and migrant political groups increasingly were able to oppose repatriation and to press instead for the principle of family reunification to be recognised. In Germany, this led to the substantive collapse of the guest-worker programme and the associated economic benefits that this conferred.

- The increased assertiveness of migrants not only applied to matters of immigration policy and family reunion; immigrant associations became increasingly concerned with the full range of social and employment benefits. One should not fall into the right-wing populist trap of believing that immigrant families over-claim all benefits – the evidence indeed inclines to a contrary assertion (Rex and Tomlinson 1979: 62). However, given the demographic profile and the special language needs of many migrant communities, increased costs arose in respect of child care, language training and education. Even if we assume only a broadly converging cost of reproduction between indigenous and migrant communities, the crucial advantage accruing to the host country and employer – a minimal or wholly displaced cost of the reproduction of labour – no longer obtained as migrant communities gradually reconstituted their family life and became permanent minorities.

- One way of understanding the economic restructuring of the period beginning in the mid-1970s is to argue in terms of new technology impelling a different industrial logic – away from mass production to small-batch production, away from labouring into independent proprietorship, away from manufacturing into services (Piore and Sabel 1984).[3] This development reduced the need to continue to employ factory hands imported from abroad.

- I alluded earlier to the remarkable consensus of opinion between official accounts and liberal and Marxist writers on the benefits conferred by the use of migrant labour. This orthodoxy is, in my view, largely correct, but some dissent was recorded at an early date by Misham (1970). His argument was both alarmist and based on his fanciful projections of inflows of migrant labour leading to a rise in the labour–capital ratio and a consequent fall in production. While his broad thesis makes unrealistic net migration assumptions, in some sectors, for example the textile industry, it is likely that working cheap, migrant labour on a 24-hour shift pattern was used as a way of holding the line against low-cost Asian textiles, thereby

---

3 The same processes also impelled a greater comparative advantage accruing to certain newly industrialising countries (for example, Hong Kong, Korea, Taiwan and Singapore), particularly in respect of low-bulk and high-value goods where the value added by the relatively cheaper labour component was significant.

avoiding the inevitable day when old machinery and tracks had to be discarded.

As Reaganomics and Thatcherism began to gain ground, and unemployment levels began to rise, arguments that importing migrants was essentially an inefficient way of reducing industrial costs became more widely heard. The political disadvantages and social costs of continuing the free importation of labour migrants also pushed the politicians into an alliance with the right wing of the European electorate which increasingly evinced extreme forms of xenophobia. In the post-1979 governments in Britain, most right-wing sentiment was contained within the Tory Party, but in France and Germany (and elsewhere in Europe too) the populist right threatened seriously to undermine conventional party allegiances. Migration issues thus moved to near the top of the political agenda in France and Germany.

Migration flows since the mid-1970s

I have given indicative, if not exhaustive, explanations for the immigration restrictions of the mid-1970s. But incomplete as this picture is, it may give the false impression that international labour migration had effectively ceased. In fact it continued – though with significant differences in the destination areas and the kinds of migrants involved. In Europe, the post-1970s migration was largely accounted for by family reunification, refugees and asylum-seekers and, to a small degree, by illegal entrants.

Illegal and irregular migrants

A much greater number of illegals have found their way to France and Germany compared to the UK, where the number is negligible. Within western Europe as a whole, the illegal population was estimated to be about 10 per cent of the foreign population, or about 0.5 per cent of the whole population (OECD 1987: 55). As Marie (1983) suggested, illegal migration serves to a degree to offset the inflexibilities of the post-restrictionist labour market:

Illegal migration has above all been a strategy adapted to a new institutional context ... [offsetting] ... the stringent restrictions on the entry of low-skilled manpower by supplying workers willing to accept low-status jobs with poor working conditions and pay. ... Recourse to illegal migrant workers may be interpreted as a movement towards replacing one category of foreigners by another contingent in a less secure position, with a view to more flexible management of the labour force.

The International Labour Office (ILO 1984: 113–14) argues forcibly that irregular migration should not be conceived as solely comprising those who cross the border fully intending to circumvent immigration or employment law. Rather, 'irregular' migrants also include those who are permitted through administrative inefficiency or convenience to enter a country, with regularisation taking place later.

The attempt by the ILO to widen the category of 'illegal' to cover the cases of other 'irregular' and 'undocumented' workers is a useful reminder to avoid premature assumptions or unjustified stigmatisation. But it is undoubtedly the case that the illegal status attaching to irregular migrants of all kinds has generated a fearful, wary segment of the population, largely helpless in the face of ruthless landlords or exploitative employers, cut off from the protection of the police and courts, and excluded from the political life and social benefits of the society in which they now live. They form part, as I shall suggest later, of an underprivileged 'helot' class that is emerging in the new Europe.

Refugees and asylum-seekers

Who is a refugee? As we have seen in earlier chapters, the relevant legal definitions derive from the 1951 international Convention which defined refugees as 'persons who are outside their country because of a well-founded fear of persecution for reasons of race, religion, nationality, membership of a particular social group or political opinion'. The 1951 Convention was drafted with the needs of the postwar displaced people of Europe firmly in mind. The modified 1967 Protocol sought to take account of events elsewhere in the world and was signed by nearly 100 countries.

Though the legal provisions appeared generous, in fact they still bore the mark of their original place of drafting. Moreover, European governments have been less than open-hearted in applying the existing provisions to those demanding entry as a result of the mass displacements occurring in the 'third world'. As a report for the Independent Commission on International Humanitarian Issues (ICIHI 1986: 33) puts it:

In the 1970s a new phenomenon emerged. Refugees from the crisis areas of Africa, Asia and Latin America began to move in increasing numbers to the industrialised countries. . . . The arrival of many refugees from geographically and culturally distant areas constituted an unprecedented challenge to the legal machinery and conscience of the receiving countries. The refugee problem, previously regarded as a factor in east–west relations, now had a north–south dimension added to it.

This succinct description can be elaborated in three respects:

- First, the volume and effects of the refugee crises were amplified as they coincided with the reduction of aid and social investment programmes to the 'third world' in response to nationalist and protectionist pressures in the industrialised countries. These pressures became politically effective precisely at the moment when many poor countries had their economic and environmental resources stretched to the limit. Increased energy costs, more expensive imports, political instability and lower commodity prices all placed a number of 'third world' countries in a position where they were unable to respond effectively to the devastation wrought by famine, war and drought.

- Second, the volume of refugee migration and potential migration expanded to such an extent (in 1993 it was estimated that there were 20 million refugees worldwide), that many potential host-states began to argue that refugees were in effect disguised economic migrants.
- Third, whereas mass displacements occurred only in the 'third world' in the 1970s and 1980s, the 1990s have ushered in a similar form of refugee migration from the former state-communist bloc. The small numbers of dissidents from communism who could be easily absorbed by the West within the framework of the Cold War rivalry, now potentially numbered hundreds of thousands, if not millions.

The combination of xenophobia and the coincidence of East–West and North–South migration have led to a mind-set in many rich countries that simply sees an undifferentiated horde of 'barbarians at the gates'. Zucker and Zucker (1987: xiv) seek to contradict this commonly and often officially held view and to develop a clear distinction between the three categories, immigrant, refugee and illegal:

Refugees are neither immigrants nor illegal migrants, although, like immigrants, they have forsaken their homelands for new countries and, like illegal migrants, they may enter those new countries without permission. But a refugee is, in the end, unlike either. Both the immigrant and the illegal migrant are drawn to a country. The refugee is not drawn but driven; he seeks not to better his life but to rebuild it, to gain some part of what he has lost. The immigrant and the migrant are propelled by hope; for the refugee whatever hope there may be must arise from the ruins of tragedy. The refugee, unlike other migrants, has lost or been denied a basic human need – the legal and political protection of a government. Accompanying that loss has been the loss, as well, of culture, community, employment, shelter – all the elements that contribute to a sense of self-worth. Refugees, whatever their origins, are in need of protection.

Beguiling as they are, such definitions depend greatly on liberal and humanist values being shared by politicians, policy-makers or immigration officials. The overall number of legally recognised refugees and the pattern of admissions do not, however, indicate wide acceptance of such views.

In Europe, the number of refugees recognised under the 1951 and 1967 Conventions varies greatly between the three countries considered here, though the pattern of increasing restriction is similar. In order to compare the German and French response to the current demands for refugee entry with the British response, I need first to describe the refugee histories and current immigration policies of the two continental countries.

Germany: refugees and foreign workers

Since its foundation in 1949, the Federal Republic of Germany ('West Germany') has provided a refuge to millions of displaced and expelled ethnic Germans. About 15 million people of German background were admitted from the Balkans and from the former German territories east of the rivers Oder and Neisse. In the minds of many German officials, politicians and the public at large, the liberal provisions for asylum of the postwar Bonn constitution were essentially directed at the German population of the East. As Blaschke (1992) puts it: 'The Stalinist policy practised in the former Eastern Territories of the Reich and in the Soviet Occupation Zone and later German Democratic Republic led in western Germany to a disastrous mixture of nationalist hyper-Germanness and concern for the protection of exiles regarded as being German.'

Despite this popular association between the right to asylum and German ethnicity, the social democratic and communist returnee politicians were strong enough to force the insertion of a universal principle in Paragraph 16 of the Fundamental Law which read, simply, 'Politically persecuted persons shall enjoy asylum.' Up to May 1993, this liberal provision served to allow a much greater refugee population from diverse backgrounds to emerge in postwar Germany compared both with France and the UK.

The relative liberality towards *refugees* has however, been superimposed on a continuing tradition of restriction on the civic status of *foreign workers*, which reaches back to the history of German industrialisation itself. As Potts (1990: 136–7) shows, as early as 1910 the 1.2 million foreign workers in Germany were subject to systematic legal constraints, including the power to expel them during periods of non-productive work. Foreign labourers were also tied to particular places of work. By 1932, with the use of scientific management techniques in the factories to reduce labour requirements and the pressures of the depression, there were only 142,000 foreign workers remaining.

The use of foreign and concentration camp labour (under conditions of severe legal regulation) again accelerated after the coming to power of the Nazis in 1933. The growth of the war machine led to the absorption of unemployed Germans into the army and, within a few years, agreements on the recruitment of foreign labour were made with foreign countries. By May 1939 there were 525,000 foreign workers in Germany and by September 1944 some 7.5 million were employed in the Reich. These served largely to replace the 11 million German men withdrawn from the labour force for military service.

The conditions of work varied between those foreign workers who were recruited from friendly or neutral countries (Italy, Slovakia, Bulgaria, etc.), those who were recruited by force in the occupied countries and those (about 1.8 million) who were actually prisoners of war. Despite the variations in treatment and conditions, the general principle for the treatment of foreign workers was announced by Sauckel, the Plenipotentiary for Labour: 'All the men must be fed, sheltered and treated in such a way as to exploit them to the highest possible extent at the lowest conceivable degree of expenditure' (cited Homze 1967: 113). As Castles and Kosack (1985: 23) explain:

> the whole German population was regularly exposed to official propaganda against foreign workers. However much the German population has repressed its experiences under Hitler since the war, the attitudes and behaviour developed then must still have some effect in shaping prejudices in modern Western Germany.

After 1945, and despite the movement of millions of ethnic Germans across the lines, the labour demands of the manufacturing and service sectors were so great that again foreign labour programmes were instituted – with Italy (1955), Spain (1960), Turkey (1961), Morocco (1963), Tunisia (1965) and Yugoslavia (1968). Again, however, there was a complex intertwining of German labour needs and refugee policy, the influx of foreign workers from southern Europe being paralleled by refugees from Salazar's Portugal, Franco's Spain, from the Greece of the colonels and from Turkey, where progressive forces were displaced by a succession of coups and subsequent military dictatorships (Blaschke 1992).

German officials explicitly referred to the use of foreign workers as *Konjunkturpuffer*, which signified their role as a shock absorber to iron out the stops and goes of the economy and to depress the supply price of labour. Foreign workers' statuses remained formally as 'guest-workers' with very limited access to civic rights. In particular, they were subject to deportation in the event of a downturn in the economy. In the period 1973–76, for example, after the oil-price crisis, the German state was able to reduce the number of foreign workers from 2.6 million to 1.9 million. However, as this figure reveals, the attempt to deter settlement and family reunification was far from successful and much less effective than the pre-1932 expulsions.

There were two main reasons for this relative failure of the German authorities. First, migrant community pressure groups, linked to progressive elements in German society, persistently asserted the right of minority workers to remain and to establish, or to re-establish, their family units. Second, laws, conventions and regulations promoted by the EC, the International Labour Organisation, the UN and the Council of Europe also served to constrain the full implementation of deportation policies (Plender 1985).

Germany: attitudes and recent policies

Within the conservative and right-wing sections of West Germany, hostility to the resident foreign population (*'Ausländerfeindlichkeit'*) was increased after the military coup in Turkey in 1980, when Turkish asylum-seekers started taking advantage of the asylum provisions of the German constitution. Other asylum-seekers arrived via East Germany. There is even some evidence that the East Germans encouraged this flow partly to raise the political temperature and partly to secure foreign exchange from passengers using the East German airline. In the early 1980s the first experiments with neo-liberalism in the eastern bloc (in Hungary and Poland, for example), coupled with conservative old-style communist counter-revolutions, led to a rapid rise in the numbers of migrants and refugees (Blaschke 1992).

The right was alarmed. To placate it, the coalition parties (the Christian Democratic Union, the Christian Socialist Union and the Free Democratic Party) introduced some changes to asylum procedures in June 1986. Chancellor Kohl also began to speak in terms that were to become a constant theme over the next few years – namely the notion of the 'misuse of asylum'. The Ministry of the Interior was the first state body to raise the issue of the annulment of Paragraph 16 of the Fundamental Law. The announcement by the Ministry seemed to give official sanction to a populist discourse that had hitherto remained unrespectable and suppressed. As Schneider (1989: 163) stated:

The tabloids and popular press wrote of the 'millions waiting at the door' and for months on end every political broadcast, radio and television programme saw politicians agitating against refugees. Even liberal newspapers began to use phrases like 'the flood of asylum-seekers' and the *Zeit* even went so far as to carry a caricature on its front page of a sewer washing asylum-seekers over the wall from East to West Berlin.

While the German government at first blanched at altering the Fundamental Law, it tightened the net against asylum-seekers in other ways. The first of two Acceleration Acts on the Asylum Procedure Act had already come into force on 1 August 1978. This limited the rights of asylum-seekers to protest against an adverse decision and decentralised the appeals procedure, thus making it more subject to local political pressures. In the second Acceleration Act, passed on 20 August 1980, asylum-seekers were no longer investigated by committees but

by individual scrutineers. As in the UK, the list of 'third world' countries whose nationals required visas was lengthened to include nearly
all those countries from which refugees emanated. (The legality of this
measure in relation to the Fundamental Law was never finally determined.)

Other measures such as forcing refugees to stay in hostels, not
allowing them to work, restricting their movement, not allowing them
to cook and reducing their entitlement to social assistance were openly
intended to act as a deterrent to any who sought to take advantage of
the asylum procedures. The work-ban on asylum applicants was especially galling to local authorities as only part of the cost of looking
after the applicants was met by the federal authorities. The hostels
could thus be targeted as homes for indigent foreigners who were not
even contributing to the costs of their maintenance.

A new law, enforced since 1 January 1987, restricted any political
activity in Germany by refugees against injustices in their home country and increased powers were given to the border police. General
disturbances in the countries of origin (such as civil wars in Sri Lanka
or Lebanon) were also no longer regarded as adequate grounds for the
grant of asylum[4] while additional delays were enforced in allowing
refugees to apply for work. Finally, increased powers of deportation
were assumed by the state (Schneider 1989: 164–5).

At one level the reunification of East and West Germany during
1990/1 provided the occasion for a fundamental restructuring of German immigration and asylum policy. Many of the implicit assumptions
in immigration law made a clear distinction between 'Germans' and
'foreigners' on the grounds of *jus sanguinis* (the law of blood). The
demolition of the Berlin Wall allowed the absorption and unification of
the largest block of ethnic Germans, though considerable numbers still
remain in the Soviet Union, in Poland and other Eastern European
countries.

The traumas of absorbing such a large population led to a reconsideration of whether asylum law should be tightened up even further so
as to restrict all asylum-seekers, be they ethnic Germans or not. On the
other hand some of the right-wing elements still nurse prewar
(*völkisch*) dreams, and wish to hang on to the possibility of the total
absorption of all ethnic Germans. The state's difficulty in responding

---

4 In contrast to the German government, Goodwin-Gill (1988: 109), formerly Senior
   Legal Adviser at the UNHCR, takes the view that, 'In any procedure relating to the
   grant, denial or termination of refuge, those fleeing civil war or inter-communal
   strife should benefit from the presumption that their life or freedom would be
   endangered by reason of generalised violence, armed conflict or massive violations
   of human rights. Such a presumption should be rebutted only by clear and
   convincing evidence that the reasons for fearing danger do not or no longer exist, or
   that the individual in question has left his or her country of origin purely for reasons
   of personal convenience.' Despite the change in the official German government
   position, in practice it did not, unlike the UK government (see Chapter 5), send
   refugees back to Sri Lanka.

to this second position is that German asylum law would have to become explicitly rather than implicitly racial in character. This would lead to conflicts with European partners, violations of international law and conventions, and the prohibition of such tiny groups as refugee Jews from the former Soviet Union – a form of restriction which will create a deep political embarrassment for the German government.

Following reunification, the difficulties occasioned by unemployment and the psychological demoralisation of people from the former East Germany have also led to a renewed interest in Nazism and the formation and revival of neo-Nazi organisations. A number of such organisations have been involved in violence directed against the hostels provided for asylum-seekers. This violence has spread from the eastern to the western parts of Germany and, according to one report 'there has been ominous evidence that young perpetrators have received tacit or even open approval from older people' (*Independent*, 7 Oct. 1991). One dramatic incident was at Hoyerswerda, in former East Germany, where a petrol bomb was thrown into a hostel, badly injuring children. Between January and September 1991, there were 99 arson attacks on foreigners' hostels, 72 of them in the last two months of that period. In August 1992 a hostel in the former East Germany was burned to the ground, with 400 local townsfolk cheering on the arsonists and preventing the police from making arrests. After five days of disturbances at the hostel, the police finally arrested 140 people.

The contemporary crisis surrounding the break-up of Yugoslavia and the mass movements of population from Romania and Albania have also revived in the minds of many European politicians, and not least the Germans, the old spectre of the 'Eastern Question'. As Marrus (1985: 50) remarked, the Eastern Question had preoccupied European diplomacy in the First World War. While there was a measure of sympathy for the Christian victims of the Ottoman Empire, 'the ferocity of the Balkan peoples towards one another was simply beyond understanding. ... Europeans were inclined to write the entire region off as a sea of barbarism and saw southern Hungary as the frontier of Europe'. This observation still pertains in so far as even the visionaries among the 12 EU countries rarely think it practical to extend the frontiers of the Community beyond Hungary. The German state is now in the 'frontline' of this argument as to whether the EU should expand – taking in the EFTA countries, Hungary and perhaps Croatia, Bosnia and Poland – or retain its western European character.

In the context of this unsettling speculation about the eastern frontier of the EU, it was easy for the political right to press further demands to alter, dilute or abolish the constitution safeguards for asylum-seekers. Roma (Gypsies) from Yugoslavia, Romania and Bulgaria bore the brunt of the increasingly restrictive asylum procedures that followed. At the same time, in the case of Polish migrants, the authorities were forced to accept that they filled key niches in the temporary and seasonal labour market, despite the high rates of unemployment in the former East Germany. Poles were exempted from visa controls and a number of agreements were concluded with the Polish government to permit contract workers, seasonal labourers, workers on short-term work permits and commuters to enter the country. From many thousands per annum, the number of Polish applicants for asylum dropped to 3,448 in 1991, while the number of legitimate Polish migrants rocketed to 170,000 people in the same year (Blaschke 1992).

German refugee policy swung uneasily between the demands for labour in particular settings, the inherited constitutional safeguards for asylum and the demand for the 'right to return' for all ethnic Germans. However, the fear of the extreme right, whose power was manifested in electoral successes early in 1993, finally decided the issue. The opposition Social Democratic Party (SPD), whose support was needed to secure the necessary two-thirds majority in the Bundestag, convinced themselves that changes to Article 16 would neutralise the far-right Republican Party and reduce the violence directed at asylum-seekers and visible minorities.

On the fateful day, 26 May 1993, with 10,000 demonstrators protesting outside, parliamentarians were brought in by helicopter to vote in the Bundestag. By the convincing vote of 521 to 132, what an SPD member of parliament called 'the utopian Article 16' was savaged by a host of amendments and conditions. The most crucial change will affect those arriving from 'safe third countries' (Poland or the Czech Republic were cited as examples) who will not be allowed to stay in Germany pending consideration of their cases. Financial help will be given to the Polish and Czech governments to house those sent back. In other cases, asylum-seekers' claims will be processed more rapidly and with fewer judicial safeguards.

It is, of course, all too easy to decry the collapse of moral fibre in Germany and to evoke the nightmare of its Nazi past. It remains a serious possibility that the extreme right will take the constitutional change as a sign of a lack of resolve by the democratic forces. Attacks on asylum-seekers and the 1.8 million Turkish minority could well be the ghastly consequence of this decision. On the other hand, German politicians have been able legitimately to point at their European partners' practices in respect of asylum-seekers, not least those in Britain. The words 'Schengen', 'Dublin' and 'Maastricht' (see below) are now used by centre and right-wing German politicians as magical incantations to avoid confronting difficult national realities and to appease their no doubt uneasy consciences. It is also pertinent to point to the mass demonstrations of liberal and left-democratic Germans who acted in solidarity with the asylum-seekers who were attacked in their hostels and who vigorously opposed the dilution of Article 16. The many Germans who have learnt from their history are a potent force in opposing the neo-Nazi right.

France: refugee history

Like post-1949 Germany, France also has an open-handed constitutional provision, though one of greater antiquity. Drawing on the stirring ideals of the Revolution, the 1793 constitution offered a haven to
those who espoused freedom and fought tyranny. The first groups
claiming asylum under this provision arrived in the period after the
Napoleonic wars when nationalist movements emerged in Italy,
Ireland, Poland and Germany mobilising under the slogans Young
Italy, Young Germany, etc. About 20,000 Spanish, Portuguese, Italian
and German refugees were granted asylum in the period before 1848.

Marrus (1985: 16) shows that one of these movements, the Young
Germany movement, drew heavily on lower-middle-class and Jewish
intellectuals. A clampdown by the state in 1819 led to many radicals
who had been attracted to the movement leaving for the safer political
climate of France. A similar impulse led the young Karl Marx to be
caught up in the heady revolutionary slogans of 1848. He fled to
France, but was forced into a second exile in the UK when the movement in France was itself suppressed.

French liberalism towards exiles and political refugees suffered a
further blow in the 1890s after the assassination of Alexander II.
Anxious to propitiate the Russians, with whom they were moving into
alliance, the French agreed to expel 'nihilist' émigrés after complaints
from the Tsar. A further 1,600 anarchists, mainly Italians, were
expelled in the period 1894–1906 (Marrus 1985: 26).

As a result of the Bolshevik victory, white Russians eventually tired
of trying to make a comeback and many, about 400,000, settled in
France – undoubtedly the political centre of anti-Bolshevik activity.
Again, France admitted 300,000 Armenians fleeing the Turkish massa-
cres of the years 1915–19 and some 400,000 Republican Spaniards
after Franco took over in 1936 (Tiberghien 1988: 3). Significant
numbers of Italians also arrived from Italy after 1926, the year in
which Mussolini consolidated his hold on the Italian state. The Fascist
ban on 'abusive emigration' only served to encourage the movement
and, as had happened in the Russian case, France became an important
centre of anti-Fascist activity.

The attitude of France towards foreign settlers of all kinds during
the interwar period was so positive that the ILO (directed by a
Frenchman, Albert Thomas) came to rely on his country as the only
country in Europe capable of taking a significant number of refugees.
The French attitude was partly conditioned by her huge losses in the
First World War. She had lost 1.5 million young productive people – 7
per cent of the population. Two out of every ten young men had died
and a further three were disabled. In the period before 1928 alone,
France absorbed 1.5 million foreign workers, many of them refugees.

After 1945, in addition to the labour migrants common in all European countries, France accepted a large number of *repatriés* from its

former colonies. These were not simply the small numbers of colonial officials and administrators, but included settlers of French origin – perhaps as many as 900,000 from Algeria alone. To those of French origin were added others of local origins who 'often sided too openly with the colonial power, perhaps to the extent of performing military service' (Husbands 1991: 173). One notable such group are the Harkis, French Muslims who were persecuted by the successful Algerian nationalists and who chose a life in France instead. The reception granted to the Harkis has been less than expected of former allies and many are complaining of being confused in the public mind with the Algerian population in general and being subject to similar forms of discrimination in housing, employment and social life. One newspaper report described the Harkis as 'swindled, deceived and forgotten' (cited Husbands 1991: 177).

France: attitudes and recent policies

Like in Britain, the question of asylum has become inextricably linked to the general politics of immigration. The success of Jean-Marie Le Pen's campaign to place immigration at the centre of the political debate has forced the conventional parties of the left and right to take up positions on three controversial matters – the accuracy of official statistics on the number of foreigners resident in France, the number of illegals present and the demographic trends in both the foreign and indigenous populations.

Despite a more liberal attitude from President Mitterrand himself, the socialist Minister of the Interior, Pierre Joxe, was forced on to the defensive in a crucial speech in the National Assembly in November 1988 (cited Husbands 1991: 189):

France does not have the means to become a country that can receive all the disinherited from developing countries. . . . Political asylum is, alas, necessary, but economic asylum is something else. The former arises from protecting human rights; the latter would amount to the French Republic taking responsibility for all the poverty in the world. There are proper procedures for Third World aid, as well as limits to it.

Though this speech is similar in content to those made by other European politicians, in France the debate on immigrants and asylum-seekers has two particular dimensions: (a) the so-called 'threshold' issue; and (b) the question of anti-Arab and anti-Muslim sentiment. The first issue has been perceptively analysed by MacMaster (1991). As he shows, politician after politician alludes to the notion of a threshold of tolerance, normally while vehemently denying that the French are in any way racist. Here is a sample of such quotes drawn from Husbands (1991) and Silverman (1991):

I am striving to disperse them [the immigrants] throughout the city in such a way that no neighbourhood surpasses a threshold of ten per cent. I believe that there is a threshold that we cannot exceed without tragedy (the Mayor of Lyon, 1981).

I refute the charge of racism against French workers. In fact, they are not racists, but, when a particular threshold is passed it provokes a rejection, as when, in the human body certain substances are present in too great a quantity (the Prefect of the Val de Marne, 1972).

The figure of 300,000 [illegal migrants] is an error. Whereas the figure has been feebly bandied about for political or racist motives, our policy consists of integrating foreigners, who have often been here for a long period, and preventing *too many* [emphasis added] of them from coming (the Minister of the Interior, Pierre Joxe, 1985).

The support for the idea of a *seuil de tolérance* crosses normal political divisions and is articulated by communist, socialist, conservative and right-wing politicians. It has more general ideological roots, but was first used in a quasi-scientific sense in 1964 by a sociologist asked to investigate the serious conflicts that had appeared in a housing estate in Nanterre between Algerian families rehoused from the *bidonvilles* and French families who had come from the Parisian slums. Subsequently, the concept was widely deployed at a municipal level by urban planners and housing managers, despite determined attempts by other sociologists to refute the scientific basis of the theory. (The highly centralised and technocratic nature of urban management in France perhaps permits a greater spread of a new orthodoxy than in other European countries.) So important had the concept become that an entire conference at Aix in 1974 was devoted to developing a searching critique.

This intellectual effort was apparently undertaken to little avail, as a mainstream right-wing news magazine, *Le Point*, restated its belief in the concept in its covering story in April 1990 (cited Husbands 1991: 193) under the title 'Immigrants: What Threshold of Tolerance?':

4,500,000 immigrants: for French people in their daily life, tension rises, sometimes beyond what can be endured. Everything goes to show that the threshold of tolerance has been reached. Although rejected by the sociologists, this notion more and more compels recognition in the face of the psychological exasperation of French people.

The second issue that is particular to France is the depth and strength of anti-Arab and anti-Muslim sentiment. Though both of these elements are present in the UK and Germany, French colonial history has left a particular legacy in this respect. The expansion of the French empire into North Africa was effectively arrested by the cultural resilience of the Muslim religion and Arabic, both of which survived *despite* French attempts to introduce the language and religion of the colonisers (an attempt never undertaken with equivalent enthusiasm in the British colonies). The defeat in Algeria (as well as the earlier defeat in Indo–China) rocked the very foundations of the French state. De Gaulle's withdrawal from Algeria and his refusal to grant a pardon to Marshal Pétain (who died in prison in 1951) inflamed the extreme right – whose demands to 'defend Christian Western civilisation' and to 'save the Fatherland' spawned a clutch of semi-clandestine extreme right-wing and anti-immigrant groups.

The doomed cause of Algérie Française gave way to the Secret Army Organisation (OAS), which in turn was supplanted by the Revolutionary Army (AR), the Occident movement and the New Order (ON) and the National Front (FN), set up in 1972 (Vaughan 1991: 214–17). By the autumn of 1983 the National Front attracted 10 per cent of the votes in local elections; a similar figure was recorded in the European elections of that year, while in the general election of 1986 its vote dipped marginally to 9.8 per cent of the votes cast. In the 1992 regional elections the socialists, with 18 per cent of the vote, were nearly humiliated by the FN.

The FN's vote was mainly fuelled by Le Pen's charismatic but contradictory personality. For example, though the Front's rallies begin with a Latin mass – thus linking it to the revival of Catholic fundamentalism – Le Pen himself has made various anti-clerical statements and is periodically linked to sexual scandals and an unseemly divorce. Despite the temporary damage to his reputation from such revelations and the story that he had acted as a torturer while in the army in Algeria, Le Pen's simple philosophy has had considerable appeal to the electorate.

Le Pen espouses a form of neo-Darwinism – that there are degrees of assimilability and trust – from family, to kin, to neighbours, to fellow-citizens, to strangers, to foes. 'If to be a reactionary is to react like an organism reacts when faced with disease, then yes, I am a reactionary. Not to be a reactionary is to sentence oneself to death. It is to let the disease or the enemy take over' (cited Vaughan 1991: 222). As Vaughan suggests, this organic analogy allows an easy identification of immigrants and asylum-seekers as the sole enemy – responsible for a host of ills like currency speculation, bad housing, unemployment, the rising crime rate, overcrowding in schools, even the spread of AIDS. A commentator in *Le Monde* (12 June 1987) put it even more crisply: for Le Pen 'everything comes from immigration, everything goes back to immigration'.

Support for the Le Pen ticket in future elections cannot be discounted, but (as in Germany and, in an earlier period, the UK) the continuing role for the far right seems to be to force the issue of immigration and asylum-seekers on to the centre of the public agenda. This certainly appeared to be the lesson from the April 1993 election when the Gaullists and the centre-right parties inflicted massive damage on the Socialists, but the National Front failed to win a single seat (despite capturing 12.5 per cent of the vote).

Realising its potential for uncontrollable social unrest, all the mainstream parties have sought to sideline 'race issues' and from time to time there have been informal understandings between social-democratic and conservative parties to play down the issue to the indigenous population, or allay the fears of the minorities when sensitive interethnic issues are raised at an international level. However, the selection of Charles Pasqua as minister of the interior, who had been previously associated with a tough anti-immigrant posture, seems to have signalled a renewed wave of racist brutality by elements of the French police. Pasqua also sought to introduce a radical immigration bill with 51 new articles, eight of which were challenged by the Constitutional Council as being unconstitutional. Only the diplomatic intervention of the Gaullist prime minister, Edouard Balladur, prevented a constitutional impasse. As with the mainstream politicians in Germany, Balladur was able to represent Pasqua's repressive measures as necessary for complying with the Schengen treaty (see below) and to reassure the right that there was 'no question of leaving France without sufficient means of protection against clandestine immigration' (*Independent*, 3 Sept. 1993). By January 1994 the constitutional crisis had passed with most of Pasqua's measures intact.

In the case of refugees, the conflation of right-wing domestic populism with immigration and refugee matters severely shook the relatively secure status of the bodies administering refugee policy. Unlike in the UK where *ad hoc* policies to refugees were developed by successive politicians and administrators at the Home Office, the French government had established a special section of the Ministry of Foreign Affairs, called the Office Français de Protection des Réfugiés et Apartides (OFPRA) in 1952, to implement the Geneva Convention of the previous year.

Founded at a moment of idealism, with a separate budget of its own and a degree of institutional solidity, OFPRA was slowly able to win the trust of refugee communities in France and a degree of independence from the immediate foreign policy pressures on successive governments. Its long pedigree also gave OFPRA recognition in negotiations with foreign governments and some clout in persuading the Ministries of the Interior and Social Security to co-operate in its schemes to settle refugees. Unlike in Germany, where the division of responsibilities between the different layers of government in the resettlement process is poorly organised, the system of reception, education, integration, training and employment devised by OFPRA gives every impression of working effectively.

Once again this shining apple cart was upset by the increased numbers of asylum-seekers demanding entry in the 1980s and the popular and political pressures to resist too many 'recognitions'. The dramatic drop in those given Convention refugee status compared to those who applied can be seen in Table 6.1. Even the absolute number recognised fell in the late 1980s, despite the much larger number of applicants.

Table 6.1: Applicants/Recognised Refugees in France

Year	No. Recognised	% Recognised
1981	14,586	77.7
1982	15,670	73.9
1983	14,608	70.0
1984	14,314	65.3
1985	11,539	43.3
1986	10,645	39.0
1987	8,704	32.7
1988	8,794	34.6
1989	8,770	28.1
1990	13,073	15.5
1991	16,112	n.a.

Source: Official figures, issued by OFPRA at a conference on Les réfugiés en France et en Europe, Paris, 11–13 June 1992.

From an examination of this table it is difficult to come to any other conclusion but that OFPRA was under increasing pressure to reduce the numbers and the percentage of recognised refugees arriving in the 1980s. As in Germany, domestic politicians sought to diminish the salience of the country's constitutional provision (and its revolutionary tradition) by blaming the all-too-convenient process of European harmonisation.

That the constraints on immigration and refugee policy were mainly domestic, not European, could be seen in the initial fence sitting by the French government at the commencement of the 1991 Gulf War. On the one hand, Mitterrand's government was anxious not to inflame Muslim sympathies or undermine French allies in the Arab world. On the other hand, the strength of anti-Islamic sentiment amongst the indigenous French population, the revival of fundamentalist Catholicism and the continuing appeal of the extreme right were starkly revealed. Even so aristocratic and respectable a figure as former President Giscard d'Estaing has stolen some of Le Pen's clothes and based his putative political comeback on the 'threshold' issue.

Mitterrand's personal unpopularity, together with a right-wing government, has made political dynamite of the immigration/refugee issue. As in Germany, for French politicians the growth of restrictive attitudes to refugees in the EU as a whole has appeared over the hill like the legendary cavalry – just in the nick of time. France's distinguished record of admitting refugees will regrettably (they will say) have to give way in the interests of harmonising European policy.

Towards Fortress Europe

As the magic date (1 January 1993) for the completion of the main elements of the EU loomed, each of the '12' states positioned itself for a significant clampdown on immigration from non-EU countries, a stance that was correctly characterised as building 'Fortress Europe' (JCWI 1989). The historically more liberal states pointed fingers at the restraints imposed by the traditionally restrictive countries in justification of their own increasingly stringent attitudes. I have provided supporting testimony from Germany and France on this point, but one might add an example from Italy. Citing constraints imposed by their European partners, the Italian government deported scores of Albanian migrants and asylum-seekers in mid-1991 and announced a package of new restrictive policies.

For their part, the 'tough-on-migrant states', notably Britain, proclaimed they would not abandon national border restrictions until all 12 moved into line with *them*. Even aspirant members of the EU have got into the act, partly in response to their own internal political pressures, but partly too to win approval from existing members of the EU and in so doing bolstering their case for entry. The Austrian government, for example, hitherto one of the most liberal in its entry policies, has been particularly active in involving the citizen army in erecting and staffing a string of new border posts. In effect, the Austrian government has shifted the Berlin Wall eastwards and is validating part of its case for EU entry by how fiercely it can police the border.

Behind the political protestations of toughness was a certain amount of official unease both as to how effectively the frontiers could be policed and whether the measures prepared could be ready in time for the moment when the free traffic of goods, services, capital *and* persons across national frontiers was due to commence. The Single European Act then linked 320 million EU nationals with the following rights in respect of freedom of movement:

- The right to enter another EU country, to visit, accept or seek employment, self-employment or provide or receive a service.
- Similar rights for spouses, children and other close relations (who do not have to be a national of a member state).
- Entrants can receive a residence permit (for a duration not less than five years).
- The Treaty of Rome had already given extensive rights to business

people to establish business or provide services in another member state.
- Students have the right to register for further and higher education (and to bring their families) provided their qualifications are recognised.

By 1992 about 15 million EU nationals out of western Europe's 320 million people already lived in other EU countries. This number is likely gradually to rise with unfathomable but, it is thought, generally benign inter-ethnic consequences. On the other hand, about 8 million non-EU nationals already legitimately reside in one or other EU country: the biggest groups being Algerians, Tunisians, Yugoslavs, West Africans, Swiss and citizens of the United States.

The rights of non-national residents vary greatly between and within countries: the Single European Act neither resolves these anomalies, nor does it guarantee freedom of movement for non-nationals. EU governments are simply left to work it out for themselves. Some non-EU nationals, no doubt, will be protected by wealth and privilege – Swiss or US business executives, for example (these I call 'denizens' below). Others will find their fate being increasingly linked to that of 'third-country nationals' from outside the EU. As the drawbridge of Fortress Europe is pulled up, some residents, it appears, may be tossed in the moat.

It is still necessary to be somewhat cautious in predicting the shape of post-1993 migration patterns within and from outside the EU. The strength of the exogenous factors propelling migration (for example in the former Soviet Union) is still unknown, while there is still a high level of discretion in operating EU guidelines inside the Community. This latitude arises from the fact that the European Parliament, the European Commission, the Council of Europe and the Council of Ministers do *not* have the power to legislate or issue binding directives with respect to immigration matters (despite various British myths to the contrary). Instead various *ad hoc* arrangements and agreements are entered into between the countries, often in an atmosphere of considerable secrecy.

One of the earliest and still largely concealed forms of European co-operation takes place through the TREVI group, founded in 1986. Even the acronym is a puzzle. Official information, or is it disinformation, has it that the idea was born in the benign (though sadly increasingly sordid) surroundings of the Trevi fountain in Rome. But Dr Markus H. F. Mohler, the Commandant of the Cantonal Police of Basel, Switzerland (who should know), says the acronym stands for Terrorism, Radicalism, Extremism and International Violence. TREVI operates under the control of the ministers of the interior (the equivalent ministry in the UK is, of course, the Home Office), supported by regular meetings of officials and police representatives. It examines questions of drug abuse, terrorism and illegal immigration. Its decisions are not legal, except in so far as the national parliaments of each member state legislate similarly. A good example is the idea of carriers, liability legislation imposing fines on airlines carrying passengers without valid passports and visas. This was discussed, it is said, at TREVI, then enacted by several European countries. The lack of any democratic checks on such a body is worrying and, from the point of view of asylum-seekers, their situation being linked to questions of drug abuse and terrorism could but prejudice any assumption that they are legitimately presenting their claims for consideration.

A body called the Ad Hoc Immigration Group (known to some in the immigration world as 'son of TREVI') has the same membership as TREVI and has generated a series of draft conventions and papers on refugees, some of which surfaced at Dublin (see below). This body was particularly active in pressing the case that European governments need not consider intercontinental movements of refugees as 'they are seldom necessary for protection reasons' and should be dealt with by a safe country in the refugees' own regions (*Independent*, 22 Oct. 1992). Another European instrument known as 'the Palma Document' standardises the level of internal security and increases the level of law-enforcement co-ordination between member states. It provides, in particular, for the co-ordination of migration policy between 'the Schengen' and 'non-Schengen' states.

Schengen and Dublin

Unlike the bodies above, the Schengen and Dublin agreements (and to a much smaller extent the Maastricht treaty) provide the open face of EU migration policy, especially as this bears on 'third country' (non-EU) nationals.

There is some irony in Schengen, a small town in Luxembourg, and Dublin, Eire's capital, being so strongly associated with the formulation of EU refugee policy, as the Grand Duchy has not received more than 100 applications for asylum each year for many years (it only received 44 in 1988), while Eire only managed an average of 20 applicants per annum over the 1980s.

Schengen

In June 1990 five of the six original members of the EU signed a convention extending and applying the 1985 Schengen agreement (Italy stayed out for a while). The 1990 meeting is also called the 'second' Schengen agreement. The close consensus reached within this grouping has generated the shorthand 'the Schengen countries', and even the expression 'Schengenland'. By 1992, eight countries (France, Luxembourg, Belgium, the Netherlands, Germany, Italy, Spain and

Portugal) had entered Schengenland, though parliamentary ratification had not yet taken place in each case.

The 1990 Schengen Convention has central chapters on aliens, refugees, privacy, security and the police. It decisively shifts the operating territorial boundaries to the external border (and to some specially designated spots inside an extended perimeter). The convention also established exclusive powers for the authorities in the fields of immigration, asylum, security and the police.

Schengen provides for a common administration and a common organisation to administer agreed regulations. Common information systems are held in Strasbourg where a list of persons to be refused entry can be accessed by any participating member's country. While its use has been delayed by software problems, even if successfully downloaded the list is simply an unchecked data base of those deemed *personae non grata* by any or all Schengen states. Schengen also provides for the common training of immigration and security officials and the common issue of visas. An (unelected) executive committee has the power to amend the working of regulations on a day-to-day basis. The ultimate object of the agreement is explicitly stated as the 'abolition' of common borders.

The suggestion of liberality that the expression 'abolition' may evoke is, however, deceptive. A Permanent Commission on International Aliens, Refugees and Criminal Law established in the Netherlands by five non-government organisations provides a much more critical view: 'There is *expansion* rather than the abolition of the border control ... the competencies, possibilities and obligations of the police and legal authorities have been extended by the Schengen regulations' (Meijers *et al.* 1992: 1–2).

Meijers cites the example of an alien wishing to enter the Netherlands. Before Schengen, he or she had to meet the conditions spelt out in the Dutch Aliens Act. Now the same alien will have to fulfil the conditions laid down by all the other signatories. This is called the principle of 'cumulation' (could this be the opposite of subsidiarity?) where everybody's law is valid and there is no agreement on a unified law and regulation.

Boeles (1992) also mounts a strong critique of the potential damage of the Schengen Agreement to the 'rule of law'. He shows that the agreement includes endless provisions for the proactive co-operation and intervention on behalf of the police and the legal authorities, but that these provisions all presume guilt and not innocence. By contrast, there is hardly any attention paid to the defence side in criminal procedure. The liberal critics also point out that throughout the Schengen Convention there is reference to treaties concluded by the Council of Europe, but the Council of Europe's Convention on the Protection of Human Rights and Fundamental Freedoms is strikingly absent. They also suggest that transferring the regulation of immigration matters from the national to the international level may mean 'a greater loss to democratic standards, parliamentary information, judicial competence and administrative openness' (Meijers *et al.* 1992: 6).

Dublin

While the UK has, of course, conspicuously and sedulously kept out of the Schengen agreements on the grounds that it wants to maintain independent checks, the British government has signed the Dublin Convention with greater enthusiasm. Called in full the Dublin Convention on the Determination of the State Responsible for Examining an Asylum Application, it was signed by all EU members, except Denmark, in June 1990.

The overriding intention of the signatories was to put an end to the phenomenon of 'multiple' ('simultaneous or successive') asylum requests, applications for asylum lodged with more than one EU state.' On one side of the argument this practice, which undoubtedly existed, was a device by asylum-seekers to exploit the weakest or most appropriate legislation: the applicant would go 'asylum shopping'. The other side of the argument attributed this phenomenon to a series of unsympathetic regimes who would refuse to process a request, be unwilling or unable to send the applicant back to a country of origin and would pass the problem on: this version gave rise to the expression 'refugees-in-orbit'.

Whether caused by the asylum-seeker or the state, the Dublin Convention intended to provide what was colloquially described as 'one-kick-at-the-can', i.e. an asylum-seeker could only make one application in the EU. It is dubious that the legal drafting actually will achieve this object. For example Article 3(1) of the convention only guarantees that a member state will examine an application from any alien for asylum. However, under the international conventions an 'application for asylum' is not the same as an 'application for protection'. Again, there are no procedures to determine which of the states is ultimately responsible and Article 3(5) refers to member states still retaining their right to act 'in compliance with the provisions of the Geneva Convention as amended by the New York Protocol'. Both treaties are incompatible with the 1951 Geneva Convention because they abandon the principle that it is incumbent on each state to determine autonomously a refugee's status.

Those who are concerned with the tendency of the Euro-technocrats to operate outside normal democratic procedures would no doubt point to the fact that parliaments have been asked to approve the contents of the Dublin Convention without the publication of the full text, there are no procedural minimum standards for the examination of the requests for asylum and Dublin (like Schengen) does not refer to any international obligations in the field of human rights.

The Single European Act, the secret agreements like TREVI and the open conventions and agreements like Schengen and Dublin will all impact on migration flows of EU nationals wishing to move, EU and non-EU nationals already legitimately in residence in their non-natal or national states and on third-country nationals seeking legally or illegally to enter the EU. The differential status that is likely to attach to each category is explored below.

The emerging European trichotomy

Immigrants, guest-workers, illegals, refugees, asylum-seekers, expatriates, repatriates, settlers – do these labels signify anything of importance? My argument that they do turns on a belief that, although there are considerable similarities between international migrants of all types, the British and other European states' policies and agreements are in the process of creating a three-tiered pattern of differentiation. Some nationals, residents and migrants are included in the body politic and accorded full civic and social rights (they become part of the 'self'), while many more are excluded from entering the gilded cage (they remain part of the 'other'). A third, intermediate type of secure, privileged foreigners also seems to be emerging.

The processes of selection for entry into one or other category have involved and been consequent on a set of massive changes to the size and shape of the gilded cages comprising post-1945 Britain, Germany and France:

- Britain saw its nationality and citizenship law fundamentally altered in 1948. Its Empire and Commonwealth citizens were reduced to aliens or given quickly fabricated and largely meaningless British citizenships. Its former Dominions established their own geopolitical priorities that were far removed from the interests of their old motherland. Aliens from the continent became fellow Europeans with bewildering speed.

- This last feature was also shared with Germany. But Germany's postwar shape and size bulged and shrank, if anything with a greater rapidity and confusion. Cut apart by the allies in 1945, the old capital, Berlin, lay stranded in the sea of the GDR, dominated by the Soviet allies. The Cold War fractured Berlin itself and Germny as a whole. After reunification an old ethnic exclusiveness reasserted itself, one which lay uncomfortably alongside Germny's commitment to the EU and its non-racial and open-handed contiution.

- France too dismembered its Empire. But because it was always possible for a so-called *évolué* to become French (through loyalty, dress, language, religion and manner), there was greater continuity between imperial and post-imperial France. Moreover, those in the smaller territories – whether in a Département d'outre-mer or Territoire d'outre-mer – remain umbilically attached to the mother country. They share a common citizenship and are formally part of Europe even though geographically they are in the Caribbean Sea, the Indian Ocean, etc. On the other hand, where the assimilationist possibility was resisted – for example in Algeria and Indo–China – a sullen, culturally alienated population arose, many with ambiguous loyalties to France. People from these areas were liable to be victims of racist attacks because of their religion, appearance or failure to accept French norms.

In short, the three states concerned fundamentally altered their sense of self-hood in the postwar period. To do this they promoted a European identity combined with an increasingly restrictive and exclusive definition of nationality and citizenship. The notion of citizenship, in particular, needs further explanation.

The important role of citizenship as a means of integrating dissatisfied members of the lower orders and including them in the core society was first explicitly recognised by Marshall (1950). For him, access to citizenship allowed everyone so favoured to be given some stake in the society, at least in respect of periodic elections, protection, and access to some social benefits. With the rise of welfare and distributive states in the postwar world – unemployment benefits, social security, housing allowances, tax credits, pensions, subsidised health care – the social wage has become a much more important symbolic and economic good. By the same token, states have sought to restrict access to the social wage by deploying workers with limited entitlements. The different statuses reflected in immigrant or guest-worker categories reflect the differential access of such groups to the social wage and to the protection afforded by the agencies of law and order.

If we consider the various categories mentioned earlier, three broad bands appear – citizens whose rights are extensive, an intermediate group (the denizens) and a group which remains a subject population akin to the ancient helots who hewed wood and toiled for the Spartans without access to democratic rights, property or protection. Some of the typical subgroups within the three different status groups mentioned are listed below.

1. *Citizens*

- Nationals by birth or naturalisation
- Established immigrants
- Convention refugees
- Repatriates

2. *Denizens*

- Holders of one or more citizenships
- Recognised asylum applicants
- Special entrants, for example, Hong Kong residents to UK/ Croatians to Germany
- Expatriates

3. *Helots*

- Illegal and undocumented entrants
- Asylum-seekers
- Overstayers
- Seasonal and temporary workers
- Project-tied unskilled workers

A few remarks on each of the three major categories will perhaps help to lend greater specificity to the labels.

Citizens

This group appears as an increasingly privileged one. Our three states have now moved from inclusive (appropriate to Empire and expansion) to exclusive definitions of citizenship. They have abandoned the principle of *jus soli* (citizenship by being born in a territory) to *jus sanguinis* (citizenship according to the parents' nationality).

In the case of the European countries that once had empires (Belgium, France, Britain, Holland) binding guarantees of citizenship to colonial subjects have frequently been ignored or circumvented by subsequent legislation. While the Dutch on the whole respected the citizenship conferred on subjects of the Netherlands, the French maintained recognition only for a small number of people in the *départements* (French Guyana, Reunion, Guadeloupe and Martinique).

The British, for their part, in the Nationality Act of 1982 stripped away the rights of residents of the colony of Hong Kong (and a few other places) and created a new citizenship of 'dependent territories' which conferred no right to live or work in the UK. Under the impact of the destabilising events in China in 1989, however, and its consequent effects on the colony of Hong Kong, Britain has been forced to guarantee the admission of up to 50,000 Hong Kong families. The intention of this guarantee is to stabilise the last years of British rule in the colony (it reverts to Chinese rule in 1997) by buying the loyalty of key officials and entrepreneurs with the offer of settlement and full citizenship in Britain. This will require amendment of the 1982 British Nationality Act and is likely to cause a major political crisis in Britain in the period leading up to the next general election.

Denizens

I conceive this group as comprising privileged aliens often holding multiple citizenship, but not having the citizenship of or the right to vote in the country of their residence or domicile. Hammar (1990) has produced a remarkable calculation that resident non-citizens living and working in European countries include 180,000 in Belgium, 2,800,000 in France, 2,620,000 in West Germany, 400,000 in the Netherlands, 390,000 in Sweden and 700,000 in Switzerland.

Many of these alien residents may be well-paid expatriates (see above) who are not particularly concerned with exercising the franchise and have compensating employment benefits – a group in short that can be seen as transcending the limits of the nation-state. However, the numbers involved in Hammar's calculations suggest that many residents have been systematically excluded from citizenship and its accompanying rights without any compensating benefits deriving from their employment. These form part of the helot category.

Helots

I have used the category 'helots' in a somewhat more inclusive way in Cohen (1987). Here I refer more narrowly to people who have illegally entered the country, people who have overstayed the period granted on their entry visas, asylum-seekers who have not been recognised under the international conventions, those who are working illegally, and those who have been granted only limited rights. A good example (cited in Castles *et al.* 1984: 77) appears in a statement given to officials as to how to operate the 1965 West German Foreigners Law:

> Foreigners enjoy all basic rights, except the basic rights of freedom of assembly, freedom of association, freedom of movement and free choice of occupation, place of work and place of education and protection from extradition abroad.

Statements such as this reveal the powerful attempt to try to exclude, detain or deport foreigners who are regarded as disposable units of labour-power for whom the advantages of citizenship, the franchise and social welfare are denied.

As Marshall (1950) argued in the case of unprivileged classes and we can now argue in terms of different categories of migrants, conferring citizenship is the key indicator of integration and acceptance within a nation state. This basic symbol of inclusion is signified by the right periodically to elect a new government. But the exercise of the vote has become of rather lesser significance than the other attendant benefits of citizenship – access to national insurance systems, unemployment benefits, housing support, health care and social security. In addition to these undoubted advantages, citizens of the European nations within the EU will soon have untrammelled rights to live, work, own property and travel within a wider Europe.

Helots and denizens are, by the same token, symbolically excluded and practically denied all the advantages just listed. In the case of the denizens, this may not be particularly burdensome – a denizen may be an employee of a multinational company with access to private medical insurance. But for a helot, the denial of citizenship is usually a traumatic and life-threatening decision. Given their vulnerability, the helots have become the key means for inducing labour flexibility and providing a target for nationalist and racist outrages.

Our trichotomy leads one to speculate that a new form of stratification has emerged which has little in origin to do with income, occupation, racial or ethnic background, gender, or a particular relationship to the means of production. Of course, there are likely to be coincidences between the different patterns of stratification. A helot is likely to be a 'third world migrant', a member of a stigmatised minority, with low income, holding an unskilled occupation and having limited access to housing, education and other social benefits. Similarly, a professionally educated, urban, middle-class, salary-earner, who happens to be a foreigner, is likely to be a denizen.

Conclusion

Migration after the 1970s to a new country will not necessarily carry the optimistic possibilities characteristic of migrants at the turn of the century. Then the 'huddled masses', at that time from Europe as well as from Asia and Africa, threw off their poverty and feudal bondage to enter the American dream as equal citizens. Equally, it was perfectly possible for English and Irish convicts to become landowners and gentleman farmers in Australia. Nowadays, one's legal or national status – whether, in my terms, a citizen, helot or denizen – will increasingly operate as indelible stigmata, determining a set of life chances, access to the kind of employment or any employment and other indicators of privilege and good fortune.

I have already identified the important legal and practical role states have in admitting immigrants and asylum-seekers. Historically, three general principles have been identified – diplomatic, use-value and nationalist/demographic reasons – in seeking to explain why governments have generous admissions policies. In the case of refugees, the role of international law has also been significant, but high levels of discretion have, until recently, still remained with the individual state.

The qualification 'until recently' refers to the increasing role of the EU in arriving at collective decisions on immigration and refugee matters. Without reviewing the detailed administrative instruments and legal technicalities again, the broad thrust of Community policy is to harmonise all migration decisions on the grounds that after 1 January 1993, when free movement within the EU will be more common, the external boundaries of Europe have to be governed by the same rules.

This increasing harmonisation of immigration and asylum policy will eventually erode the distinctive British tradition described in earlier chapters and the German and French traditions described above. This prospect is more a medium- than a short-term one. For example, unlike the other two countries discussed Britain has stayed out of the Schengen Treaty grouping France, Germany, Italy, Spain, Portugal and the Benelux countries in a common system of regulation. Within the constraints of the Schengen agreements, Germany is preoccupied with the massive problems of unemployment and uneven development consequent on reunification. As shown above, Germany has also had to reconcile the aborted nationalism of earlier periods which resulted in pro-ethnic German policies, labour market gaps and the fear of a massive influx of migrants from Yugoslavia and other former communist states.

France is perhaps politically more ready to bury its distinctive immigration history and its old desire for independent big-country status in favour of the benefits of European integration. Even in France, however, there are special difficulties. These arise from the growth of fundamental Catholicism and the consequent attacks on the Muslim and Arab populations as being 'non-French' and incapable of assimilation. (Even the long-settled Jewish population has been drawn into this maelstrom.) But anti-Islamic sentiments are gradually penetrating the EU as a whole – in Spain and Italy as an aspect of anti-North African feeling; in Germany as a part of anti-Turkish sentiment; and in Britain as witnessed by the controversy surrounding the publication of Salman Rushdie's *The Satanic Verses*.

In this sense, the French have simply ignited a latent but now emerging European consciousness which has its roots in the driving of the Ottomans from the Danube and the Moors from southern Spain. The Holy Roman Empire lives again, though this time it appears more dedicated to the worship of Mammon than God.

CHAPTER   7

Theoretical implications
and conclusion

> [The Englishman's] . . . spoken sense is next to nothing, nine-
> tenths of it palpable *non*-sense: but his unspoken sense, his
> inner silent feeling of what is true, what does agree with fact,
> what is doable and not doable, – this seeks its fellow in the
> world. A terrible worker; irresistible against marshes, moun-
> tains, impediments, disorder, incivilisation; everywhere van-
> quishing disorder, leaving it behind him as method and order.
> – cited C. Hall (1992: 283)

In my opening quote written in 1833 the Scot, Thomas Carlyle,
contrasted the virtues of the practical English with the voluble French.
There was not much point in asking John Bull to give his opinion on
anything for, he claimed, the English were doers not talkers. The
'silent English' were like the 'silent Romans'. Their epics were written
on the surface of the earth – unlike the 'ever-talking, ever-gesticulating
French'. Nowadays, it would be impossible in scholarly circles to get
away with the grand generalisations about national character that were
permissible in Carlyle's day (though popular idiom is probably still
quite close to his way of thinking). The academic objections to his, and
similar, observations are threefold:

- First, there can be no 'essential' national character because this in-
  conceivably assumes a single genetic blueprint radically different
  to that of other nations, or a set of traumatic historical experiences
  that affected the whole nation uniformly.
- Second, Carlyle is atemporal. Were the English always as he
  describes? Just the same, for example, when they were daubing
  themselves with woad or as they approach the twenty-first century?
  Rather, was not his panegyric to the English simply a contingent
  reflection of their commercial and colonial success during the nineteenth centuy?
- Third, if thre first two objections to Carlyle's notion of 'Englishness' are valid, how much more valid would they be when discussing 'Britishness'? Immediately we are forced to consider the
  constitutive identities involved. What about the differences
  between Welsh, Scottish, Irish and English national characters and
  their complicated congruencies and contiguities? What about sub-
  identities based on regional, class and gender differences? And, in
  the late twentieth century, what about ethnically specific identities

held by black or brown Britons, or the European identity all Britons
are invited to share with others on the continent?

Faced with these or similar objections to national essentialisms, historians, social theorists and literary scholars have in recent years developed a large theoretical armoury with which to bombard the problem
of national identity. I cannot hope to do full justice to the rich array of
possible alternatives, but want none the less to relate my account of
British identity to five broad strands of relevant and stimulating theory.
The five strands comprise discussions of: (a) racism, (b) otherness and
difference, (c) boundary formation, (d) nationalism and (e), the
construction of social identities.

What do we mean by racism?

In my introductory chapter and from time to time throughout the text, I
have indicated my caution in equating all expressions of an exclusive
British identity with the notion of 'racism'. It is time now to be more
explicit. I fully accept that when people experience discrimination
because of racial appearance or assumed biological differences
(technically, labelling through phenotypification or genotypification),
using the term 'racist' to describe the perpetrators of the discriminatory
acts is perfectly proper and appropriate.

Difficulties in deploying the term arise, however, when differences
and prejudices are acknowledged to be *socially*, *culturally* or *ideologically* constructed – either by the social actors themselves or by observers and commentators – without explicit reference to appearance or
biology. The proliferation of meanings of 'racism' in such contexts has
led two well known scholars to provide a divided entry in a *Dictionary
of Race and Ethnic Relations* ('Racism' in Cashmore 1988: 247–51).
Both accept that 'the word has been used in so many ways that there is
a danger of it losing any value as a concept' but, whereas Michael
Banton is content to abandon the term in modern settings, Robert
Miles wants to continue to employ the term, with the following explanation: '[Racism] is the attribution of social significance (meaning) to
particular patterns of phenotypical and/or genetic difference which,
along with the characteristic of additional deterministic ascription of
real or supposed other characteristics to a group constituted by descent,
is the defining feature of racism as an ideology' (p. 250). Additionally,
these characteristics must be evaluated negatively and justify unequal
treatment of the defined group.

I found this definition difficult to operationalise. Moreover, in addition to overtly racist acts, this book is concerned about forms of
exclusion which did not obviously or instinctively seem to fit the
'racism' label, even if we treat 'racism' as a generalised ideology of

difference. Before the big waves of non-white migration from the New Commonwealth after the Second World War, anti-Catholicism, anti-Semitism and anti-Irish prejudice were the main forms of group discrimination. It seems doubtful that the word 'racism' – used in English only from the 1940s – can retrospectively be deployed to describe these forms of discrimination. In modern Britain, I discussed deportation and exclusionary asylum policies directed against people who are phenotypically similar to most of the host population. Finally, some of the strongest discriminatory sentiments – for example, anti-Muslim feeling – deploy cultural and religious categories to target their victims with little or no allusion to colour or descent.

Of course, anti-Semitism, anti-Muslim sentiments, or the exclusion of the Irish, the Cypriots and potential migrants from behind the old Iron Curtain can all, with a degree of theoretical inventiveness, be rerendered as forms of 'racism'. Indeed, a number of authors have sought to do so in some or all of the cases mentioned. They usually rely on the power of simile to make their case. The argument would go something like this: of course the Irish, etc. are not a separate 'race' (but we all know that 'races' are artificial social constructs anyway), but as they are *treated* like a different race and *alluded to* in race-like ways, they are 'racialised' and can thus be considered the victims of 'racism'. In short, we can have 'racism' without 'race'.

Other authors have sought to reduce all cognate phenomena to 'race' or 'racism' by a process of rather indiscriminate aggregation. One example is provided by Sarup (1991: 89), who writes: 'It is evident that many racists have the capacity to link the discourses of Englishness, Britishness, nationalism, patriotism, militarism, xeno-phobia and gender difference into a complex system which gives "race" its contemporary meaning.' It is greatly to be hoped that this tendency has now reached its apogee in the subtitle to a recent book, namely: *Racialised Boundaries: Race, Nation, Gender, Colour and Class and the Anti-racist Struggle* (Anthias and Yuval-Davis 1993)

The aggregation procedure is not so much flatly wrong as it is tenu-ous – stretching the elastic band of 'racism' around a fatter and fatter bundle of related (yet importantly distinct) phenomena so thinly that the band is in grave danger of snapping and flying off out of sight. Frankly, so certain was I that this line of thinking could not be of much significance in interpreting my subject-matter, that at first I resolved not even to have a discussion of 'racism'. However, my mind was changed after reading two innovative and insightful accounts.

In the first account considered, Bauman (1991: 62–82) seeks to refute Taguieff's notion that racism and heterophobia (fear of differ-ence) are closely related phenomena. Instead, he proposes a suggestive trichotomy: (a) *heterophobia*, a phenomenon of unease, anxiety, discomfort and a sense of loss of control commonly (and normally in the sense of sanely) experienced when confronted by the unknown; (b) *contestant enmity*, a form of antagonism and hatred generated by the social practices of identity-seeking and boundary-drawing (see my later discussion of these practices). Here, the contestants dramatically separate, or keep a required distance from one another. Separation is necessary precisely *because* the alien threatens to penetrate the opposing group and to blur the distinction between the familiar and the strange; (c) *racism*, which differs from contestant enmity by not admitting any possibility for a certain group of human beings to become part of the rational order. Endemic blemishes and deficiencies make the group unreachable by scientific, technical or cultural manipulation. Racism demands territorial exclusion or (in the case of the Holocaust Jews) extermination.

Without developing a full critique of Bauman, I would simply add that heterophobia may be mediated by curiosity[1] and contestant enmity by mutual interest. Only racism proper (in his sense) is beyond rational challenge. While Bauman's trichotomy can generate a set of rich logical possibilities, in practice my data did not fit all that well. Heterophobia may have characterised (for example) turn-of-the-century reactions to eastern European Jews. But it is an increasingly unlikely phenomenon in modern Britain, if for no more prosaic a reason than that humanity's full variation is displayed – even if imperfectly and through a distorted lens – on the television set (97 per cent of British households have at least one). Other evidence in the book suggests that the processes of 'identity-seeking' and 'boundary-drawing' do indeed occur, but they rarely lead to strong forms of separation. Indeed, as I argued in Chapter 1, the frontiers of identity formation, with the exception of the alien–British boundary, are 'fuzzy' and permeable. On the other hand, my demonstrations of exclusionary conduct go well beyond his two racist possibilities (territorial exclusion or extermination). Included in my discussion are deportations, detentions, nationality, citizenship and other legal restrictions, asylum refusals, hostility against sanctuaries and those seeking to cross identity frontiers, and anticipatory exclusions such as visa controls and fines imposed on carriers of aliens. These provide a much richer array of possible forms of boundary maintenance and exclusion and suggest that the distinction between Bauman's second and third categories is much less clear than he surmises.

The second innovative account of racism that I want to allude to is Goldberg's *Racist Culture* (1993), a treatment by a philosopher who is closely aware of the comparative experience of racism in South Africa, Europe and the USA. A lengthy book is not going to be easily summarised for my purposes, but I take Goldberg's principal starting

---

1   A brief personal experience may be illustrative. When I lived in Nigeria, I had occasion to walk in the poorest streets of the city of Ibadan. The children had clearly never seen an *oyimbo* (white man) close up before and darted in and out pinching me while furiously rubbing at my skin with a wild mixture of excitement, inquisitiveness and consternation. They hoped, their parents explained, to rub off the lighter colouring to reveal the proper skin underneath.

point to be that race and racial thinking have become increasingly normal and diffused among many social actors in most societies. Therefore, whatever the scientific, technical or logical difficulties, we (i.e. commentators or academics) encounter in using the terms 'race', 'racism' etc., it is our job to trace the way in which the notion is inscribed in people's consciousness and lends meaning and direction to their everyday conduct.

Like a tenacious tracker dog, Goldberg himself makes a creditable job of following all the labyrinthine trails and tracks where his rabbit of racism leads. Sometimes he doubles back on himself, sometimes he seems to lose the scent. On many occasions he closes in, but perhaps inevitably never manages to catch the creature by its throat and shake it to death. In the manner of a Bugs Bunny of the conceptual forest, Goldberg's rabbit of racism somersaults free, then multiplies, appearing again and again in different guises – one time as the anthropological 'primitive' or 'tribal', on the next occasion as 'the third world', on the third occasion as an urban 'underclass'. Although Goldberg would probably be unhappy at the medical comparison, I could not help thinking of a free floating virus, where the particular disease contracted is contextually specific and takes different forms, but the virus itself remains potent and continually mutates.

If I have understood Goldberg correctly (and I am not sure I have), he posits the idea of a free-floating set of exclusionary possibilities which attach themselves to different objects ('hosts' in my analogy), and are therefore expressed in different discourses and forms. When sufficiently distinct they become different 'racisms' (with emphasis on the plural). This notion would work quite well with my subject matter as a theoretical explanation of, for example, the way in which different groups have been targets of detention or deportation at different periods. Whereas most historians would insist on providing a causal chain specific to each period and group, Goldberg's analysis of different, but logically connected racisms would allow an underlying pattern to emerge. He is himself aware of the danger of attributing a timeless functionalism to racisms and argues that, although success is not guaranteed, resistance to racisms is possible, even if only along the lines of a gruelling guerrilla campaign (pp. 224, 226):

Resistance to racisms consists in vigorously contesting and disputing exclusionary values, norms, institutions and practices, as well as assertively articulating open-ended specifications and means for an incorporative politics. Where racisms are openly and volubly expressed, it is likely a matter of time before a more or less organised resistance by its objects, often in alliance with other antiracists, will be promoted in response. ... Antiracist means may include confrontation, persuasion, punishment for racist expressions, or sometimes imaginatively rewarding anti- or even nonracist expression.

.

Otherness and difference

A different strand of theory arises from notions of 'Otherness' and 'difference' which, though often vague, have been used with dramatic effect by literary theorists and cultural anthropologists to show how Eurocentric views of the world came to be dominant. For example, Pratt (1986), a scholar of comparative literature, shows how travellers' descriptions of the San of southern Africa (called 'Bushmen') codified difference and fixed 'the Other' in a timeless present. All actions and reactions are thought to be habitual and predictable. The ethnographic present gives a history to the observer (characteristically the European, the insider 'the Self'), but denies coevalness to the observed (the outsider, the alien, 'the Other'). Such an atemporal attribution can be bent to a positive depiction of national character – as in Carlyle's description of the English – but is also highly amenable to racism in the sense used by Bauman. By suggesting that members of 'the Other' are incapable of change, they become unamenable to reason, incapable of change, adaptation or assimilation. This notion of a fixed and negative Other is, as I have shown in my account, very close to the thinking of the hidden frontier guards at the Home Office who, as late as the 1920s would, for example, have found it inconceivable that seven or eight of the descendants of the 'unassimilable' Slavs and Jews would become ministers in Mrs Thatcher's cabinet sixty years later. There is a similar essentialism in (say) Enoch Powell's descriptions of British people of Caribbean descent, who are assumed to be incapable of change in their new environment despite half of their number being born and raised in Britain (according to the 1991 census).

Useful then in showing how those outside the charmed circle are denied an historical consciousness, 'the Other' has also been used to show how Europe distanced itself from other world regions. This process was probed brilliantly by Said in *Orientalism* (1991: 1–3) who argued that the Orient had a special place in Europe's experience as its main cultural contestant and a source of rival civilisations, languages and cultures. The Orient was the source of Europe's 'deepest and most recurring images of the Other. . . . European culture gained in strength and identity by setting itself off against the Orient as a sort of surrogate and even underground self.' If the Orient represented a redoubtable yet ultimately subordinated enemy, Africa and the indigenes of the Americas were so easily enslaved, conquered or infected with European diseases, that their inhabitants (and descendants) became lodged in the European consciousness as inferior beings placed on the lowest rungs of a static hierarchy of racial excellence.

Yet despite the degrading heritage of disparagement, Europeans sensed some affinity with Africans even if they sought to deny and repress their attraction. Missionaries were terrified of being converted by the heathen, Victorian scholars like Burton provided prurient ethnographic descriptions and Rider Haggard's heroes were always being tempted by magnificent and sensuous women, sometimes diplomatically transmogrified into paler-complexioned examples, as in *She* ('who must be obeyed'). As Brantlinger (1986: 215) shows, Kurtz in Conrad's *Heart of Darkness* displays many of the resultant contradictions. In his unrestrained lust and hunger for power he displaces his own 'savage' impulses onto Africans. As Victorians penetrated the heart of darkness 'only to discover lust and depravity, cannibalism and devil worship, they also discovered, as the central figure in the shadows, a Stanley, a Stokes, or a Kurtz – an astonished white face staring back.'

This unexpected twinning of anthropos, this recognition of commonality behind the difference, is paralleled in psychoanalytical writings by Freud's discovery of the unconscious and Jung's theory of subconscious archetypes. These represented a collective personality manifested in dreams, myths and religions (and also in the fantasies of the psychotic). It is notable that Jung's work on archetypes was based on fieldwork among native Americans and Kenyans. In both the literary and psychoanalytical articulations of the Other with the Self, the Self is on a journey of discovery which turns into a quixotic, reflexive and surprising journey of self discovery. The externalised becomes internalised, because it had always been there.

My own initial hypothesis in this book was that 'one only knows who one is by who one is not'. Although expressed in a very simple form, this proposition fits well with the more complex discussion of the Self–Other relationship I have highlighted. As the asylum-seeker, foreigner, stranger or alien is silhouetted and identified, the British are, so to speak, delineating one or other aspect of themselves. Their national identity is thereby being continually defined and redefined. The processes of exclusion and rejection uncover and reveal and become constitutive of the national identity itself.

Despite their allusive, metaphorical and literary quality, discussions of Otherness are inherently more heuristic, subtle and optimistic than many discussions of racism (or 'racisms', to accept Goldberg's corrective). The latter are often pessimistic and denying of the human spirit and characteristically assume that dominant groups are likely always to maintain their hegemony. While it is true that some writers seek to articulate an anti-racist strategy, their nostrums remain ultimately unconvincing because of the overwhelming sense of the inevitability and ubiquity of 'racism' that they have previously depicted. On the other hand, discussions of Otherness easily admit more liberating possibilities of self-examination and auto-critique. Psychological insights can expose the aspects of the Self that resemble the Other or how the Self displaces and projects onto the Other. Equally, an appeal to conscience, common humanity or self-interest can be used to reduce perceived difference. The ethical and progressive possibilities of this strand of theory are particularly marked in Sampson's (1993: 175) plea to commence *Celebrating the Other*, the title of his recent book:

We are obliged to work together with others in a responsible way because who and what we are and who and what they are are intimately and inextricably linked. We cannot be us, nor can they be they without one another: our responsibilities, then, are not simply to avoid the other but of necessity and in recognition of this inherent bonding, to work together on our collective behalf.

Boundary formation

A closely-related strand of theory looks at the processes of boundary formation. In trying to describe how some distinctive objects are made by the mind, Said (1991: 54) suggested that a group of people living on only a few acres of land will set up boundaries between their land, its immediate surroundings and the territory beyond, often designated as 'the land of the barbarians'.[2] It is not required that the barbarians accept the 'us–them' label for the distinction to work. The difference may be arbitrary or fictive: it is enough that 'we' have set up the boundaries of 'us', for 'them' to become 'they'. 'They' have a culture or an identity incompatible with ours. As Said reasons, 'To a certain extent, modern and primitive societies seem thus to derive a sense of their identities negatively.'

Said's contention can be greatly extended by reference to an anthropological debate started by Barth's (1969) notion of ethnic boundaries. For Barth, boundaries can be real or symbolic, visible or invisible. The markers that divide can include territory (see my discussion of nationalism below), history, language, economic considerations, or symbolic identifications of one kind or another. But there are a number of other potential markers – perhaps, Wallman (1986: 230) notes, as many as fourteen. She further avers that once having listed the range of boundary-markers, the problem still remains as to when, whether and which markers the social actors will choose.

In addressing this question Barth had used the metaphor of a boundary 'vessel'. The contents of the vessel would determine the firmness or weakness of the boundary and the significance of the diacritica which differentiated the 'us' from the 'them'. Wallman's important addition to this tradition is to suggest that differences between peoples only turn into ethnic boundaries when 'heated' into significance by the identity investments of either side (irrespective of the actors' consciousness or purpose). In the case of the boundary between the British and the Others, I would suggest that the diacritica include race, religion, language, ethnicity, nationalism and symbolic identifi-

2 This three-fold distinction corresponds well to my notion of family-, cousin-, and stranger-hoods (discussed in Chapter 1) and to the related boundary distinctions between a core identity, a fuzzy frontier and the harder frontier separating off the alien- from the core identity.

cations of many sorts (dress, appearance, accent, manner, the flag, the monarchy, etc.) on the part of the British. However, the temperature of these markers are significantly heated by the social actors I have called 'the open frontier guards'. While politicians like Mr Powell, Lady Thatcher, Lord Tebbit, Winston Churchill Jr, Peter Lilley or Michael Portillo are the stokers, the engineers are 'the hidden frontier guards' at the Home Office, some of whose hitherto covert actions I have spotlighted in this book.

The tradition pioneered by Barth essentially considered ethnic group boundaries without reference to state formation. Parallel work by historians and political philosophers has made useful inroads into the supposed 'naturalness' of national boundaries. One historical account by Sahlins (1992) focuses on the Cerdanya region of Catalonia, divided between France and Spain in 1659. His micro study reveals just how problematic is the assumption that nationality is (or should be) coincident with territory. Locals found themselves insiders, outsiders, then insiders again in bewildering mixes. They became 'political amphibians', donning two or three masks of nationality – sometimes finding that when they sought to discard one or other, their assumed identity embarrassingly 'stuck to their skins.'

The political philosopher, Onara O'Neill (1993a), is equally convinced that far from normally being coincident, boundaries and national identities are characteristically permeable and variable. Boundaries can be made more or less permeable while national identities 'can be reshaped, reformed and recombined.' Her and Sahlins's stress on the indeterminacy, malleability and variability of identity boundaries perhaps goes rather further than I have suggested in the case of the British frontiers of identity, but I share their arguments that boundaries are legitimated not legitimate, that key political and social actors selectively construct the walls that separate, or selectively permit access through the turnstiles and gateways linking the inner and outer worlds. Such selectivity is often supported by an economic ideology, as in the stunning neo-liberal hypocrisy that defends transboundary free trade and capital flows but restricts population mobility (cf. Barry and Goodin 1992). Again, as O'Neill (1993b) emphasises, moral philosophy could not defend an interpretation of sovereignty that constitutes an arbitrary limit to the scope of justice. Yet that is precisely what a national boundary does. It constrains crossing (whether for asylum, travel, migration, abode, work, settlement, or to take up citizenship) but permits transnational economic interaction without transnational powers of taxation or a convincing transnational programme to relieve poverty. In short, there are such things as *just* (fair) borders. Generalised claims to impermeable boundaries made by nationalists cannot therefore be ethically sustained.

Nationalism

The attempt to make the boundaries of nationality and identity coincide is, of course, the nationalists' project. I cannot begin to analyse the thousands of scholarly tracts on the fourth strand of theory considered here, namely nationalism. But it is relevant to notice that an influential book (B. Anderson 1983) treats the nation as an imaginary identity-construct, as real in people's minds as it is in the world. For Anderson (pp. 15–16), the nation is an 'imagined community' with four principal qualities: It is *imagined* because the members of even the smallest nation will never know the most of their fellow members, yet in the minds of each is the image of their commonality. The nation is imagined as *limited* 'because even the largest of them has finite, if elastic boundaries beyond which lie other nations'. (No nation claims to be coterminous with humankind.) It is imagined as *sovereign* in that it displaces (or at least severely undermines) the legitimacy of organised religion or the monarchy. Finally, it is imagined as a *community* because regardless of actual inequality, the nation is conceived of as a deep horizontal comradeship.

This last element of nationalism is a particularly potent explanation for the extraordinary loyalty that the idea of nationalism can command. Men and women apparently willingly die for their nations and go through endless sacrifices to get a nation-state (a territorialised identity) of their own. One can hardly look at a newspaper's front page without seeing an example of this phenomenon, be it in ex-Yugoslavia, the former Soviet Union, Africa, Asia or Europe. The progress of the idea (but some might add also its dilution) over the last half-century can be measured by a simple head count of those nations who have acquired recognised status. When the UN was formed after the Second World War, its membership comprised 50 nation-states, by 1994 there were 184 members, by the end of the century about 200 nation-states will be signed up.

How was a British identity formed and how does it change with the ebb and flow of nationalism at home and abroad? Here the more conventional historians come into their own. Colley (1992: 5–6), for example, makes a convincing case that the British only came to define themselves as a single people after 1707. This was not because of any political or cultural consensus at home, but because of the threat from abroad. She follows Benedict Anderson in accepting that Great Britain was an invented nation superimposed onto much older loyalties and alignments, but adds:

It was an invention forged above all by war. Time and time again, war with France brought Britons, whether they hailed from Wales or Scotland or England, into confrontation with an obviously hostile Other and encouraged them to define themselves collectively against it. They defined themselves as Protestants struggling for survival against the world's foremost Catholic power. They defined themselves against the French as they imagined them to be, superstitious, militarist, decadent and unfree. And, increasingly, as the wars went on, they defined themselves in contrast to the colonial peoples they conquered, peoples who were manifestly alien in terms of culture, religion and colour.

Colley's account is totally compatible with the idea of the British nation as a social construct, a territorialised identity embodying a web of affiliations that are manipulated, modified, elevated or even sometimes abandoned by leading historical actors. Nationalism is evoked in response to a real or perceived external threat (Spain, France, Catholicism, or nowadays South–North and East–West migration); or, the point that Colley misses, an external opportunity (empire, gold mines, the route to the Far East).

This second and historically later aspect of British nationalism, the expansive rather than defensive form of nationalism, largely accounts for the way in which patriotism lost its pre-eighteenth century association with political radicalism and became a property of the conventional right. In the nineteenth century, jingoism substituted for a defence of the (imagined) traditional liberties of the 'freeborn'. Even for the people, and not just for the toffs and the militarists, jingoism brought the ideology of empire, which imparted a source of national pride and a sense of racial and cultural superiority. The empire tradition can still be milked by unscrupulous politicians, as in the Falklands/Malvinas war, but it clearly lost its diminishing significance as the pace of decolonisation grew.

In a sense Britain's post-empire nationalism had nowhere to go to – other than into the arms of the New Right. As Sarup (1991: 91) has argued, essentially Enoch Powell, and later Roger Scruton, Peregrine Worsthorne and the like, articulated a racially based theory of nationalism, where 'the process of national decline is often presented as coinciding with the dilution of once homogeneous stock by alien strains'. 'Race' and 'Nation' have now become elements in a rhetoric of order through which modern conservatism can voice populist protest against Britain's post-imperial plight.

Other historians, with more domestic concerns, have emphasised the nationalist responses to migration from areas not formally in the British Empire. Samuel (1989: xi–xii), for example, points to the crucial role of the Irish in the making of a British national identity:

The Irish formed a distinct underclass in nineteenth-century towns and cities, living in ethnic streets and clustered around their chapels, funeral parlours, and pubs. They suffered a double opprobrium, as the bearers of an alien religion and as a source of cheap labour, and their recalcitrance to authority invited the hostile attention of the Poor Law and the police. The civil war between 'Saxon' and 'Celt' (as it was called at the time of the 1868 election) became a normal feature of the mill towns of Lancashire, the great seaports of the west, and even of such remote districts as the Fife coal field.

While not seeking to deny the important influence of the colonial and imperial heritage in structuring the British identity, Colin Holmes's (1988) magisterial survey of immigration to Britain over the period 1871–1971 includes the graduations and stereotypes developed about European, Chinese and Jewish immigrant groups. By providing a full conspectus he is able to develop a more sophisticated understanding of the role of black Commonwealth immigration in shaping British xenophobic and nationalist responses.

Despite the more nuanced views of the historians the New Right commands some attention in the press, in the Conservative Party and in popular opinion because of its barely concealed references to New Commonwealth migration. It has also provided intellectual support for the 'gut conservatism' of the frontier guards by defending instinctive and inarticulate prejudice in the name of the preservation of 'the culture' of a race, society or nation. In an interesting echo of Carlyle's praise for the tongue-tied English, Roger Scruton, the editor of the *Salisbury Review* and perhaps the most influential of the New Right thinkers, thought that 'illiberal sentiments'

seem to arise inevitably from social consciousness: they involve natural prejudice, and a desire for company of one's own kind. That is hardly sufficient ground to condemn them as 'racist' or to evoke against them those frivolous fulminations which have aptly been described as 'death camp chic' (cited Dummett and Nicol 1990: 239).

Through such taunting of the liberal intelligentsia, the New Right has given a new lease of life to some of the most reactionary forms of British nationalism. At the same time it is important not to exaggerate its appeal. It seems to me doubtful that the New Right can defend for much longer the pretence that Britain once was, or once again can be, racially or culturally homogenous. It is also unlikely that a snobbish appeal to exclusiveness (even if made in the name of the inarticulate) will provide a viable contemporary alternative to patriotism or jingoism. At the level of British decision-makers (who are having increasingly to cope with European and global concerns) nationalist appeals are increasingly anachronistic. And, as far as popular white opinion is concerned, the New Right has about as much genuine rapport with the working classes as the commissars of old had with their rank-and-file.

Another way of understanding the apparent revival of nationalist sentiment in Europe is provided by Husbands (1994) who revives the notion of a 'moral panic' first proposed by Stanley Cohen (1972) to characterise public overreaction, fanned by a news-hungry media, to deviant youth movements. Husbands suggests that anxieties about national identities in Britain, Germany and the Netherlands (and, by inference, France) have analogous features to a moral panic. Sensitivities about Muslim fundamentalism, political asylum and illegal migration have fostered fears of a 'cultural dilution' of the majority's cherished ways and threatened the collective psychic wellbeing. As Husbands concedes, there is not a perfect fit between the upsurge of national moral panics and changes in economic and social conditions which would help give the concept some predictive force. None the less a creative use of the concept provides a useful way of coming to grips with the exaggerated responses to the characteristically minor threats posed by the presence of non-nationals in European societies.

While panics by their very nature flare up then evaporate, I would surmise that in countries like Britain, France and Germany – locked into regional blocs and tied by their dependence on world trade and capital flows – undiluted nationalism will not provide a long-term palliative for anti-foreigner fears, particularly if the ideologues seek to offer the 'nation' as an *exclusive* focus of loyalty and identity. This is because in mature nation-states a Pandora's box of multiple loyalties and identities – nationalist, ethnic, religious, linguistic, cultural and gender based – has already been opened. All compete for attention and affiliation. It is to the marketplace of these identities that I next turn.

The construction of social identities

In recent years, the study of identity has been greatly enhanced by cross-cultural studies in history, sociology, anthropology and psychology. The key point of departure for much discussion is the 'real world' observation that nationalist, regional, racial and ethnic mobilisations are occurring globally and pervasively. At the same time, within (and to some degree between) national, racial or regional units of identification, are other kinds of social groupings – organised often on the axes of age, disability, gender or class. These too are claiming rights or advantages in the name of their particular social affiliation. Such are the persistence, universality *and* simultaneity of these claims, that some academics argue that the construction, reproduction and reshaping of identity is the crucial preoccupation of our era.

These scholarly observations have yielded four major insights which have informed my use of the notion of identity:

- First, in the modern (and what some insist on calling the 'postmodern') world, identity is *fragmented*, a process that starts with the fragmentation and humbling of the human ego itself. Whereas some Eastern philosophers welcomed this insight, the fragmentation of identity proved too threatening for the children of the Enlightenment. In their attempt to recover their identities, or to overcome identity irresolution, groups lash out, often violently, at other neighbouring groups. This is what makes the fragmentation of modern identity-constructs both so important and so potentially dangerous.[3]

- Second, in seeking to overcome fragmentation, there is an important class of identity-constructs which focuses on exclusive *territorial* claims. These I have considered as 'nationalism' and have discussed earlier.

- Third, the modern study of identity has yielded convincing evidence that the phenomenon of *multiple social identities* is much more common than previously had been assumed. These data have dished the old 'essentialisms' – for example, the Marxist idea that all social identity could *essentially* be reduced to class identity. This does not mean that class consciousness does not exist, but rather that there are other competing claims for affiliation that cannot be reduced to epiphenomena. Thus, gender, age, disability, race, religion, ethnicity, nationality, civil status, even musical styles and dress codes, are also very potent axes of organisation and identification. These different forms of identity appear to be upheld simultaneously, successively or separately and with different degrees of force, conviction and enthusiasm.

- But how do individuals attach themselves to, or withdraw from, any one label or category? This question leads to the fourth major insight I deployed in my test – the notion of *situational identity*. The basic idea here is that an individual constructs and presents any one of a number of possible social identities, depending on the situation. Like a player concealing a deck of cards from the other contestants, the individual pulls out a knave – or a religion, an ethnicity, a lifestyle – as the context deems a particular choice desirable or appropriate.

There are obvious limits to the manipulative use of situational identity. It is relatively easy to change a religion or one's clothes. It is less easy to change one's accent, manner and language, though Eliza Doolittle

---

3 Virtually all the major intellectual breakthroughs of the modern world have threatened simplistic notions of self-regard and the over-inflation of our egos. This process probably started with Galileo, who decentred the earth itself when he demonstrated that the planets and the sun did not revolve around us. His compatriots sought to hang him for this bad news. Equally, Darwin showed that man was not a uniquely privileged creature, but simply one species that survived. Other dominant species preceded us, others may follow us. For his pains, the fundamentalists and creationists ban Darwin's work or anyone who adheres to his theory. In his insightful article, Hall (1991) lays emphasis on four other sources of the fragmentation of identity – Marx, Freud, Saussure and post-modernism itself. In each a process of decentring, of humbling and rendering humankind into relative insignificance, takes place – in Marx through the power of economic forces, in Freud through the role of the unconscious and in Saussure through the underlying system of language. Although post-modernists would have to deny this, I would suggest that post-modernism is itself largely the recognition of these unambiguously *modernist* insights into the human condition.

managed it in G. B. Shaw's *Pygmalion*. It is very difficult to alter one's physical appearance, one's phenotype.[4]

The fragmentation, territoriality, multiplicity and situationally specific aspects of British identity have all gained expression in my account. One way of understanding racist and nationalist claims is that they seek to simplify complexity, reduce diversity to singularity and provide an artificial unity in the face of plurality. I see my data as confirming, explaining and demonstrating complexity, diversity and plurality without collapsing into the moral vacuum of total relativism or the grosser absurdities of postmodernist discourse.

Having considered five strands of theory concerned with how a national identity might be construed, I want to turn next to the issue of whether outsiders have a particular role in understanding such an issue.

The stranger: a personal note

In his own attempt to understand the England of the 1930s Felix de Grande-Combe (1933: 303) ended with this admonition to his French compatriots:

If it should happen that you do not understand an English custom, blame only your lack of intelligence, but if after repeated efforts you are still nonplussed, just take a long look at a map of the world and tell yourself that it may well be that what you fail to grasp is possibly the very reason that accounts for the immensity of the British Empire.

His remarks still serve as a warning against the *hubris* of a foreigner. Something that seems offensive, idiosyncratic or illogical may well have a productive, but hidden, social function that the naive observer cannot yet discern.

Many strangers have attempted to understand the societies in which they have found themselves through fate or election. Schutz's (1944: 499–507) classic social-psychological essay highlights two aspects of the stranger's interaction with a host society. The first is an apparent

---

4   Difficult, but by no means impossible – as is demonstrated by the large sales of skin and hair-altering products and by the successful strategy of 'passing', even in such racially divided societies as the USA and South Africa. There are some cultures where the possibility of mistaking one phenotype for another has led to mutilation at an early age to inhibit cross-identification (the facial marks of the Yoruba of south-western Nigeria is one example).

obsession with objective reasoning, less because he[5] has a greater propensity to judge, than because of his

> bitter experience of the limits of 'thinking as usual'. . . . Therefore the stranger discerns, frequently with a grievous clear-sightedness, the rising of a crisis which may menace the whole foundation of the 'relatively natural conception', while all those symptoms pass unnoticed by members of the in-group, who rely on the continuance of their customary way of life.

Schutz's second observation is that the home group sees the stranger's objectivity as criticism, or even a display of disloyalty. The stranger is thought ungrateful because he fails to acknowledge and affirm the culture that has given him shelter and protection. (What the in-group does not understand is that the stranger is unable initially to consider the host-culture as a welcoming sanctuary, but rather sees it, as Schutz avers, 'as a labyrinth in which he has lost all sense of his bearing'.)

One popular axiom that stresses the *positive* side of the stranger's plight is the idea that the spectator sometimes sees more of the game than the player. This aphorism was triumphantly realised in de Tocqueville's *Democracy in America* (1899), a work widely acknowledged as a key insight into the workings of US political institutions.

Britain has also had its fair share of outside commentators, though the reception granted to such observers' writings has normally been less than enthusiastic. Perhaps the only major exception to this rule is the welcome accorded to Hungarian-born George Mikes's book, *How to be an Alien*. First published in 1946 and reprinted and republished 24 times before Mikes's death in 1987, it contains poignant and beguiling vignettes of how to adjust to the manners and customs of his adopted country. There can be few book-buying newcomers to the UK who did not learn to locate some basic cultural landmarks from Mikes's insights.

To the British themselves the book had another function. It was beautifully judged, falling just short of overt criticism and cleverly depicting quite wide differences between the writer and his hosts as charming idiosyncrasies on their part. As this conformed exactly to two elements of the national self image – a sense of humour and tolerance towards eccentricity – the book was a great success. Mikes was embraced by the establishment and, according to the obituary by his publisher André Deutsch, 'he had an enormous circle of friends and was one of the most popular members of the Garrick.'

I am afraid my own account of the formation and reshaping of the British national identity does not match Mikes's formula. For a start there is not much humour ('What d'you mean, there's not any!'); though I hope some gentle irony is visible now and again. More worry-

---

5 'He' in the original, so let me dispense with formal gender equality. 'He', in any case, is closer to 'me' in this instance.

ingly, after I had finished the book I suddenly felt uneasy that it may
be thought to have been written in a vindictive spirit. At any event, for
the record I most vehemently deny any malicious intention. Puzzle-
ment, concern, disappointment, indignation, yes – I had all these
reactions as I dug deeper into the relationship between those who
spoke for 'the British' and those who at various times constituted 'the
Other'. But I have no wish for the book to be read as a generalised
anti-British or anti-English tract. Such a stereotyped critique of total
nations is decisively not what *Frontiers of Identity* is about.

In the book itself I have quoted Queen Victoria on religious tolerance approvingly and applauded the current monarch for her pro-Com-
monwealth stance. I have written of the MPs who defended those
caught in the web of immigration laws, the journalists who exposed
abuses of power, the judges who tried to stop the erosion of *habeas
corpus*, the refugee agencies who pleaded for the mitigation of harsh
asylum laws, the priests and imams who gave sanctuary to those
threatened with deportation and the British friends, neighbours and
relatives who protected those they saw as unjustly victimised by the
immigration authorities.

Beyond the book I think of the many people who work for humanitarian causes, racial justice and religious tolerance. I think of the Rock
Against Racism concerts and the tens of thousands of students who
turned out in anti-apartheid marches. But, I emphasise, my admiration
of many British people is not confined to the '*Guardian*-reading
public', as the 'progressive' forces in Britain are so often caricatured.

I think, for example, of the district officer in Nigeria who spent half
a lifetime drawing the botanical specimens of that country; of the
medical officer in St Helena patiently explaining health care to young
mothers; of the honest British copper in Hong Kong trying to keep out
of the graft that surrounded him; of the pink-faced British official at
the Council of Europe trying to apologise for the boorishness of a well
known Northern Ireland politician; of the senior citizens with bright,
quick eyes who came to my lectures on colonial nationalism in the
small halls of the London Co-operative Society in the early 1960s.
There is no way my book is an attack on any of these fine British
people, or the millions like them.

At the same time, I do not pretend to be making bloodless, neutral
judgements of particular institutions or individuals and, with Schutz, I
feel that I have detected some more alarming general symptoms of a
rising crisis – whether with 'grievous clear-sightedness' or not I will
not presume to say. I trust the evidence adduced in the body of the
book provides enough empirical ballast to convince the reader that my
observations and conclusions transcend mere prejudice.

Observations: institutions and individuals

First, I am opposed to the open frontier guards like Enoch Powell, Margaret Thatcher and Norman Tebbit who openly defend a narrow nationalism and seek to delineate 'the Other'. Of course it is important to understand the varying nuances of their positions – for example, Thatcher is a fervent Atlanticist, while Powell sounded like a Trotsky- ist when he talked of the USA. I am opposed too to politicians like Peter Lilley who run campaigns against 'foreigners scrounging off our welfare services' or Michael Portillo, the son of a Spanish Republican exile to Britain, who propounded the bizarre notion to Southampton university students that 'If any of you have got an A level it is because you have worked to get it. Go to any other country, and when you have got an A level you have bought it' (*Daily Telegraph* 5 Feb. 1994). Some of these inane sentiments no doubt arise from political panic. But such crabby, mean-spirited statements do much more harm than is commonly acknowledged. By playing to the populist gallery, to ata- vistic heterophobia and modern xenophobia, these 'open' frontier guards lend a veneer of respectability to intolerant ideas and encourage the exercise of covert power against the outsider.

A number of defences of British nationalism are closely analogous to Le Pen's ideas, with a peculiar notion of 'culture' substituting for the role of biology. The classical bias of the New Right English intelli- gentsia contrasts with the natural science bias in France: but both are building elaborate bastions against invasive alien forces. I simply res- pond to such notions by pointing to the naive, ahistorical and monochromatic ideas of the nation to which such thinkers apparently subscribe. Society and nation (like culture and biological organisms) have always been, and continue to be, enriched and invigorated by diversity and difference.

Of course one has to concede the ultimate possibility that the ad- mixture of strangers can eventually fundamentally alter and even subvert a host culture. But in both Britain and France we normally are talking of small fractions of the population (under 6 per cent of the population are of New Commonwealth origin in the UK and a similar figure obtains for residents of Arab origin in France). The implication that the adults of these minorities share nothing in common with Euro- pean society is wholly fallacious and, of course, the children of such minority groups are already strongly socialised into the language and social norms of their host societies. To proclaim intellectually that hostility to such small groups is legitimate and 'natural' is the moral equivalent of celebrating the virtues of a bully in a playground.

Second, I am against the exercise of discretionary power – in all arms of government – but of course I have been concerned particularly with the 'hidden' frontier guards at the Home Office. The argument here is more finely balanced. I personally know of a number of Asian, African or Caribbean people and refugees from other countries who have been treated sympathetically after representations to officials. This is the justification for such powers – allowing a humane judgement to temper the rules where they do not exactly cover the situation. But I am persuaded by the contrary argument i.e. a better mode of government starts with a clear statement of the limits to delegated authority and places such authority under strict parliamentary control and judicial supervision.

I find this alternative preferable for two reasons. Time and again, as I have shown in the book, the 'hidden' frontier guards (the Troups and Pedders of this world) are working with narrow or outdated outlooks and secretly bending the will of parliament to their own preferences. The other reason is drawn from what may be an unexpected source, David (now Lord) Waddington. While minister of state at the Home Office responsible for immigration and later as home secretary, he complained angrily that he would not give special consideration to the cases of those who were supported by public campaigns or MPs' representations, on the grounds that those who were *not* so supported also needed their cases fairly considered. This seems to me to be an irrefutable argument for the equal and, where possible, open consideration of all immigration cases. What one loses by the exercise of sympathetic discretion in individual cases, one more than gains by even-handedness and justice being seen to be done in all cases.

Third, I am disheartened at the norms that seem to have grown up in the Immigration Service Union, the body that organises the 'functionary' frontier guards. It is natural that a group doing an unpopular and difficult job draws into itself and tries to maintain an *esprit de corps* in the face of the angry people with whom they often have to deal (think of traffic wardens, prison officers or the mainland troops in Northern Ireland). But in no way can this justify the evidence of special lobbying by the union I adduced in Chapter 3, or the clear and irrefutable findings of a formal investigation by the Commission for Racial Equality[6] (CRE 1985: 130–1, 132) that 'members of some racial groups were considerably more likely to be closely examined'.

So alarmed was it at the evidence of discrimination at the ports of entry that the Commission recommended 'a new ethos to be generated and to permeate the system, affecting procedures, training and all management and supervision systems'. Because they are the first representatives of the British nation that outsiders meet, it is vital that immigration officers should be welcoming, have irreproachable characters, be representative of white and non-white Britons and do their jobs precisely according to the book.

Fourth, the Conservative government's mania for privatising everything has gone 'over the top' in the case of the use of private security guards at immigration detention centres. I have quoted reports and

---

6 The Home Office applied to the High Court to stop this investigation from ever taking place, but failed in its bid.

have observed in my visit to the *Earl William* detention ferry that these guards are wholly untrained in inter-personal skills, have no relevant language capacities, and are generally unsympathetic even to people who are clearly in a state of considerable distress. It is, perhaps, just possible to argue that private security firms could back up trained staff at the SEAs and airport detention centres – which are essentially temporary holding pens for those who are alleged to be illegal entrants. But to use such staff in detention centres for asylum-seekers – detainees who, after all, have committed no crime and may have just experienced torture, seen their loved ones killed or their homes destroyed – this clearly is unconscionable.

The French authorities use the Croix Rouge to support such people when they first arrive. We[7] should also use the Red Cross, the St John Ambulence Brigade, the Red Crescent and equivalent voluntary bodies. The desired ambience should suggest care, concern and therapy, not suspicion and punishment. By treating asylum-seekers as criminals, we are presuming their 'guilt' (as 'illegal entrants' or 'economic migrants') before their cases have been heard. This rupture of our much admired judicial tradition of assuming innocence before the proof of guilt has the dangerous prospect of spreading to other stigmatised groups.

Fifth, during the course of preparing this study I have had to read hundreds of clippings of legal judgements on immigration matters. I have drawn attention to some of the most important cases where the judiciary acted to restrain the abuse of administrative power, including the judgement that Kenneth Baker, while home secretary, acted in contempt of court. But, as I read the clippings, I could not help thinking of my birthplace, South Africa, in the 1960s, with the government 'plugging loopholes' as they called it, with extra legislation and bolder administrative diktats every time the courts found against it. We desperately need leading members of the judiciary, as a body, to protest against the erosion of *habeas corpus* and appeal rights in immigration and asylum cases. Again, if unbridled executive authority gets its way here, there is a danger of a malignant spread to the citizenry as a whole.

Sixth, among the progressive forces which can serve to build bridges between the British and the 'others' are the orthodox religions. The revival of sanctuary in the 1980s provided a golden opportunity to

---

7 The alert reader may have noticed that, truly unconsciously, I slipped for the first time into the use of 'we', rather than 'the British people', 'the British government', etc. Schutz (1944: 502) was there before me: 'The approaching stranger, however, is about to transform himself from an unconcerned onlooker into a would-be member of the approached group. The cultural pattern of the approached group, then, is no longer a subject matter of his thought, but a segment of the world that has to be dominated by actions. . . . Jumping from the stalls to the stage, so to speak, the former onlooker becomes a member of the cast, enters as a partner into social relations with his co-actors, and participates henceforth in the action in progress.'

celebrate the Church's more elevated past and to create a dialogue between the Christian and the other faiths. Christianity, in particular, has the capacity to transcend mere phenotype; the deep Christian convictions of the British-Caribbean population could be used to counteract the racial consciousness that still isolates the population of Caribbean origin and descent.

While much has been done at the parish level and in bodies like the British Council of Churches, the dignitaries of the Church seem to be wedded to having full coffers and empty pews. I doubt that I am the only middle-aged fogey that believes religion should be about morality and taking intrepid ethical positions. (I also believe, though this is incidental to my purpose, that such stands will pay off in terms of attracting new adherents to a faith.) The treatment of asylum-seekers in modern Britain seems to me to call for an unambiguous moral pronouncement, a clarion call from the top leadership of all the Christian churches. Instead the hierarchy seem to believe that the bad odour that attaches to their vestments and mitres will miraculously dissipate if they remain perfectly silent and totally invisible.

Seventh, as argued in Chapter 5, the conventional left- and anti-racist protestors have often found themselves shouting inappropriate slogans representing past causes. The reception and treatment of asylum-seekers in Britain has long superseded any simple notion of white versus black. By clinging to the vague solidarity implied by the word 'black', those who oppose the harsh treatment of foreigners will not be talking the same language as the Vietnamese, Hong Kong Chinese, Kurds, Iranians, Cypriots and Africans who have already suffered grievously. They will be unable to relate their present claims for justness and fairness to Britain's pre-1945 history. Moreover, their precognition will be unable to take account of the likelihood that the next wave of victims will be white refugees from eastern Europe, not black Commonwealth and Pakistani migrant workers.

The pamphleteers and sloganeers have also been slow to recognise that the European context of much immigration law and practice will increasingly mean effecting alliances with sympathetic groups on the continent and not seeking always to fight the good fight on their own parochial patch with their own half-forgotten formulae.

Eighth, sections of the popular press are simply so ill-informed and misleading in their coverage of immigration and refugee matters that their victims should be allowed a compulsory right of reply. In their anti-foreigner paranoia some newspapers make no attempt whatever to distinguish between family visitors, tourists, students, intending immigrants, dependants and asylum-seekers. The cartoons they carry are frequently vicious or crass and reproduce offensive and dated racial stereotypes. Their editorials are often so prejudiced as to be debasing to the human spirit. There is now a widely accepted argument that those whose lives have been disrupted by irresponsible reporting (and who cannot afford the gagging writs and libel actions that protect all the rich and powerful, except royalty) should have some recourse against the press. Equally, where provocative and misleading racial slurs are made, there should be the right for responsible bodies like the CRE to correct erroneous or offensive reports with counter-information occupying equivalent space and prominence. The resulting turgid prose will soon stop any further abuse of press power. (Can this be another joke?)

Symptoms, recommendations ... and a bit of evangelism

Let me return under this heading to some final thoughts on what Schutz identified as 'symptoms' of a 'rising crisis' that may through over familiarity go unnoticed, but if left unresolved threaten to undermine our conventional moorings and the very substance of our British identity.

My first suggestion is that there should be continuing public pressure to 'solve the Irish problem'. The debates about Scottish devolution and Welsh nationalism will take their course in a peaceful if not entirely painless way. But the running sore of Northern Ireland is simply not responding to the same dogged remedies of the politicians. This remains an unresolved frontier of identity, with lethal consequences for many innocent Britons.

Seen in the terms used in the first chapter of this study, the Protestant settlers in Ireland are essentially similar to the white Britons in the rest of the British diaspora, and they will have to face the same ultimate choice – repatriation or the adoption of the local citizenship. The carving out of Northern Ireland in 1921 so that a Protestant majority was artificially created served to delay the choice, but will not finally obviate it.

A second symptom which menaces the underpinnings of the British identity is the alarming collapse of individual rights and the increasing capacity of the prime minister of the day to use automatic parliamentary majorities to ram through legislation threatening historic freedoms. I have alluded to this issue already in my comment on the shaky status of *habeas corpus* and appeal rights in immigration cases. But the continuing impasse in Northern Ireland is also brutalising the army and police force, thus adding greatly to the demoralising picture of the UK as the country with the most human rights violations in Europe (see Table 7.1).

If this table is not a strong enough inducement to constitutional reform, I do not know what will be. With Lord Scarman, Lord Chief Justice Taylor and others, I see no reason why the European Convention on Human Rights should not be fully incorporated into our domestic law. This will serve as a strong disincentive to vainglorious politicians and serve to restrain the arbitrary use of bureaucratic authority. Immigrants, aliens, asylum-seekers and British citizens alike will all be better protected.

Table 7.1 *Human Rights Violations in Europe to 1987*

Country	No. of violations found by Committee of Ministers	No. of violations found by European Court of Human Rights
Austria	4	11
Belgium	3	10
France	0	1
Germany	1	7
Greece	1	0
Eire	0	2
Italy	0	10
Netherlands	1	8
Portugal	0	2
Sweden	1	2
Switzerland	3	4
UK	37	19
Total	51	76

Note: No violations have been found against Denmark, Iceland, Liechtenstein, Luxembourg, Malta, Norway or Spain.

Source: *Independent* (30 Nov. 1988) citing official data.

My third concern is that we have retreated from our obligations and turned our backs on our friends in the Commonwealth much too harshly and much too precipitously. Most of the supporting argument for this view has already been made in Chapter 1, so let me just quickly summarise. We cannot once again assume the white man's burden. (For a start, that would offend the 50 per cent of our people who are women and the 6 per cent who are black.) But issues like environmental damage, poverty, famine, human rights abuses, the transfer of intermediate technology, gender and development or the spread of democracy are at the top of many British youngsters' political agendas.

The Commonwealth, particularly its poorer members, could become a focus for their idealism and enthusiasms. Instead of encouraging such an identification, the government of the day has cold-shouldered the poor Commonwealth, to the point that even Lady Chalker, the Tory minister for overseas development, was constrained to protest loudly at our miserly aid allocation.

Fourth, given the evidence of the abuse of power by civil servants and politicians in the case of asylum-seekers, there is a good case to establish a quasi-independent Office for the Recognition, Protection and Welfare of Refugees, along the lines of the French OFPRA. Since 1979, the main forms of abuse have been two: the immediate rush to legislation or judicial appeal whenever the courts have found against the actions of an official or a minister and second, the sense of an unscalable and united wall of IOs, Home Office officials, police and media. Such agents and agencies should not be in sole charge of evaluating asylum claims.

My proposed office would have the role of *deciding* on the grant of refugee status on evidence and argument presented *both* by the Home Office and the asylum-seeker alike. The office would also have the power to call for independent medical advice and expert testimony concerning conditions in the country of departure.

Finally, I trust it is not being *too* evangelical or idealistic to say that a nation needs to have a self-image and a role – a part of its national identity – that transcends the mere money-grubbing individualism of recent years. Mrs Thatcher's notorious and ignorant comment that 'there is no such thing as society' exposed her own lamentable and desiccated *Weltanschauung*. Talking tough to foreigners, talking big about very modest economic achievements, sending British troops to 'bash the Argies' – this is a phoney and vulgar voice of 'Great' Britain. It furnishes faint echoes of our stirring imperial past, but is a pathetic, Disney World, plaster copy of it.

The real greatness in Great Britain lies in the rule of law; its (relative) tolerance to strangers; its (again relative) acceptance of other religions; the free, independent and critical parts of its press; the independence of its broadcasting authorities; the amusing self-denigration of its talking classes; its sparkling drama; its pragmatic tradition of problem solving; the genius of its research scientists wresting Nobel prize winning solutions out of Heath Robinson equipment, its rich vibrant language, its traditions of fair play and due process; its heritage of Empire and Commonwealth. . . .

These are the key components of British identity that we should be diffusing in Europe and sharing with our co-citizens on the continent as we jointly explore the frontiers of our emerging European identity. It behoves us also to remind ourselves forcibly that beyond the cosy European club of 'fat cats' is a wider potentiality and an even greater challenge – the elaboration and construction of a global identity and citizenship.

REFERENCES

A–DWG [Anti-Deportation Working Group] (1985) *The Right to be Here*, London: A–DWG.

AFA–DC [Andy and Farida Anti-Deportation Campaign] (n.d.) *A Long, Sharp Shock: Racism, the Criminal Law and the Threatened Deportation of Andy Anderson*, Manchester: AFA–DC.

AI [Amnesty International] (1990) *Memorandum to the Governments of Hong Kong and the United Kingdom Regarding the Protection of Vietnamese Asylum-seekers in Hong Kong*, London: AI International Secretariat.

Anderson, Benedict (1983) *Imagined Communities*, London: Verso.

Anderson, Perry (1992) *English Questions*, London: Verso.

Angier, Carole (1992) *Jean Rhys: Life and Work*, London: André Deutsch.

Anthias, Floya and Nina Yuval-Davis (1993) *Racialised Boundaries: Race, Nation, Gender, Colour and Class and the Anti-racist Struggle*, London: Routledge.

Barry, Brian and Robert E. Goodin (eds) (1992) *Free Movement: Ethical Issues in the Transnational Migration of People and Money*, New York: Harvester Wheatsheaf.

Barth, Frederick (1969) *Ethnic Groups and Boundaries*, Bergen: Universitetsforlaget.

Batsleer, Janet (1988) 'The Viraj Mendis Defence Campaign: Struggles and Experiences of Sanctuary', *Critical Social Policy*, 22, Summer, 72–9.

Bauman, Zigmunt (1991) *Modernity and the Holocaust*, Cambridge: Polity Press.

Bean, Philip and Joy Melville (1989) *Lost Children of the Empire*, London: Unwin Hyman.

Berghahn, Marion (1984) *German–Jewish Refugees in England*, Leamington Spa: Berg Publishers.

Bindoff, S. T. (1961) *Tudor England*, Harmondsworth: Pelican.

Blaschke, Jochen (1992) 'Refugee Policy and East–West Migration in the Federal Republic of Germany', Paper for a conference organised by the Office Français de Protection des Réfugiés et Apartides, Paris, 11–13 June.

Boeles, P. (1992) 'Schengen and the Rule of Law' in Meijers *et al. q.v.*, 135–46.

Böhning, W. R. (1972) *The Migration of Workers in the United Kingdom and the European Community*, London: Oxford University Press.

Brantlinger, Patrick (1986) 'Victorians and Africans: The Genealogy of the Myth of the Dark Continent' in Henry Louis Gates Jr *q.v.*, 185–222.

BRC [British Refugee Council] (1985) *Refugee Adviser's Handbook*, London: BRC.

—— (1987) *Settling for a Future: Proposals for a British Policy on Refugees*, London: BRC.

Butcher, Ivor J. and Philip E. Ogden (1984) 'West Indians in France: Migration and Demographic Change' in Philip E. Ogden (ed.) *Migrants in Modern France: Four Studies*, Occasional paper 23, Department of Geography and Earth Science, Queen Mary College, University of London.

Cashmore, E. Ellis (ed.) (1988) *Dictionary of Race and Ethnic Relations*, London: Routledge.

Castells, Manuel (1979) 'Immigrant Workers and Class Struggles in Advance Capitalism: the Western European Experience' in R. Cohen *et al. Peasants and Workers: the Struggles of Third World Workers*, New York: Monthly Review Press, 353–79.

Castles, Stephen and Godula Kosack (1985) *Immigrant Workers and the Class Structure in Western Europe*, Oxford: Oxford University Press, 2nd edition [first edition 1973].

Castles, Stephen *et al.* (1984) *Here for Good: Western Europe's New Ethnic Minorities*, London: Pluto.

CCCS [Centre for Contemporary Cultural Studies] (1982) *The Empire Strikes Back*, London: Hutchinson.

CCWAG [Cypriot Community Workers' Action Group] (1982), *Compulsory Deportations: The Case of Cypriot Refugees Living in the United Kingdom*, London: CCWAG.

Cesarani, David (1987) 'Anti-Alienism in England after the First World War', *Immigrants and Minorities*, 6 (1), 5–29.

—— (1992) 'Barred from Fortress Britain', *Times Higher Educational Supplement*, 3 Jan.

Charter '87 (1990) Newsletter of Charter '87: A Charter for Refugees, Cambridge, March.

Chesnais, Jean-Claude (1990) 'Migration from Eastern to Western Europe, Past (1946–1989) and Future (1990–2000)', Paper presented to second meeting of senior officials entrusted with the preparing of the Conference of Ministers on the Movement of Persons Coming from Central and Eastern European Countries, *Council of Europe*, Strasbourg, 8–9 Nov.

Cohen, Robin (1987) *The New Helots: Migrants in the International Division of Labour*, Aldershot: Gower.

Cohen, Stanley (1972) *Folk Devils and Moral Panics*, London: MacGibben and Kee [new ed. 1980].

Cohen, Steve (1987) *It's the Same Old Story: Immigration Controls against Jewish, Black and Asian People with Special Reference to Manchester*, Manchester: Manchester City Council Public Relations Office.

—— (1988) *A Hard Act to Follow: The Immigration Act 1988*, Manchester: South Manchester Law Centre and the Viraj Mendis Defence Campaign.

Colley, Linda (1992) *Britons: Forging the Nation 1707–1837*, New Haven: Yale University Press.

CRE [Commission for Racial Equality] (1985) *Immigration Control Procedures: Report of a Formal Investigation*, London: CRE.

Cross, Malcolm (1988) 'Migrants and New Minorities in Europe' , unpublished paper, Coventry, Centre for Research in Ethnic Relations, University of Warwick.

Cross, Malcolm and Han Entzinger (eds) (1988) *Lost Illusions: Caribbean Minorities in Britain and the Netherlands*, London: Routledge.

CRRU/BCC [Community and Race Relations Unit/British Council of Churches] (n.d.) *Why Sanctuary? An Information and Discussion Pack*, London: British Council of Churches.

Cunningham, W. (1969) *Alien Immigrants to England*, with a new Introduction by C. Wilson, New York: Augustus M. Kelley [first edition 1897].

Dasent, J. R. (1890) *Acts of the Privy Council of England, New Series, Vol. VII, AD 1558–1570*, London: HMSO.

Deedes, William (1968) *Race Without Rancour*, London: Conservative Political Centre.

de Grande-Combe, Felix (1933) *England This Way! Tu Viens en Angleterre*, London: Ivor Nicholson & Watson.

de Tocqueville, Alexis (1899) *Democracy in America*, 2 vols., New York: The Colonial Press [first published in 1835].

Diller, Janelle M. (1988) *In Search of Asylum: Vietnamese Boat People in Hong Kong*, Washington, DC: Indochina Resource Action Center.

d'Orey, S. (1984) *Immigration Prisoners: a Forgotten Minority*, London: Runnymede Trust.

Dowty, A. (1987) *Closed Borders: The Contemporary Assault on Freedom of Movement*, New Haven: Yale University Press.

Duffield, Mark (1988) *Black Radicalism and the Politics of Deindustrialisation*, Aldershot: Gower.

Dummett, Ann and Andrew Nicol (1990) *Subjects, Citizens, Aliens and Others*, London: Weidenfeld and Nicolson.

ECRE [European Consultation on Refugees and Exiles] (1983) *Asylum in Europe: A Handbook for Agencies Assisting Refugees*, London: ECRE, 3rd edition.

Fawcett, J. E. S. (1969) *The Application of the European Convention on Human Rights*, Oxford: Clarendon Press.

Foucault, Michel (1979) *Discipline and Punish: The Birth of the Prison*, Harmondsworth: Penguin.

Freeman, Gary P. (1979) *Immigrant Labor and Racial Conflict in Industrial Societies: The French and British Experience, 1945–1975*, Princeton: Princeton University Press.

Gates, Henry Louis Jr (ed.) (1986) *'Race', Writing and Difference*, Chicago: University of Chicago Press.

Gillman, Peter and Leni Gillman (1980) *'Collar the Lot!' How Britain Interned and Expelled its Wartime Refugees*, London: Quartet Books.

Gilroy, Paul (1987) *'There Ain't No Black in the Union Jack': The Cultural Politics of Race and Nation*, London: Hutchinson.

Glazer, Nathan and Daniel P. Moynihan (1963) *Beyond the Melting Pot: The Negroes, Puerto Ricans, Jews, Italians and Irish of New York City*, Cambridge, Mass.: Massachusetts Institute of Technology Press.

GMIAU [Greater Manchester Immigration Aid Unit] (1990) Newsletter, 3, Summer.

Goldberg, D. J. and J. D. Raynor (1989) *The Jewish People: Their History and Religion*, Harmondsworth: Penguin.

Goldberg, David Theo (1993) *Racist Culture: Philosophy and the Culture of Meaning*, Oxford: Blackwell Publishers.

Goodwin-Gill, G. S. (1978) *International Law and the Movement of Persons Between States*, Oxford: Clarendon Press.

—— (1983) *The Refugee in International Law*, Oxford: Clarendon Press.

—— (1988) '"Nonrefoulement" and the New Asylum-seekers' in D. A. Martin (ed.) *The New Asylum Seekers: Refugee Law in the 1980s*, Dordrecht: Martinus Nijhoff.

Gordon, Paul (1981) *Passport Raids and Checks: Britain's Internal Immigration Controls*, London: Runnymede Trust.

—— (1985) *Policing Immigration: Britain's Internal Controls*, London: Pluto Press.

Goulbourne, Harry (1991) *Ethnicity and Nationalism in Post-Imperial Britain*, Cambridge: Cambridge University Press.

Grahl-Madsen, A. (1972) *The Status of Refugees in International Law, vol. II*, Leiden: A. W. Sijthoff.

Green, Penny (1990) *Private Sector Involvement in the Immigration Detention Centres*, London: Howard League for Penal Reform.

Hall, Catherine (1992) *White, Male and Middle Class: Explorations in Feminism and History*, Cambridge: Polity Press.

Hall, Stuart (1991) 'Ethnicity: Identity and Difference', *Radical America*, 23 (4), 1991, 9–20.

Hammar, Tomas (1990) *Democracy and the Nation State*, Aldershot: Avebury.

Hansen, Emmanuel (1977) *Frantz Fanon: Social and Political Thought*, Columbus: Ohio State University Press.

Herskovitz, M. (1958) *The Myth of the Negro Past*, Boston: Beacon Press.

Hoch, Paul K. (1985) 'No Utopia: Refugee Scholars in Britain', *History Today*, Nov., 53–6.

Holmes, Colin (1988) *John Bull's Island: Immigration and British Society, 1871–1971*, Basingstoke: Macmillan.

—— (1991) *A Tolerant Country: Immigrants, Refugees and Minorities in Britain*, London: Faber & Faber.

Holt, Richard (1990) *Sport and the British: A Modern History*, Oxford: Oxford University Press.

Home Office Statistical Bulletins (various years).

Homze, E. L. (1967) *Foreign Labor in Nazi Germany*, Princeton: Princeton University Press.

Husbands, Christopher T. (1991) 'The Mainstream Right and the Politics of Immigration in France: Major Developments in the 1980s', *Ethnic and Racial Studies*, 14 (2), April, 170–98.

—— (1994) 'Crises of National Identity as the "New Moral Panics": Political Agenda-Setting about Definitions of Nationhood', *New Community*, 20 (2) Jan., 191–206.

ICIHI [Independent Commission on International Humanitarian Issues] (1986) *Refugees: Dynamics of Displacement*, London: Zed Books.

ILO [International Labour Office] (1984) *World Labour Report, vol. 1*, Geneva: ILO.

IND [Immigration and Nationality Department of the Home Office] (various years) *Report*, London: The Home Office.

James, Brian (1988) 'The Myth of a "Martyrdom"', *The Times*, 2 Aug., 9.

James, C. L. R. (1963) *The Black Jacobins*, New York: Vintage Books.

JCWI [Joint Council for the Welfare of Immigrants] (1989) *Unequal Migrants: The European Community's Unequal Treatment of Migrants and Refugees*, London and Coventry: JCWI and the Centre for Research in Ethnic Relations, University of Warwick.

Joly, Danièle (1989) 'Resettling Refugees from Vietnam in Birmingham', in D. Joly and R. Cohen (eds) *q.v.*, 76–95.

—— (1993) 'Political Decisions on Asylum', Paper to an International Seminar on Emerging Trends and Major Issues in Migration and Ethnic Relations in Western and Eastern Europe organised by UNESCO and the Centre for Research in Ethnic Relations, University of Warwick, Coventry, 5–8 Nov.

Joly, Danièle and Robin Cohen (eds) (1989) *Reluctant Hosts: Europe and its Migrants*, Aldershot: Avebury.

Jones, Peter R. (1982) *Vietnamese Refugees: A Study of their Reception and Resettlement in the United Kingdom*, Research & Planning Unit Paper, 13, London: Home Office.

Kasinsky, Renee (1976) *Refugees from Militarism*, New Brunswick: Transaction Books.

Kay, Diana and Robert Miles (1992) *Refugees or Migrant Workers? European Volunteer Workers in Britain, 1946–1951*, London: Routledge.

Kaye, Ronald and Roger Charlton (1990) *United Kingdom Refugee Admission Policy and the Politically-Active Refugee*, Research Papers in Ethnic Relations, No. 13, Coventry: Centre for Research in Ethnic Relations, University of Warwick.

Kindleberger, Charles P. (1967) *Europe's Post-war Growth: The Role of Labor Supply*, Cambridge: Harvard University Press.

Kosmin, Barry (1981) 'Exclusion and Opportunity: Traditions of Work amongst British Jews' in P. Braham *et al.* (eds) *Discrimination and Disadvantage in Employment: The Experience of Black Workers*, London: Harper & Row in association with the Open University Press, 185–98.

Lafitte, F. (1940) *The Internment of Aliens*, Harmondsworth: Penguin.

Lal, Victor (1990) *Fiji, Coups in Paradise: Race, Politics and Military Intervention*, London: Zed Books.

Landa, M. J. (1911) *The Alien Problem and its Remedy*, London: P. S. King & Son.

Layton-Henry, Zig (1990) (ed.) *The Political Rights of Migrant Workers in Western Europe*, London: Sage Publications.

LCHMT [Lords Commissioner of His Majesty's Treasurer under the direction of the Master of the Rolls] (1929) *Acts of the Privy Council of England*, London: HMSO.

—— (1930) *Acts of the Privy Council of England*, London: HMSO.

Lerner, J. and R. Roy (1984) 'Numbers, Origins, Economic Value and Quality of Technically-Trained Immigrants into the United States', *Scientometrics*, 6 (4).

Lévi-Strauss, Claude (1977) *Tristes Tropiques*, Harmondsworth: Penguin.

Little, Kenneth (1947) *The Negroes: A Study of Racial Relations in English Society*, London: Kegan Paul, Trench, Trubner & Co.

MacMaster, N. (1991) 'The "seuil de tolérance": The uses of a "Scientific" Racist Concept', in M. Silverman *q.v.*

Marie, C. G. (1983) *L'immigration clandestine et travail clandestin*, Paris: Ministère des Affairs Sociales et de la Solidarité Nationale.

Marrus, Michael R. (1985) *The Unwanted: European Refugees in the Twentieth Century*, New York: Oxford University Press.

Marshall, T. H. (1950) *Citizenship and Social Class and Other Essays*, New York: Cambridge University Press.

Marx, Karl (1976) *Capital*, (Vol. 1), Harmondsworth: Pelican in association with New Left Review.

May, Roy and Robin Cohen (1972) 'The Interaction between Race and Colonialism: A Case Study of the Liverpool Race Riots of 1919', *Race and Class*, 16 (2), 111–26.

Meijers, H. *et al.* (1992) *Schengen: Internationalisation of Central Chapter on the Law on Aliens, Refugees, Security and Police*, Utrecht: W. E. J. Tjeenk Willinck for the Permanent Commission on International Aliens, Refugee and Criminal Law.

Mikes, George (1946) *How to be an Alien*, London: André Deutsch.

Miller, S. C. (1974) *The Unwelcome Immigrant: The American Image of the Chinese, 1785–1882*, Berkeley: University of California Press.

Misham, E. J. (1970) 'Does Immigration Confer Economic Benefits on the Host Country' in Institute of Economic Affairs, *Economic Issues in Immigration*, London: IEA.

Moore, Robert (1977) 'Migrants and the Class Structure of Western Europe' in R. Scase (ed.) *Industrial Society: Class Cleavage and Control*, London: Allen & Unwin.

Morgado, Cosme (1989) *The Role of Members of Parliament in Immigration Cases*, Policy Papers in Ethnic Relations, No. 14, Coventry: Centre for Research in Ethnic Relations, University of Warwick.

Mount, Ferdinand (1992) *The British Constitution Now*, Oxford: Heinemann.

Nairn, Tom (1977) *The Break-up of Britain: Crisis and Neo-nationalism,* London: Verso.

—— (1992) 'A Party Putsched Back into Power', Review of Mount (*q.v.*), *Guardian Weekly*, 31 May.

Nicol, Andrew (1981) *Illegal Entrants*, London: Runnymede Trust and the Joint Council for the Welfare of Immigrants.

Northam, Gerry (1987) 'The Clergyman Who Gave Refuge to a Communist', *Listener*, 25 June, 7–8.

OECD [Organisation for Economic Co-operation and Development] (1987) *The Future of Migration*, Paris: OECD.

O'Neill, Onara (1993a) 'Permeable Boundaries, Multiple Identities', Paper to the Fabian Society Philosophy Group, London School of Economics, Dec.

—— (1993b) 'Justice and Boundaries', Paper to the Fabian Society Philosophy Group, London School of Economics, Dec.

Patterson, Sheila (1969) *Immigration and Race Relations in Britain, 1960–1967*, London: Oxford University Press for the Institute of Race Relations.

Peach, Ceri (1968) *West Indian Migration to Britain: A Social Geography*, London: Oxford University Press.

—— (1990) 'The Caribbean in Europe', Paper for the Conference on the Caribbean in the 1990s, Institute of Commonwealth Studies, University of Oxford, 10 Jan.

Piore, M. J. and C. F. Sabel (1984) *The Second Industrial Divide: Possibilities for Prosperity*, New York: Basic Books.

Plender, Richard (1985) 'Migrant Workers in Western Europe', *Contemporary Affairs Briefing*, 2 (14) April, 1–7.

Potts, L. (1990) *The World Labour Market: A History of Migration*, London: Zed Books.

Power, Jonathan (1979) *Migrant Workers in Western Europe and the United States*, Oxford: Pergamon Press.

Pratt, Mary Louise (1986) 'Scratches on the Face of the Country; or, What Mr. Barrow Saw in the Land of the Bushmen' in Henry Louis Gates Jr *q.v.* 138–62.

PRT/JCWI [Prison Reform Trust and Joint Council for the Welfare of Immigrants] (1984) *Immigration Prisoners Project: A Law unto Themselves: Home Office Powers of Detention*, Paper No. 1, London: PRT/JCWI.

Refugee Council (1991) *At Risk: Refugees and the Convention Forty Years On*, London: Refugee Council.

Rex, J. and Sally Tomlinson (1979) *Colonial Immigrants in a British City: A Class Analysis*, London: Routledge & Kegan Paul.

Richardson, P. (1984) 'Coolies, Peasants and Proletarians; the Origins of the Chinese Indentured Labour in South Africa 1904–7' in S. Marks and P. Richardson (eds) *International Labour Migration: Historical Perspectives*, London: Maurice Temple Smith for the Institute of Commonwealth Studies.

Ringer, Benjamin B. (1983) *'We the People' and Others: Duality and America's Treatment of its Racial Minorities*, New York: Tavistock Publications.

Roche, T. W. E. (1969) *The Key in the Lock: A History of Immigration Control in England from 1066 to the Present Day*, London: John Murray.

Rodney, Walter (1981) *A History of the Guyanese Working People, 1871–1905*, London: Heinemann.

Sahlins, Peter (1992) *Boundaries: The Making of France and Spain in the Pyrenees*, Berkeley: University of California Press.

Said, Edward W. (1991) *Orientalism: Western Conceptions of the Orient*, Harmondsworth: Penguin.

Samora, Julian and P. V. Simon (1977) *A History of the Mexican–American People*, Notre Dame: University of Notre Dame Press.

Samuel, Raphael (ed.) (1989) *Patriotism: The Making and Unmaking of British National Identity, Vol. II, Outsiders*, London: Routledge.

Sampson, Edward E. (1993) *Celebrating the Other: A Dialogic Account of Human Nature*, Hemel Hempstead: Harvester Wheatsheaf.

Saperstein, David (ed.) (1987) *Providing Sanctuary: The Jewish Role: A Practical Guide for Congregations and Individuals*, New York: Union of American Hebrew Congregations for the Commission on Social Action of Reform Judaism.

Sarup, Madan (1991) *Education and the Ideologies of Racism*, Stoke-on-Trent: Trentham Books.

Schierup, Carl-Ulrick (1990) *Migration. Socialism and the International Division of Labour*, Aldershot: Avebury.

Schneider, Robin (1989) 'Asylum and Xenophobia in West Germany' in Danièle Joly and Robin Cohen *q.v.*, 162–8.

Schutz, Alfred (1944) 'The Stranger: An Essay in Social Psychology', *American Journal of Sociology*, 49 (6), 499–507.

Seeley, Sir John (1883) *The Expansion of England*, Cambridge: Cambridge University Press.

Sherman, A. J. (1973) *Island Refuge: Britain and Refugees from the Third Reich, 1933–9*, London: Paul Elek.

Shutter, Sue (1992) *Immigration and Nationality Law Handbook*, London: Joint Council for the Welfare of Immigrants.

Siebold, Martin (1934) 'Sanctuary', *Encyclopaedia of the Social Sciences*, 534–7.

Silverman, M. (ed.) (1991) *Race, Discourse and Power in France*, Aldershot: Avebury.

Smith, Anthony D. (1991) 'The Nation: Invented, Imagined, Reconstructed?', *Millennium: Journal of International Studies*, 20 (2), 353–68.

Smith, David (1977) *Racial Disadvantage in Britain: The PEP Report*, Harmondsworth: Penguin.

Solomos, John (1988) *Black Youth, Racism and the State: The Politics of Ideology and Policy*, Cambridge: Cambridge University Press.

—— (1989) *Race and Racism in Contemporary Britain*, Basingstoke: Macmillan.

Speier, H. (1969) *Social Order and the Risks of War*, Cambridge, Mass.: Massachusetts Institute of Technology Press.

Stastny, Charles (1985) 'The Roots of Sanctuary', *Refugee Issues*, 2 (4), British Refugee Council and Queen Elizabeth House Working Papers on Refugees, 19–39.

Stenton, D. M. (1965) *English Society in the Early Middle Ages*, Harmondsworth: Pelican.

Thompson, Mel (1990) 'Migrants from the Caribbean to Britain: A Case Study of the West Midlands', Ph.D. thesis, University of Warwick.

Thornberry, C. (1963) 'Dr Soblen and the Alien Law of the United Kingdom', *International & Comparative Law Quarterly*, 12(2) pt 2, 414–74.

Tiberghien, F. (1988) *La Protection de réfugiés en France*, Aix-en-Provence and Paris: Presses Universitaire d'Aix-Marseille and Economica.

Tinker, Hugh (1974) *A New System of Slavery: The Export of Indian Labour Overseas, 1830–1920*, London: Oxford University Press.

—— (1984) 'Into Servitude: Indian Labour in the Sugar Industry, 1883–1970', in S. Marks and P. Richardson (eds) *International Labour Migration: Historical Perspectives*, London: Maurice Temple Smith for the Institute of Commonwealth Studies.

Troup, Sir E. (1925) *The Home Office*, London: G. P. Putnam & Sons.

UK–HO [United Kingdom Government – Home Office] (various dates) *The Home Office Statistical Bulletin*, Croydon: Home Office.

UKIAS [United Kingdom Immigration Advisory Service] (1985) *Annual Report, 1984–5*, London: UKIAS.

van Hear, Nicolas (1991) 'Forced Migration and the Gulf Conflict, 1990–1991', *Oxford International Review*, 3 (1), 17–21.

Vaughan, M. (1991) 'The Extreme Right in France: "Lepénisme" or the Politics of Fear' in L. Cheles *et al.* (eds) *Neo-Fascism in Europe*, London: Longman, 211–33.

Visram, Rozina (1986) *Ayahs, Lascars and Princes*, London: Pluto Press.

VMDC [Viraj Mendis Defence Campaign] (1988a) *Viraj Mendis: Life or Death*, Manchester: VMDC.

—— (1988b) *Viraj Mendis: Life or Death: The Evidence Supporting a Full Review of the Case*, Manchester: VMDC.

VMDC–RSG [Viraj Mendis Defence Campaign – Religious Support Group] (1988) *Sanctuary: Manchester Perspectives*, Manchester: VMDC–RSG.

Wallman, Sandra (1986) 'Ethnicity and the Boundary Process in Context' in J. Rex and D. Mason (eds) *Theories of Race and Ethnic Relations*, Cambridge: Cambridge University Press.

Weller, Paul (n.d.) 'Sanctuary as Concealment and Exposure: The Practice of Sanctuary in Britain as Part of the Struggle for Refugee Rights', Unpublished Paper.

—— (1987) *Sanctuary: The Beginning of a Movement?*, London: Runnymede Trust.

────── (1989) *The Multi-Faith Dimensions of Sanctuary in the United Kingdom*, Canterbury: Centre for the Study of Religion and Society, University of Kent.

Wenden, Catherine de (1990) 'The Absence of Rights' in Zig Layton-Henry *q.v.*, 27–44.

Williams, Colin H. (ed.) (1982) *National Separatism*, Cardiff: University of Wales Press.

Williams, Eric (1964) *Capitalism and Slavery*, London: André Deutsch.

World Economic Forum (1992) *World Competitiveness Report*, Lausanne: WEF.

Wrench, John (1991) 'Employment and the Labour Market', *New Community*, 17 (4), 617–23.

Zolberg, Aristide R. *et al.* (1986) 'International Factors in the Formation of Refugee Movements', *International Migration Review*, 20 (2), 151–69.

────── (1989) *Escape from Violence: Conflict and the Refugee Crisis in the Developing World*, New York: Oxford University Press.

Zucker, Norman L. and Naomi F. Zucker (1987) *The Guarded Gate: The Reality of American Refugee Policy*, San Diego: Harcourt, Brace, Jovanovich.

Newspapers and weeklies cited

Asian Times
Daily Express
Daily Mail
Daily Star
Daily Telegraph
Die Zeit
European
Financial Times
Glasgow Herald
Guardian
Guardian Weekly
Independent
Jewish Chronicle
Le Monde
Listener
Manchester City News
Morning Post
New Society
New Statesman and Society

Northern Echo
Observer
Pall Mall Gazette
People
Punch
Scotsman
Spectator
Standard
Sun
Sunday Dispatch
Sunday Express
Sunday Telegraph
The Times
Times Higher Educational Supplement
Weekly Journal
Western Daily Press
Yorkshire Post

INDEX

200, 203, 209-10
frontiers, 1, 2-3, 5, 7, 9, 12-15,
18-19, 21-2, 25, 27-8, 33-7, 42,
44-6, 50-2, 62, 68, 75, 82-3,
86-7, 90, 97-100, 104, 107,
109, 125-6, 128-30, 155, 157,
159-60, 163, 173, 181, 195,
197, 200, 203, 208-10, 213,
215
fuzzy frontiers (concept of), 7, 12,
18-19, 25, 28, 34-5, 107, 195
Gardner, Joy, 53
Gatwick airport, 112
Geneva Convention, 54, 72, 84,
86, 137, 157, 179, 185
George v, HRH, 44
Germany/German, 3, 14, 17, 25-
31, 33, 43-4, 46-8, 67, 69, 71-5,
77-8, 92, 94, 100-4, 110, 128,
131, 133, 142, 161-6, 169-75,
177-81, 183, 186, 188-9, 191,
203-4, 214
East German/East Germany,
163, 171, 173-4
ethnic German, 71, 163, 169,
170, 172, 174, 179
immigration policies, 171-74
refugees and foreign workers,
169-71
West German constitution, 69,
71, 171
Ghana/Ghanaians, 81, 83, 91,
117, 160
Gillman, Peter and Leni, 47, 73,
104, 105
Gilroy, Paul, 49
Goldberg, David, 195-8
Goodin, Robert E., 200
Goodwin-Gill, Guy, 110
Gordon, Major Evans, 43
Gordon, Paul, 42, 121, 126-7
Goulbourne, Harry, 23, 50, 79
Grant, Bernie, 53, 66-7
Greece/Greeks, 32, 37, 54, 76,
123, 131, 135, 170, 214
Green, Penny, 117, 119-20, 147
Grenville, William Wyndham, 40
Gulf War, the, 93, 105-6, 116,
120, 128, 180
gurdwaras (Sikh), 133
Gypsy/Gypsies, 43, 67, 173
Hall, Catherine, 13, 14, 192

Hammar, Tomas, 189
Harkis, 71-2, 176
Harmsworth, Vicount, 21
Harrison, David, 66
Hart, Judith, 77
Harwich, 99, 112, 116-18
Hastings, Governor General
Warren, 22
Hattersley, Roy, 91-2, 139-40
Heathrow airport, 17, 58, 85, 88,
90-1, 93, 99, 112
helots, 3, 167, 187, 189-90
Hoare, Sir Samuel, 102
Hoch, Paul, 75
Holmes, Colin, 43, 44, 45, 74-5,
104, 203
Holt, Richard, 10
Holy Roman Empire, 33, 191
Home Office, 2, 3, 18, 40, 42-8,
52-66, 75, 77-8, 81-7, 89, 96,
99-102, 104-9, 111-12, 114-16,
118-25, 127, 133, 135-6, 138,
141-5, 148-59, 197, 200, 209-
10, 215
Homeward Bound Fund, 66
Homze, E.L. 170
Hong Kong, 24, 54-6, 76, 78-80,
90, 159, 188, 208, 212
Hosenball, Mark, 52-3, 58
Huguenot[s], 35, 70, 72
human rights, 106, 109, 111, 128,
131, 146, 149, 176, 184-5, 213-
14
Hungary/Hungarians, 44, 71, 76,
94, 171, 173, 207
Hurd, Home and Foreign
Secretary Douglas, 13, 82-3,
86, 88, 118, 125, 137-8, 140,
144-5, 156
Husbands, Christopher T., 176-7,
203-4
Illegal Immigration Intelligence
Unit (IIIU), 126-7, 134
imagined community (concept
of), 201
Immigration Act Detainees
(IADs), 99, 125, 129
Immigration and Nationality
Department (IND), 54-5, 59-61,
65, 77, 81-2, 88-9
immigration officer[s] (IO), 41,
48, 51, 58, 60, 62, 64-6, 84, 87-